# Managing Manufacturing Using Microsoft Dynamics AX 2009

Other books by Scott Hamilton

*Managing Information: How Information Systems Impact Organizational Strategy* (with Gordon B. Davis), Business One Irwin (1993), an APICS CIRM textbook

*Maximizing Your ERP System,* McGraw-Hill (2003)

*Managing Your Supply Chain Using Microsoft Navision,* McGraw-Hill (2004)

*Managing Your Supply Chain Using Microsoft Axapta,* McGraw-Hill (2004)

*Managing Your Supply Chain Using Microsoft Dynamics AX,* Printing Arts (2007)

*Managing Your Supply Chain Using Microsoft Dynamics AX 2009,* Printing Arts (2009)

# Managing Lean Manufacturing Using Microsoft Dynamics AX 2009

Scott Hamilton, Ph.D.

Copyright © 2009 by Scott Hamilton. All rights reserved. Printed in the United States of America. Except as permitted under the United States Copyright Act of 1976, no part of this publication may be reproduced, stored in a retrieval system, or transmitted, in any form or by any means, electronic, mechanical, photocopying, recording, or otherwise, without the prior written permission of the author.

ISBN 978-0-9792552-1-2

*To my parents, Glenn and Goodie*

# Contents

*Foreword* ix
*Preface* xi

**Chapter 1** **Introduction**    **1**
Applicability of Lean Manufacturing Approaches    2
Maturity Stages in Lean Manufacturing    4
Summary of New Constructs for Lean Manufacturing    5
A Baseline Model of Operations    8
Summary of Scenarios Used Throughout the Book    9
Executive Summary    9

**Chapter 2** **Lean Scenarios and Traditional Approaches**    **11**
Make-to-Stock Products    12
S&OP Approaches for Make-to-Stock Products    14
Make-to-Order Products    19
S&OP Approaches for Make-to-Order Products    21
Lean Accounting and Maturity Stages    23
Case Studies    24
Executive Summary    25

**Chapter 3** **Fixed Kanbans**    **27**
S&OP Approaches for Fixed Kanbans    30
Fixed Purchasing Kanbans    33
Fixed Replenishment Kanbans (for Component Picking Purposes)    42
Fixed Manufacturing Kanbans    48
Floor Stock Management Approaches    57
Managing Engineering Changes When Using Fixed Kanbans    63
Variations in Using Fixed Kanbans    65
Managing Non-Lean Items    74
Case Studies    75
Executive Summary    77

**Chapter 4** **Fixed Kanbans with Subcontract Manufacturing**    **49**
Subcontract Manufacturing with a Discrete Kit of Supplied Components    81
Subcontract Manufacturing with Consigned Inventory of Supplied Components    90
Variations of Subcontract Manufacturing    94
Executive Summary    97

## Contents

**Chapter 5  Work Cell Considerations    99**
Use of Routing Data for Costing Purposes    99
Takt Time Metrics for a Work Cell    100
Drumbeat for a Work Cell    103
Case Studies    104
Executive Summary    105

**Chapter 6  PTO Replenishment Kanbans    107**
PTO Replenishment Kanbans for Shipping Purposes    108
PTO Replenishment Kanbans for Component Picking Purposes
    (for Fixed Manufacturing Kanbans)    116
Executive Summary    118

**Chapter 7  PTO Kanbans for Make-to-Order Items    119**
S&OP Approaches for PTO Kanbans    122
PTO Manufacturing Kanbans    123
PTO Replenishment Kanbans (for Component Picking Purposes)    134
PTO Purchasing Kanbans    138
Managing Engineering Changes When Using PTO Kanbans    140
Variations in Using PTO Kanbans    140
Case Studies    142
Executive Summary    143

**Chapter 8  Lean Accounting    145**
Product Costing    145
Order-Based Costing    146
Value Stream Costing    147
General Ledger Considerations    150
Executive Summary    151

**Chapter 9  Lean Order Schedules    153**
Terminology for Using a Lean Order Schedule (LOS)    155
Using a LOS for PTO Manufacturing Kanbans    156
Using a LOS for Fixed Manufacturing Kanbans    171
Case Studies    175
Executive Summary    175

**Chapter 10  Alternative Approaches for the Lean Scenarios    179**
Alternative Approaches to the Baseline Model    179
Alternative Approaches to Fixed Kanbans    183
Executive Summary    185

**Chapter 11  Summarizing the Transition to Lean    187**

**Appendix A  Dynamics AX Terminology and Synonyms    193**
**Appendix B  Purposes of Work Center and Routing Data    199**
**Appendix C  Purposes of Work Cell Data    205**

*Index*    209

# Foreword

My involvement with lean manufacturing has spanned three decades, which includes almost 10 years in designing and implementing the lean manufacturing functionality now incorporated into Microsoft Dynamics AX. When I set out to create a system that supported lean principles for manufacturing and distribution organizations, I did not realize the length and at times the frustration of the journey. ERP systems today still depend, almost exclusively, on planning engines with increasingly higher levels of complication and so-called rich functionality. I go to exhibitions where I see advanced planning engines with lovely looking graphics that show, at this moment in time, the product can be made and shipped perfectly. I am shown a wealth of technology innovations that will ensure the product is made on time. It is almost as if the computer system not only performs this planning but actually makes the product as well! In producing Lean Enterprise for Dynamics AX as part of the eBECS organization, I hoped to produce something useable that conforms to the way people and organizations do lean. We produced the solution to customer pull in an attempt to make sure we gave customers value.

This book represents the first valid attempt to take all the ideas that the market has "pulled" and put them in one place with a degree of structure. The book enables the reader to see how lean and ERP can work together, and provides a platform to help readers in their waste reduction ventures. I commend it to you.

The software functionality for lean manufacturing is also a lean journey. The current functionality within Dynamics AX is not the end of the journey. I firmly believe that simplicity is the name of the game, and hope that simplicity guides the future.

Andrew Rumney<br>
Solutions Director, eBECS Limited<br>
www.ebecs.com<br>
www.leancentreofexcellence.com

The Microsoft Dynamics Lean Centre of Excellence serves as an educational outreach/training facility for organizations that require training on the lean capabilities in order to further their lean initiatives. Microsoft recognizes that a successful lean implementation is not simply about providing the right software tools; as important are the skills of the team that architect and deliver the solution. See **www.leancentreofexcellence.com** for more information.

eBECS are specialists in the design and delivery of world-class lean and agile business solutions. Working with customers across manufacturing, distribution, and the extended supply chain, eBECS utilizes Microsoft Dynamics AX and related technologies to build practical and effective solutions that streamline and integrate processes, minimize waste, optimize the supply chain, and manage demand-driven operations. See **www.ebecs.com** for more information.

# Preface

The target audience for *Managing Lean Manufacturing Using Microsoft Dynamics AX 2009* consists of those individuals involved with supply chain management in lean manufacturing operations. In particular, it is focused on those implementing or considering Microsoft Dynamics AX[1] as their ERP system for managing lean manufacturing. My involvement with this target audience and Dynamics AX provided the motivation for writing this book. There were three motivating factors.

First, I would have liked a guidebook about how lean manufacturing actually works with an ERP system such as Dynamics AX. The literature provides a wealth of theoretical viewpoints, but rarely addresses prescriptions for actual software functionality to support supply chain management in lean manufacturing. I wanted something that could explain ERP software functionality to support lean manufacturing scenarios, especially for handling kanbans and the different maturity stages of lean.

The second motivating factor involved a desire to facilitate system implementation and on-going usage. My efforts to train and consult with firms involved in the lean journey, and an ERP system like Dynamics AX, often involve explanations about how to effectively use the system to model typical lean scenarios and solve critical problems. This book represents a baseline of knowledge about how Dynamics AX solves common and unique business problems in lean manufacturing.

The third motivating factor involved a desire to assist those providing services related to Dynamics AX and manufacturing firms. They are charged with providing knowledgeable service across all interactions with their customers and suggesting solutions to business problems. This book reflects my experience in working alongside these people. Our working relationship typically involved training and joint efforts at selling, consulting, and customer support.

This book focuses on the lean manufacturing functionality within the latest version of Dynamics AX 2009. A previous book covered the traditional approaches to supply chain management in AX 2009.[2] This book provides footnotes to relevant information within the previous book, which helped reduce book length.

---

[1] Dynamics AX is a registered trademark of Microsoft Corporation.

[2] *Managing Your Supply Chain Using Microsoft AX 2009* is available on Amazon.com.

The prior research for writing about lean manufacturing built on my previous efforts for understanding Dynamics AX and the target audience. For example, the prior research covered the available documentation and training materials, presentations at various conferences, discussions with current users, and talking with knowledgeable experts at partners and Microsoft. My learning process was supplemented by thousands of hands-on simulations to understand how the system really worked and how it solves the business problems of various lean environments. Most importantly, my learning process was facilitated by numerous discussions with Andrew Rumney. Andrew was the original architect of the lean manufacturing functionality, and he shared the wealth of his experience with system implementations and lean practices.

In terms of understanding the target audience, the prior research involved gaining an in-depth knowledge of various types of lean manufacturing operations and the management team responsible for those operations. In this respect, the prior research built on my face-to-face consulting engagements with over a thousand manufacturing and distribution firms.[3] Many of these firms were undertaking lean manufacturing initiatives. These engagements primarily focused on supply chain management and effective ERP system usage. Each engagement required interviews with the management team to gain an in-depth understanding of how they currently run (and want to run) their business, and facilitative discussions about ways to improve operations and system effectiveness. These engagements covered the spectrum of operations, company size, levels of ERP expertise, terminology, geographies, and cultures across six continents. Each engagement required explanations that accounted for these variations in the target audience.

Other venues have also provided opportunities to understand the target audience and attempt to provide meaningful explanations through teaching and written materials. These other venues included teaching training seminars, conducting executive seminars, software user group presentations, MBA classes at several major universities, and classes for vocational-technical colleges and APICS certification. Attempts to provide written explanations have included my responses to hundreds of RFPs (requests for proposals) related to ERP systems, as well as writing software user manuals,

---

[3] Syntheses of these consulting engagements and related case studies have been published in two previous books. *Managing Information: How Information Systems Impact Organizational Strategy* (Irwin, 1993, with Gordon B. Davis) was one of the textbooks for the Certificate in Information Resource Management by the American Production and Inventory Control Society (APICS). *Maximizing Your ERP System: A Practical Guide for Managers* (McGraw-Hill, 2003) focuses on supply chain management in manufacturing firms. Other consulting engagements have been summarized in my previous books about Microsoft AX and NAV.

books, and scholarly articles based on field research and secondary research.[4] The opportunities to consult with firms implementing or considering Microsoft Dynamics AX have supplemented the foundation of prior research. The case studies within this book reflect some of these consulting engagements.

A critical issue in writing this book involved the choice of topics, and the sequence and level of detail for explaining these topics. The topics focus on key software functionality that supports the dominant business practices in lean manufacturing environments. The topics reflect those use cases actually tested and proven to work. Not all use cases could be tested or proven, and these use cases are not included in the book. The linear presentation sequence was shaped by what worked most effectively in previous writing, teaching, and consulting efforts for the target audience. The presentation employs a baseline model of operations to simplify the explanatory approach. Variations in this baseline model are covered using an anchor-and-adjustment approach to the explanations. The explanations include scenarios and case studies illustrating different types of business practices.

A second critical issue in writing this book involved the evolving nature of software package functionality. The standardized functionality covered in this book reflects the AX 2009 version. It is the author's intention to publish new editions as new releases become available, along with additional case study examples.

The book reflects my interpretation of how to use Microsoft Dynamics AX 2009. Errors of omission and commission, and any misunderstandings, are hopefully minimized.[5] Corrections and suggestions are welcome, as well as additional case study examples. Please send to **ScottHamiltonPhD@aol.com**. The intended goal is to provide an overall understanding of how it all fits together so readers can accelerate their learning process about managing their lean manufacturing operations.

Each day of writing was started with the following prayer:

> Creator of all things, give me a sharp sense of understanding, a retentive memory, and the ability to grasp things correctly and fundamentally. Grant me the talent of being exact in my explanations, and the ability to express myself with

---

[4] Examples of relevant articles range from "Requirements of Smaller Manufacturers for Computer-Based Systems" (published in the *APICS Quarterly*, Winter 1984) to "Trends Affecting Manufacturers and ERP" (published in *TechnologyEvaluation.com*, October 2003). More academic-oriented articles include an annual summary of MIS doctoral dissertations since 1973 (published in *MIS Quarterly*).

[5] The book is for information purposes only. The author, publisher, and Microsoft make no warranties, expressed or implied, in the presentation of information.

thoroughness and charm. Point out the beginning, direct the progress, and help in the completion.

Many people helped in completing this book, especially Jan DeGross in editing and typesetting, and Deb Skoog and Debbie Pearson in printing the book. Invaluable feedback was obtained from several reviewers, most notably Andrew Rumney but also Mark Hermans, Darren Hogg, and others. The book is dedicated to my parents, who provided guidance, feedback, and support throughout their lives.

# Chapter 1

# Introduction

An integrated supply chain management (SCM) system represents a critical success factor for effective implementation of lean manufacturing. The SCM system supports development and consensus for the demand plan, integrates engineering and sourcing information, manages changes associated with continuous improvement, and ensures supply–demand synchronization with demand pull techniques. The SCM system also defines product structure and costing information, provides the basis for financial information and reports, and provides a single source of the truth for decision making.

Many have argued that traditional SCM/ERP systems do not apply to lean manufacturing. One argument is that the weekly time increments associated with sales and operations planning, and the resulting supply orders, represent a blunt instrument that does not support the details of day-to-day coordination required by demand pull techniques. A second argument is that many SCM/ERP software packages lack the new constructs such as kanbans needed to support lean manufacturing. These limitations have often necessitated the use of manual systems, such as physical containers or cards to represent kanbans and a manually maintained schedule board. However, the manual kanban systems have their own difficulties such as lost cards and lack of information integration and visibility.

Most of the published literature provides few prescriptions about actual software functionality to support SCM for lean manufacturing. In addition, the lean enthusiasts emphasize new conceptual models and a new vocabulary which contributes a sense of mystique for those only familiar with the traditional SCM approaches.

This book covers the SCM software functionality to support lean manufacturing scenarios, as defined by functionality within the latest release of Microsoft Dynamics AX 2009. It also covers the traditional SCM approaches to these same scenarios, as defined in a previous book *Managing Your Supply Chain Using Microsoft AX 2009.* The book explains how to transition from traditional to lean approaches. In particular, it explains the incremental conceptual differences between the lean and traditional SCM approaches.

The targeted reader includes those individuals implementing or considering Dynamics AX to support their lean manufacturing initiatives, as well

|  |  | Distribution or Manufacturing Firm | Solution Provider |
|---|---|---|---|
| **Overall Goals** | | Improve understanding of how SCM software can support lean manufacturing | |
| | | Improve firm performance through effective supply chain management systems for lean manufacturing | Improve firm performance through effective customer service |
| System Implementation Life Cycle | **System Selection** | Reduce selection risk<br>Evaluate system fit and needed customizations<br>Provide vision of an integrated system to support lean manufacturing initiatives | Accelerate learning process<br>Reduce new employee ramp-up time<br>Improve solution-selling techniques<br>Improve training and consulting efforts<br>Support gap/fit analyses<br>Improve customization capabilities |
| | **Implementation** | Accelerate learning process<br>Reduce implementation costs and time<br>Reduce user resistance to change | |
| | **On-Going Operation** | Suggest changes to improve system usage<br>Revitalize a wayward implementation | |

Figure 1.1 Reasons for Reading Book

as those providing sales and implementation services. Figure 1.1 summarizes the reasons for reading this book for each of these audiences. The book is especially targeted at those people trying to understand the new conceptual models associated with lean manufacturing approaches, where they already have familiarity with traditional approaches to supply chain management.

## Applicability of Lean Manufacturing Approaches

Lean manufacturing approaches generally apply to the use of a manufacturing cell that produces a family of products (or a single product) with certain characteristics. These favorable characteristics include a higher certainty of demand, linear demand patterns, higher usage rates, higher component costs, shorter component lead times, and stable product structures with similar components. These favorable characteristics can apply to make-to-stock and make-to-order environments. In contrast, the lean approaches do not generally apply to products with the opposite characteristics, such as low certainty of demand, erratic demand patterns, low usage rates, long lead time components, and dynamically changing product structures. These characteristics represent special challenges to lean approaches that are more cultural than system related. The traditional SCM approaches tend to work better for products with these opposite characteristics. Vendor-managed inventory may also be considered for low-cost high-usage components such as nuts and bolts.

Lean manufacturing approaches have been especially applicable in two basic scenarios as described below.[1]

- Make-to-stock products with a small finished goods inventory. This example reflects the classic Toyota system approach with a short order-to-ship lead time and manufacturing cycle (ranging from hours to 1 or 2 days). Finished goods inventory can be stocked in a shipping area or at the final work cell, where the inventory levels typically reflect a day of supply (depending on the volatility of demand). The choice of a location for finished goods inventory affects the choice of a kanban approach. Fixed kanbans can replenish finished goods inventory at the shipping area, whereas pull-to-order kanbans (for the sales order quantity) can pull inventory at the final work cell to the shipping area. The book's baseline scenarios for Scenario #1 and Scenario #3 illustrate the different locations for finished goods inventory.

  An additional benefit of locating the finished goods inventory at the final work cell is that production personnel can easily see their inventory position and act accordingly.

- Make-to-order products with no finished goods inventory. This example reflects the Dell Computer approach where sales order visibility exceeds the manufacturing cycle. The customer provides forward visibility by placing sales orders with future delivery dates or by accepting a promised sales order delivery date in the future. The pull-to-order kanban quantities typically reflect the precise quantity and mix of products specified in the sales order. Alternatively, a pull-to-order kanban can be expressed as multiple kanbans with a quantity that reflects the item's normal container size.

Many make-to-order products are built from stocked components, where the stocked components may be purchased or manufactured. The stocked components are typically placed in a stockroom (or kept at the producing work cell) based on fixed kanbans, and pulled to the relevant work cell based on sales order demands. This approach employs pull-to-order replenishment kanbans to move a stocked component to its point of use. The book's baseline scenario for Scenario #4 illustrates a lean environment for make-to-order products.

A product may be completely make-to-order, such as a custom product or a rarely produced product. Pull-to-order kanbans can be used for every item in the product structure, including purchased components.

---

[1] These two lean scenarios were described in the book *Lean Transformation* by Bruce Henderson and Jorge Larco (Oaklea Press, 2000).

The lean manufacturing approaches to supply chain management reflect a number of lean techniques. Techniques such as kanbans and positioning required resources at the production area have special relevance, but other techniques also apply. These include value stream mapping, quality at the source, total productive maintenance, setup reduction, batch size reduction, standardized work, work balancing, production leveling, visual performance data, and continuous improvement.[2]

## Maturity Stages in Lean Manufacturing

Most companies begin their lean journey with a pilot project approach, which represents the first of three maturity stages in lean manufacturing.[3] The pilot project focuses on shop floor processes and implementing lean methods at one or more work cells. The project may involve changes in the factory layout based on value stream mapping. Illustrative changes include the definition and design of work cells, supermarkets for floor stock areas, and a reduction in bottlenecks. The pilot project uses kanbans for manufacturing and visual coordination tools, and typically supports tracking of floor stock inventory and an order-based approach to costing. A supplier has been identified for each purchased item (along with quality at the source initiatives), but purchasing kanbans are not typically used because suppliers are not ready for this type of coordination. Figure 1.2 summarizes this first stage and the other maturity stages of lean manufacturing.

The pilot project stage can also be characterized by several other lean techniques that are summarized in the figure. Once the pilots are working well, the lean methods are rolled out across the plant and into other areas of the business.

With the second stage, the biggest change involves value stream costing. Components are issued to the value stream, and end items are received from the value stream and the component inventory in floor stock locations is typically not tracked. Other changes include the widespread use of manufacturing kanbans and selective use of purchasing kanbans. The third stage involves organizing the company by value stream, and extending the lean practices throughout the company and with customers/suppliers.

These three maturity stages are reflected in variations of using the lean manufacturing functionality within Dynamics AX. For example, the supports the transition from traditional SCM approaches to lean, the transition from order-based costing to value stream costing, and the transition from detailed tracking to no tracking of floor stock inventory. Chapter 11 summarizes the transition from traditional to lean.

---

[2] Kenneth W. Dailey's book, *The Lean Manufacturing Pocket Handbook* (DW Publishing Co., 2003) provides an excellent yet brief summary of lean manufacturing techniques.

[3] The brief description of maturity stages draws heavily on the comprehensive explanations provided in the book *Practical Lean Accounting* by Brian Maskell and Bruce Baggaley (Productivity Press, 2004).

| Maturity Stage | Primary Characteristics | Other Characteristics |
|---|---|---|
| Preparing for Lean | Initial efforts to model lean scenarios using traditional approaches<br>Gain understanding of lean approaches | Initial efforts to change factory layout |
| Stage #1 — Lean Pilot Projects | Focus on shop floor processes<br>Use of kanbans for manufacturing<br>No purchasing kanbans for suppliers<br>Visual coordination tools<br>Tracking of floor stock inventory<br>Order-based approach to costing | Making to takt time<br>Drumbeat scheduling<br>Quick changeover and SMED<br>Standardized work<br>Quality at source and self inspection<br>Continuous improvement teams |
| Stage #2 — Manage by Value Stream | Focus on value stream<br>Widespread use of kanbans for manufacturing<br>Use purchasing kanbans for some suppliers<br>Eliminate tracking of floor stock inventory<br>Value stream approach to costing | |
| Stage #3 — Lean Enterprise | Organize company by value stream<br>Extend lean practices throughout company<br>Extend lean practices with customers/suppliers | |

Figure 1.2 Maturity Stages of Lean Manufacturing

## Summary of New Constructs for Lean Manufacturing

The conceptual model for lean manufacturing involves new constructs concerning kanbans and work cells. These constructs are introduced now, and subsequent chapters provide more detailed explanations.

**Kanbans (aka Kanban Orders)** A kanban has a unique identifier (aka kanban order number), and each variation of a kanban order has a slightly different life cycle and associated status (aka kanban order status). The terms *kanban* and *kanban order* will be used interchangeably; they both refer to a pull signal for coordinating supply chain activities. The replenishment policies for a kanban order are specific to an item, warehouse, and container.[4] Stated another way, a kanban order inherits a set of replenishment policies that reflect its source of supply such as purchased or manufactured, and whether it is directly linked to a pull signal such as a sales order. The linkage to a pull signal differentiates the two basic types of kanbans—a fixed kanban and a pull-to-order kanban (aka PTO kanban).

---

[4] A container has other synonyms such as tote or pallet. A printed kanban ticket typically accompanies the container as part of the visible pull signal. Alternatively, an electronic version of the kanban ticket (aka the kanban order) can act as the pull signal without accompanying a physical container.

- *Fixed Kanban.* A fixed kanban communicates a pull signal using a fixed container quantity and multiple containers. The fixed kanbans are not linked to actual sales orders. They reflect anticipated rates of demand based on the current sales backlog or sales forecasts for end items, plus bill of material (BOM) information for components.
- *PTO Kanban.* A PTO kanban is closely linked to a pull signal such as a sales order demand or the component demand for producing a manufactured item. A single PTO kanban is typically generated for the required quantity. However, a required quantity can also be satisfied with multiple PTO kanbans that reflect multiple containers (and a fixed quantity per container) that add up to the required quantity.

Variations in kanban orders reflect these two basic types (fixed kanbans and PTO kanbans) and the sources of supply (manufacturing, purchasing, and replenishment). Each variation has a slightly different approach for defining replenishment policies and creating kanban orders. In addition, each variation has a slightly different life cycle of kanban order transactions and status, and different coordination tools.[5]

The book's explanation of kanban variations will employ consistent terminology to minimize possible confusion. Figure 1.3 summarizes the terminology for fixed and PTO kanbans. The book will sometimes shorten the terminology for fixed kanbans by dropping the word "fixed," since the alternative is already differentiated by the words "PTO kanban." The figure illustrates this shortened term by displaying the word [Fixed].

The new constructs related to kanban orders replace the traditional SCM approaches that involve purchase orders, production orders, and picking lists. They can also work in parallel with the traditional approaches, typically because lean manufacturing has only been implemented for selected product lines, for selected portions of a product structure, or for selected trading partners in the supply chain.

A manufacturing kanban order supports coordination of production activities, but it does not support cost accumulation for actual costing purposes. When order-based costing is required, each receipt of a manufacturing kanban can automatically generate an associated production order. The autodeduction of components (and routing data) for this production order supports the actual costing capabilities within AX.

**Work Cell**  A work cell represents a group of equipment and workstations in a bounded area to facilitate small-lot continuous flow production. Compo-

---

[5] The replenishment policies and life cycle transactions for these kanban orders have many similarities with traditional production orders, purchase orders and picking lists. The kanban orders also employ alternative coordination tools that have similarities with traditional tools. An understanding of these similarities helps to bridge the change in conceptual models and vocabulary for lean manufacturing.

| Kanban Terminology | | |
|---|---|---|
| | **For Fixed Kanbans** | **For PTO Kanbans** |
| Term | [Fixed] Kanban or<br>[Fixed] Kanban Order | PTO Kanban or<br>PTO Kanban Order |
| Status | Kanban Status or<br>Kanban Order Status | Kanban Status or<br>Kanban Order Status |
| Identifier | Kanban Order Number | Kanban Order Number |
| Printed Document | Kanban Ticket | Kanban Ticket |
| Types Of Kanbans | [Fixed] Purchasing Kanban | PTO Purchasing Kanban |
| | [Fixed] Replenishment Kanban* | PTO Replenishment Kanban* |
| | [Fixed] Manufacturing Kanban | PTO Manufacturing Kanban |
| | [Fixed] Manufacturing Kanban<br>with Subcontracting | PTO Manufacturing Kanban<br>with Subcontracting |

*A Fixed Replenishment Kanban is only used for component picking purposes, whereas a PTO Replenishment Kanban can be used for component picking purposes or shipping purposes.

Figure 1.3 Terminology for Kanbans

nent inventory is located in a floor stock area near the work cell, along with other required resources, to support a point-of-use strategy.

A work cell represents a simpler alternative for modeling lean scenarios in comparison to the use of Dynamics AX work centers and routing data. You indicate the work cell for producing an item as part of the kanban policies for a fixed or PTO manufacturing kanban. The list of empty kanbans by work cell provides a coordination tool. Takt time metrics provide a measure of work cell performance, and the work cell's drumbeat can support sales order delivery promises based on available capacity.

The simpler alternative of a work cell does not currently support value-added costs related to direct manufacturing and overhead allocations. Most lean scenarios focus on direct material costs so the limitation is not an issue. However, some lean scenarios require value-added costs to support calculation of a manufactured item's cost and suggested sales price. Autodeduction of these value-added costs supports an order-based costing approach for manufacturing kanbans. In this case, routing data must be used to support the costing purposes. Chapter 5 explains several work cell considerations, including the use of routing data for costing purposes.

**Other New Constructs** Kanbans and work cells represent the primary constructs for managing lean scenarios. Other new constructs represent advanced functionality covered in separate chapters. This includes the new construct of a lean order schedule (Chapter 9) and the alternative approaches to fixed kanbans (Chapter 10).

## A Baseline Model of Operations

This book employs a baseline model of operations and several baseline scenarios to simplify explanations. The baseline model focuses on standard products (identified by an item number) that must be tracked by site and warehouse area. Additional characteristics of the baseline model are listed below.

- ❖ Work cells within a single physical site. The work cells for lean manufacturing may comprise some or all of the manufacturing processes within a single physical site.[6] A work cell can also represent a subcontract manufacturer.
- ❖ Warehouse areas without bin locations. Examples of warehouse areas include a stockroom, the floor stock area next to a work cell, and a shipping area. Inventory balances are not tracked by bin location within a warehouse area, since the layout and low inventory minimize this requirement. The floor stock areas for components, and the stockroom areas, are often termed supermarkets as a reflection of their efficient organization.
- ❖ Focus on direct material costs. Most lean scenarios focus on direct material costs, and (when applicable) the outside operation costs for subcontract manufacturing.
- ❖ Focus on standard costing. Most lean scenarios focus on standard costing for inventory valuation purposes. However, some lean scenarios require actual costing, which involves an order-based costing approach to manufacturing kanbans. In this case, each receipt of a manufacturing kanban order can create a behind-the-scenes production order with autodeduction of components (and routing data) to support actual costs.
- ❖ No routing data, although the selected use of AX routing data for costing purposes may be employed. The costing purposes include the calculation of a manufactured item's cost and sales price based on routing data, and the cost accumulation (via autodeduction) against a production order to support actual costing.
- ❖ No inventory tracking of batch or serial numbers.
- ❖ No use of the item variant fields such as color, size or configuration id.
- ❖ No quarantine orders or quality orders.

Variations to the baseline model are described in Chapter 10; they reflect alternative approaches for handling lean scenarios.

---

[6] The AX solution approaches for modeling single-site and multisite operations are described on pages 351-355 in the AX 2009 book.

## Summary of Scenarios Used Throughout the Book

The book employs several baseline scenarios to illustrate lean manufacturing and simplify the explanations. These lean scenarios are initially described in terms of traditional SCM approaches (in Chapter 2), and subsequently described in terms of lean SCM approaches using fixed kanbans, PTO kanbans, and lean accounting. This provides an anchor-and-adjustment approach to learning. The primary scenarios are listed below; some scenarios have variations.

- Scenario #1: Make-to-stock products with internal manufacturing
  - Single level product
  - Multilevel product (Scenario #1a)
  - Multilevel product and black hole warehouses (Scenario #1b)
- Scenario #2: Make-to-stock products with subcontract manufacturing
  - Using a discrete kit of supplied components
  - Using consigned inventory stocked at subcontractor (Scenario #2a)
- Scenario #3: Pull-to-order shipping area for stocked end items
  - Pull-to-order floor stock area for stocked components
- Scenario #4: Make-to-order products
  - Single level product
  - Multilevel product (Scenario #4a)
- Scenario #5: Value stream costing

The variations to a scenario reflect different business practices. For example, Scenario #2 covers the dominant approach to subcontract manufacturing, and Scenario #2a covers an alternate approach. The case studies at the end of each chapter highlight additional variations of lean scenarios.

Each scenario highlights the nature of coordination tools such as kanbans or traditional supply orders. Each scenario also highlights a point-of-use strategy of placing components in a floor stock area for a work cell, which must be reflected in BOM information for the warehouse source of components. The diagram for each scenario illustrates the bill of material information and the work cell information. The diagrams also highlight sales orders triggering the creation of PTO kanbans.

## Executive Summary

The software functionality to support supply chain management in lean manufacturing employs kanbans to support make-to-stock and make-to-order production strategies. Kanbans provide a different approach to SCM coordination in comparison to traditional approaches employing purchase orders, production orders, and picking lists. However, many companies must employ both kanbans and traditional supply orders in the early maturity stages of lean manufacturing.

This chapter reviewed the applicability of lean manufacturing approaches and the associated maturity stages. It introduced the new constructs concerning kanbans and work cells, where work cells replace the use of AX work centers and routing data. It described the baseline model of operations used throughout the book to simplify explanations, and also summarized the baseline scenarios used to illustrate common lean environments.

# Chapter 2

# Lean Scenarios and Traditional Approaches

The typical lean scenarios provide a starting point for explaining supply chain management, and for assessing the applicability of traditional approaches. Chapter 1 discussed the applicability of lean manufacturing approaches for a family of make-to-stock and make-to-order products that are internally manufactured, although the manufacturing process may also involve outside operations. This chapter starts with several lean scenarios for make-to-stock products, and then covers scenarios for make-to-order products.

Make-to-stock products typically have a small level of finished goods in a lean scenario. The completed products can be (1) stocked in a shipping area or (2) stocked at the final work cell and then pulled to a shipping area based on sales orders. The sales and operation planning (S&OP) approach for make-stock products can be based on sales forecasts, the pipeline of actual sales orders, or both. These characteristics can be grouped into three basic lean scenarios, as summarized in Figure 2.1. They are labeled Scenario #1, Scenario #2, and Scenario #3.

| | | S&OP Approach | | |
|---|---|---|---|---|
| | | Make-to-Stock Items and Stocked Components | Make-to-Order Items Indirectly Linked to Sales Orders | Make-to-Order Items Directly Linked to Sales Orders |
| | | Kanban Approach: Fixed Kanbans | | PTO Kanbans |
| Lean Scenario Characteristic | Internal Manufacturing | Scenario #1 | | Scenario #4 |
| | Subcontract Manufacturing | Scenario #2 | | Subcontract manufacturing also applies to make-to-order items |
| | Pull-to-Order Shipping Area | Scenario #3 | | N/A |
| | Lean Accounting and Value Stream Costing | Scenario #5 | | |

Figure 2.1 Summary of Lean Scenarios

11

Make-to-order products have no finished goods inventory, and they often involve sales order delivery promises based on material and capacity constraints. The capacity constraints can be expressed in terms of drumbeat availability at a work center. These characteristics constitute Scenario #4. Scenario #5 involves the use of value stream costing and black hole warehouses to support more mature stages of lean manufacturing.

This chapter describes the traditional approaches for handling each lean scenario, and consists of the following sections:

- Make-to-Stock Products
  - Scenario #1: Internal Manufacturing
  - Scenario #2: Subcontract Manufacturing
  - Scenario #3: Pull-to-Order Shipping Area
- Make-to-Order Products
  - Scenario #4: Internal Manufacturing
- Lean Accounting and Maturity Stages
  - Scenario #5: Value Stream Costing and Black Hole Warehouses

The traditional approaches often employ work centers and routing data, and these terms (rather than the term *work cell*) are reflected in this chapter's explanation of lean scenarios.

## Make-to-Stock Products

The lean scenarios for make-to-stock products involve a work center that produces a family of similar products. They may also involve a series of work centers in a multilevel product structure, or a work center representing a subcontract manufacturer. The explanation for each scenario starts with a representative product structure, and a discussion of the sales and operations planning (S&OP) approach and traditional coordination tools.

### Scenario #1: Internal Manufacturing

The representative make-to-stock product shown in Figure 2.2 reflects one product within the family produced by a final assembly work center. It has a multilevel product structure with several characteristics, as described below.

- *End Item.* The demand plan for the end item drives supply chain activities, such as the production orders to produce the end item at the final assembly work center. The demand plan may consist of a sales forecast, sales orders, or both. Components are delivered to the work center's floor stock area to support each day's production orders. For example,

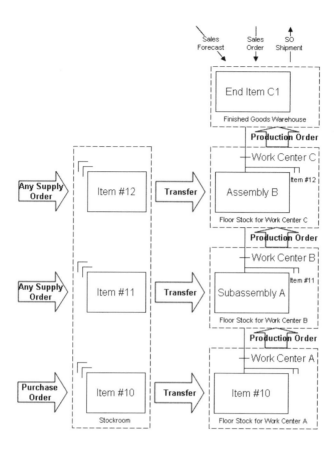

Figure 2.2  Multilevel Product with Internal Manufacturing

a consolidated picking list coordinates the transfer of stocked components from the stockroom. Completed end items are placed in a finished goods warehouse, and the receipts trigger component backflushing.
* *Purchased Components.* Purchase orders for components are received into a stockroom, and then transferred to the relevant floor stock areas to support production activities. Other supply orders such as transfer orders are similarly received and issued.
* *Manufactured Components.* Production orders coordinate each work center's activities for manufactured items, which are produced from components stocked at a corresponding floor stock area. A consolidated picking list coordinates the transfer of stocked components from the stockroom. Completed parent items are placed in the floor stock area for the next work center, and the receipts trigger component backflushing.
* *Routing Information.* The routing information for a manufactured item provides the traditional approach to defining the relevant work center.

In a lean scenario, however, you typically use a simplified definition of routing data to support very limited purposes. These purposes include the identification of the work center producing an item, and the grouping of production orders by work center to support coordination efforts. The simplified routing data can optionally provide the basis for work center consumption logic regarding the warehouse source of components.[1]

The simplified routing data may be used for costing purposes, such as calculating the value-added costs (and suggested sales price) for a manufactured item. It may also be used for sales order delivery promises based on available capacity, where production orders consume capacity. Appendix B describes the simplified approaches for defining and using routing data.

The production pool associated with an item (and its production orders) provides an alternative for grouping production orders, so that routing data may not be required to support coordination efforts.

The bill of material information indicates the warehouse source of components. It also provides the basis for cost roll-up calculations. Each item in the product structure has a cost that typically reflects direct material costs. Other costs such as labor or overhead are not typically included in a manufactured item's cost.

## S&OP Approaches for Make-to-Stock Products

The demand plan represents a key aspect of the S&OP approach. The demand plan for make-stock products can reflect three options: sales forecasts, the pipeline of actual sales orders, or both. These three options for a demand plan are explained below. The planning calculations use the demand plan to generate planned orders and coordinate supply chain activities.[2]

- ❖ *Sales forecasts.* The sales forecasts can be expressed for individual items within the product family. They could also be expressed for an item group and a planning bill (aka *item allocation key*), so that the product mix percentages disaggregate the forecast. As a general guideline, the sales forecast must be entered in weekly increments in the near-term horizon, and monthly increments in the longer term horizon. The master plan policies determine whether sales forecasts will be included in the planning calculations.
- ❖ *Pipeline of sales orders.* The pipeline of sales orders provides a better foundation for producing to actual demand.[3] This requires a pipeline that

---

[1] The options for defining a component's warehouse source are described on pages 52-54 in the AX 2009 book.

[2] A demand plan and the planning calculations are described on pages 142-152 in the AX 2009 book.

[3] The pipeline of sales quotations can also be considered as demands, as defined by the master plan policies.

exceeds the cumulative manufacturing cycle time, otherwise a combination of sales orders and forecasts must be used. The production orders for end items are indirectly linked to these sales orders, as reflected in the due dates and quantities.
* *Both.* The combination of sales orders and forecasts involves considerations about how to handle forecast consumption.

The planning calculations use the demand plan to suggest planned orders that "chase the demand." The planned orders apply to every item within the product structure, and provide a key coordination tool for supply chain activities. The planned orders reflect each item's planning data.[4] Figure 2.3 summarizes the two variations of a demand plan—using sales forecasts versus sales orders—and their traditional S&OP approach.

With make-to-stock products and forecasted demand, the planning calculations generate a set of forecast plan data (using the forecast scheduling task) and a set of master plan data (using the master scheduling task). A sales forecast may not be required for make-to-order products indirectly linked to sales orders.

The planned orders within the set of master plan data can be used to calculate the number of fixed kanbans for stocked items, as illustrated in Figure 3.3 and described in the next chapter.

The traditional approaches to managing supply chain activities involve planned orders and other coordination tools, as described below.

* *Purchasing.* The primary coordination tools include planned purchase orders for each item's preferred vendor, the actual purchase orders, and action messages.[5] Another tool includes an arrival overview of scheduled receipts.
* *Production.* The primary coordination tools include planned production orders, the actual production orders, the picking list associated with a production order, a production schedule by production pool, and action messages. When routing data has been defined, the additional tools include a capacity versus load analysis, a production schedule by work center, and a Gantt chart.[6] However, the production orders must be scheduled or started to be displayed on many of these coordination tools.
* *Transfers.* The primary coordination tools include planned transfer orders for each item's warehouse source, the actual transfer orders (or transfer journals), and action messages.[7]

---

[4] The AX 2009 book describes the key planning data for purchased items (pages 23-32), manufactured items (pages 74-79), and transfer items (pages 356-359).
[5] The coordination tools for purchasing are described on pages 251-254 in the AX 2009 book.
[6] The coordination tools for production are described on pages 322-327 in the AX 2009 book.
[7] The coordination tools for transfers are described on pages 363-365 in the AX 2009 book.

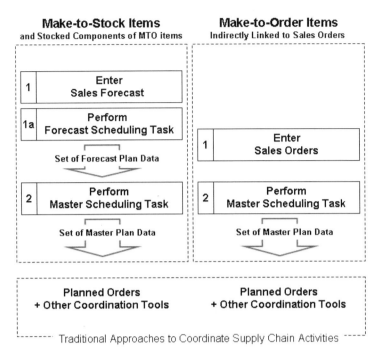

Figure 2.3  Traditional S&OP Approaches to Make-to-Stock Products

- *Sales Orders and Delivery Promises.* The delivery promises can reflect capable-to-promise (CTP) logic, which accounts for material constraints and capacity constraints (when routing data exists).[8]
- *Shipping.* The anticipated shipments provide one coordination tool, along with the order-based or consolidated picking lists.[9]

The traditional approach typically reflects the S&OP time increments (such as weekly), so that a production order or a purchase order often represents a week's worth of demand. A weekly time increment does not support the details of day-to-day coordination required by demand pull techniques. Other problems with these traditional approaches include the noise level of action messages, even with tolerance settings to minimize the number of messages. The messages tend to be ignored. A traditional approach may employ routing data, which sometimes requires considerable effort for data maintenance. In lean scenarios, you typically autodeduct the routing operations on production orders to eliminate the collection and analysis of actual time reports.

---

[8] Delivery date promises are described on pages 182-183 in the AX 2009 book.

[9] The coordination tools for handling shipments are described on pages 270- 282 in the AX 2009 book.

A variation of the above-described traditional approaches comes closer to modeling a lean scenario. In this variation, the demand plan and the planned orders reflect daily increments, and near-term planned orders provide the only coordination tool since they represent "empty kanbans." They are never firmed up. Each "kanban receipt" involves minimal transaction processing, such as an orderless production receipt (via the BOM journal) or a purchase receipt (which automatically creates and receives a purchase order against a blanket purchase order). It is feasible to use the item's order quantity modifiers so that multiple planned orders have a fixed quantity equal to the normal kanban quantity. However, these planned orders still reflect an approximation of the detailed day-to-day coordination in a lean scenario.

## Scenario #2: Subcontract Manufacturing

Subcontract manufacturing involves an outside operation using supplied components. The Dynamics AX approach to modeling subcontract manufacturing involves a separate item to represent the outside operation, and specifying the item as a BOM component with a component type of vendor[10] It is termed the *outside operation component*. For example, the item description might be "outside operation to produce parent item x." It specifies the value-added costs and indicates a purchase requirement. You can optionally define a routing operation for an external work center, but it is not required.

The simplest approach to subcontract manufacturing involves a single operation in the production process, so that the BOM components define the supplied material to produce the parent item. The supplied material can be handled as a discrete kit sent to the subcontractor, or as consigned inventory stocked at the subcontractor. Figure 2.4 summarizes these two methods using an illustrative product structure that does not include a routing operation for the external work center.

Scheduling a production order for the end item will automatically create the purchase order for the outside operation component. This purchase order must be received and then invoiced. There are several differences to the two methods for handling supplied material.

❖ *Discrete kit method.* The kit of supplied components is picked and sent to the subcontractor after the production order has been started. The components' inventory is not tracked within Dynamics AX, and you report a production order receipt when the subcontractor sends the end item back.

---

[10] Subcontract manufacturing using the outside operation component is described on pages 68-71 in the AX 2009 book.

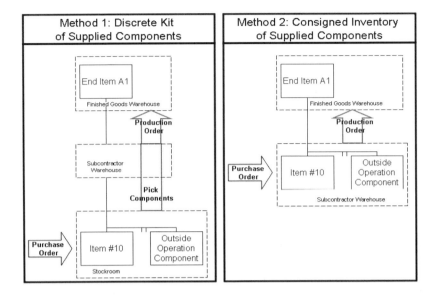

Figure 2.4 Traditional Approaches to Subcontract Manufacturing

* *Consigned inventory method.* The supplied components are directly delivered to the subcontractor via purchase orders, or transferred via transfer orders, so that their inventory is tracked within Dynamics AX. You report a production order receipt for the end item, which autodeducts component inventory at the subcontractor.

There are other variations to subcontract manufacturing, such as stocking the end item at the subcontractor or sending the end item to another subcontractor.

## Scenario #3: Pull to Order Shipping Area

Completed end items are often placed in a floor stock area at the final assembly work center, and then pulled to a shipping area based on sales order demand. This reflects the lean philosophies about minimizing inventory and providing visibility within a value stream, such as the work cell visibility of their inventory position.

The consolidated picking list within Dynamics AX provides one solution approach for a pull-to-order shipping area.[11] It generates a picking list for one or more sales orders assigned to a shipment, and the picked materials are placed in a bin location that represents the shipping area. The shipment can

---

[11] The use of a consolidated picking list is described on pages 271-278 in the AX 2009 book.

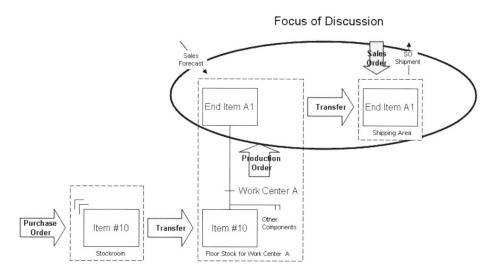

Figure 2.5  Pull-to-Order Shipping Area

then be sent, which generates a packing list update for the relevant sales orders.

An alternative solution approach employs transfers from the floor stock area(s) to the shipping area based on sales order demand. Figure 2.5 summarizes this approach with an illustrative product structure, and highlights the focus of discussion.

Within the illustrative product structure, the end item's sales forecast has been defined for the warehouse representing the floor stock area. Actual sales orders (for the shipping area warehouse) trigger planned transfer orders, and transfers can be recorded as transfer journals.

## Make-to Order Products

The lean scenarios for make-to-order products involve a work center that produces a family of similar products. They may also involve a series of work centers in a multilevel product structure, or a work center representing a subcontract manufacturer. The distinguishing characteristic is that the production order for the end item is generated from the sales order, and scheduling this production order automatically generates the reference orders for its make-to-order and buy-to-order components. The explanation starts with a representative product structure, and a discussion of the sales and operations planning (S&OP) approach and traditional coordination tools.

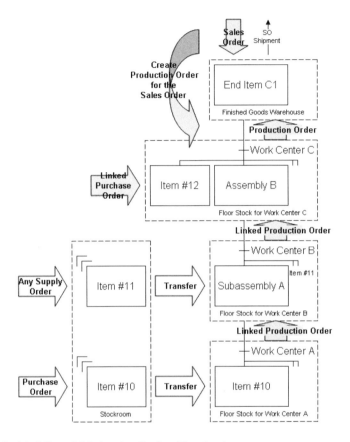

Figure 2.6  Multilevel Make-to-Order Product

## Scenario #4:  Make-to-Order Products

The representative make-to-order product shown in Figure 2.6 reflects one product within the product family produced by a final assembly work center. The product structure reflects several make-to-order and buy-to-order components, as well as several stocked components. It has several distinguishing characteristics, as summarized below.

❖ *Sales order and production order for the end item.* You can immediately create a production order for a sales order line item, as shown by the arching arrow in Figure 2.6. Or you can subsequently firm up the end item's planned production order corresponding to the sales order. The linkage between the two is displayed in the reference fields for each order. However, this represents a loose linkage, since changes to the sales order (such as a quantity or date change) do not automatically update the production order, and vice versa.

- *Make-to-order component.* Each make-to-order component must be identified in the bill of material with a component type of *production* rather than *normal*.[12] This means that its production order will be automatically generated after you "release" the end item's production order, and the two will be directly linked. The directly linked production order is termed a *reference order* or linked production order. The linkage between the two is displayed in the reference fields for each order. The reference orders can span multiple levels in the product structure based on the production component type assigned to lower level assemblies. Figure 2.6 illustrates two levels of linked production orders, which are delivered to the floor stock areas representing their point of use. Changes to the end item's production order quantity, date and status can automatically update its reference orders.

  The concept of "releasing" the end item's production order can be accomplished by changing its status from created to scheduled, released, or started. You can also reset this production order status (such as resetting it to created), which will delete its reference orders.

- *Buy-to-order component.* Each buy-to-order component must be identified in the bill of material with a component type of *vendor* rather than *normal*.[13] This means that its purchase order will be automatically generated after you "release" the end item's production order, and the two will be directly linked. The directly linked purchase order is termed a *reference order* or *linked purchase order*. The linkage between the two is displayed in the reference fields for each order. A linked purchase order must be delivered to its point of use. Figure 2.6 illustrates one linked purchase order for Item #12, which is delivered to the floor stock area representing its point of use. Changes to the end item's production order quantity and date can automatically update its linked purchase orders.

## S&OP Approaches for Make-to-Order Products

The key aspects of the S&OP approach consist of the sales orders and the corresponding production orders for end items. As shown in Figure 2.7, you create a production order for each end item specified on a sales order line. The sales order demand will be used in planning calculations to generate and display planned orders for stocked components. Releasing the production order for the end item will automatically generate the reference orders for make-to-order and buy-to-order components.

The traditional approaches to managing supply chain activities for stocked components were described in the previous section. The same coordination tools apply to a buy-to-order or make-to-order component, except

---

[12] The impacts of component type are described on pages 47-49 in the AX 2009 book.
[13] The impacts of component type are described on pages 47-49 in the AX 2009 book.

Chapter 2

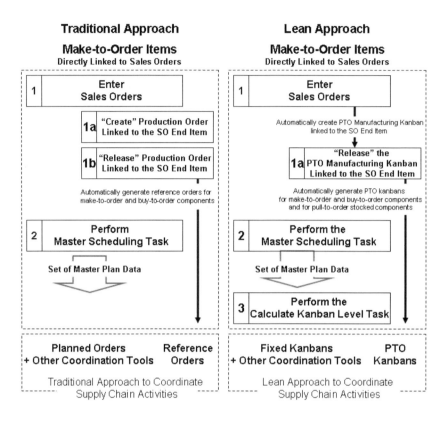

*Figure 2.7 S&OP Approaches for Make-to-Order Products*

that you do not firm up a planned order because the reference orders are created by releasing the production order for the end item.

The lean S&OP approach for make-to-order items is shown side-by-side in Figure 2.7 to emphasize several similarities and differences.

❖ *Similarities in the S&OP approach.* The concept of a production order linked to a sales order is replaced by a PTO manufacturing kanban, and you similarly "release" this PTO manufacturing kanban to automatically generate PTO kanbans for make-to-order and buy-to order components. The PTO kanbans replace the use of reference orders. The planned orders generated by the master scheduling task can coordinate non-lean items in the product structure. They can also be used to calculate the number of fixed kanbans for stocked components.

❖ *Differences in the S&OP approach.* The PTO manufacturing kanban is automatically created for the sales order line item; it does not require a separate step. In addition, it is directly linked to the sales order, so that it will be automatically updated by changes to the sales order quantity, date, or ship-from warehouse. The types of coordination tools are different, such as using the kanban manufacturing and kanban purchasing forms. The replenishment kanbans replace the concept of a production order picking list.

## Lean Accounting and Maturity Stages

The three maturity stages of lean manufacturing were summarized in Chapter 1. The pilot stage is often characterized by an order-based approach to actual costing, which is supported by the traditional use of production orders. This requires a detailed tracking approach to floor stock management, since the component inventory quantities must be backflushed to correctly assign actual costs to each production order.

The detailed tracking approach generates unnecessary inventory transactions for components to support order-based costing. An alternative approach employs backflushing of component value to assign costs to each production order. This alternative approach employs the cost substitution concept to calculate the total value of components, and generate an appropriate entry for the picking list journal. It means that component inventory quantities will not be autodeducted when you report the receipt of a manufactured item. This alternative to order-based costing is not supported by traditional functionality within Dynamics AX.

The second and third stages of lean maturity are characterized by a shift to value stream costing and the use of black hole warehouses. The traditional AX functionality partially supports value stream costing and the black hole concept, as described in the breakout box for Scenario #5.

### Scenario #5: Value Stream Costing and Black Hole Warehouses

A value stream is typically represented by a financial dimension, so that all costs (such as material, labor and other costs) can be charged to the financial dimension. Traditional functionality within AX supports the assignment of a financial dimension to items, thereby supporting the concept of value stream costing by product family.

Value stream costing for internal production typically involves no tracking of inventory quantities in floor stock areas. Components are issued to the value stream, and end items are received from the value stream. This approach has been termed the *black hole concept*. However, the pull signals associated with empty kanbans are still required at various stages of the production process to coordinate activities within the black hole.

Traditional functionality within AX can partially support the black hole concept. For example, you can use the inventory journal transactions to issue components (and receive end items) and charge the relevant financial dimension for the value stream. As another example, you can turn off inventory tracking for an item (using the Inventory Model Group assigned to the item), and production orders can still be used to coordinate production activities.

## Case Studies

### Case 1: Production Orders as PTO Manufacturing Kanbans

A transportation equipment manufacturer produced a multilevel custom product, where each custom product (quantity of one) was configured via a rules-based configurator. The factory layout involved a final assembly area consisting of three sequential work cells and a 90 minute takt time per work cell. The time requirement for each work cell was reflected in a master routing with three operations. Each work cell's hourly costs reflected its average crew size and overhead factors. Several supporting work cells produced the customized subassemblies, which were identified in the bill of material with a component type of production. Each subassembly was assigned a master routing with one routing operation that specified its corresponding work center, its time requirement, and its hourly costs. Use of the product configurator generated a unique BOM version for the item number representing the custom end item, and for the item numbers representing customized assemblies. The product configurator also assigned the relevant master routing to each manufactured item. The company currently employed Dynamics AX and the product builder capabilities.

Use of the product configurator provided a realistic promised delivery date to each sales order based on capable-to-promise logic. This finite scheduling logic reflected the drumbeat of the final assembly work center. A production order was created for the sales order line item after completing and approving the product configuration of the end item. Scheduling this production order for the end item automatically generated the reference orders for the customized subassemblies. These production orders were directly linked to their parent production order, and acted as pull signals. Changes in sequencing of the final assembly schedule automatically synchronized these reference orders. After reporting a production order as started, one employee from a work cell team reported the actual time expended at the work cell. This approach supported the requirements for actual costing. A completed subassembly was placed in the floor stock area for the next work cell.

Each configuration consisted of purchased components obtained on the basis of planned purchase orders. The planned purchase orders reflected the sales order pipeline, and purchases were received into the stockroom. These purchased components were issued to floor stock areas via production order picking lists. In many cases, a configuration required buy-to-order material identified in the bill of material with a component type of vendor. This meant that the purchase orders were automatically created after scheduling the production order for the end item, and the purchases were received into the relevant floor stock areas.

**Case 2: Kit Items Requiring Final Assembly** This case study illustrates a manufacturing company that has embraced lean techniques in a pilot stage, and wanted to compare their current-but-traditional SCM approach to the potential use of kanban orders. The analysis suggests both approaches work, but their traditional approach seems to work best.

A surgical kit manufacturer produced standard and custom kits at a final assembly work cell based on sales orders that represented next-day requirements for performing surgeries. Each standard kit was identified by an item number and bill of material. A custom kit was identified by a generic item number (a modeling-enabled item), and an option selection process defined the kit contents as a unique BOM version which was assigned to the sales order line. Each kit was priced and sold as a single sales order line item, but required actual production order costing based on the kit components.

With the traditional approach, the order entry person created a production order (at a started status) for each sales order line item. The production order acted as the pull signal for the final assembly work cell, and the production order pick list acted as the pull signal for transferring purchased components from the stockroom to the floor stock area. Purchase orders for specialty components were automatically created (with direct linkage to the end item's production order) and then received to the floor stock area. The production order receipt autodeducted the component quantities from the floor stock area, and the completed kit was then shipped against the sales order.

With a kanban approach, the end items would be assigned kanban policies for a PTO manufacturing kanban. The sales order would automatically generate a corresponding PTO manufacturing kanban, the PTO replenishment kanbans for its components, and the PTO purchasing kanbans for specialty components. The receipt of a PTO manufacturing kanban would autodeduct the component quantities from the floor stock area, and the completed kit could then be shipped against the sales order.

# Executive Summary

Dynamics AX supports several traditional SCM approaches to lean manufacturing scenarios for make-to-stock and make-to-order products. The traditional approaches can be used in the early maturity stages of lean manufacturing when kanban coordination has only been established for a selected product family, or for some of the components in a product structure. The traditional approach to production order costing may also be used in an early maturity stage to support order-based costing associated with kanban orders.

Some lean manufacturing scenarios can be supported by the traditional approaches within AX. Make-to-order products linked to sales orders, for example, can employ the traditional AX approaches to closely mimic PTO manufacturing kanbans using production orders for the end item and reference orders for its make-to-order components. This was illustrated in Case 1. In contrast, the traditional AX approaches for handling make-to-stock products (or make-to-order products indirectly linked to sales demand) cannot easily mimic fixed kanbans. For example, the near-term planned orders loosely mimic fixed kanbans, but they do not provide the detailed day-to-day coordination between supplies and demands in a multilevel product structure. However, the traditional approach to an S&OP game plan for make-to-stock products can still be used to calculate the number of fixed kanbans, as described in the next chapter. The same S&OP game plan can also be used to generate planned orders for components not yet managed by kanban coordination.

# Chapter 3

# Fixed Kanbans

Fixed kanbans provide a lean approach for supply chain coordination of stocked items, whether they represent make-to-stock products or stocked components in make-to-order products. Fixed kanbans also apply to make-to order products with indirect linkage to actual demands. The number of fixed kanbans for each item in the product structure reflects the anticipated rate of demand, which can be calculated from a sales forecast or from the pipeline of sales orders respectively. In contrast, pull-to-order (PTO) kanbans support make-to-order products with direct linkage to sales orders.

This chapter focuses on using three types of fixed kanbans: purchasing, manufacturing, and replenishment. Fixed replenishment kanbans support component picking purposes by moving stocked items to their point of use. The chapter starts with two scenarios for a single level and a multilevel product to illustrate use of fixed kanbans, and the first section explains S&OP approaches for fixed kanbans. Subsequent sections cover each type of fixed kanban in terms of the policies for creating a kanban, the life cycle of a kanban, and the relevant coordination tools. Kanban policies for each item and warehouse must be defined in order to create fixed kanbans, and one kanban policy (the active flag) determines whether the newly created kanbans can be used.

Additional sections cover the approaches for managing engineering changes, variations in floor stock management (to support order-based and value stream accounting), and variations in using fixed kanbans. The chapter concludes with the approaches for managing non-lean items within the product structure, which are characteristic of early maturity stages in lean manufacturing. The chapter consists of the following sections:

❖ S&OP Approaches for Fixed Kanbans
❖ Fixed Purchasing Kanbans
❖ Fixed Replenishment Kanbans (for Component Picking Purposes)
❖ Fixed Manufacturing Kanbans
❖ Floor Stock Management Approaches
❖ Managing Engineering Changes When Using Fixed Kanbans
❖ Variations in Using Fixed Kanbans
❖ Managing Non-Lean Items

A variation of a manufacturing kanban involves an outside operation, as described in the next chapter on subcontract manufacturing (Chapter 4). Another variation involves stocking finished goods at the work cell, and transferring inventory to a shipping area to support sales order shipments, as described in the chapter about PTO replenishment kanbans for shipping (Chapter 6).

## Scenario #1: Single Level Product and Fixed Kanbans

A single level product provides the simplest viewpoint for illustrating fixed kanbans. Figure 3.1 depicts a single level product produced from purchased components, where purchases can be coordinated using purchasing kanbans or normal purchase orders for non-lean items. This scenario illustrates use of a finished goods warehouse for the small inventory of completed products. This inventory could have been kept in a floor stock area by the final work cell, as illustrated in a subsequent scenario (Scenario #3).

Sales order shipments for the end item consume inventory of its kanbans in the finished goods warehouse, resulting in empty kanbans that communicate a production requirement for the work cell. The subsequent receipt

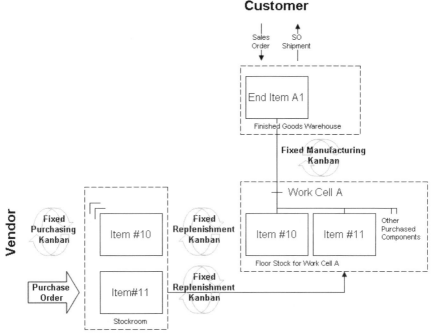

Figure 3.1 Single Level Product and Fixed Kanbans

of the manufacturing kanban places inventory back in the finished goods warehouse. The kanban receipt also triggers component backflushing when using a detailed tracking approach to floor stock management. In a similar fashion, an empty replenishment kanban will pull component material from the stockroom to the floor stock area. An empty purchasing kanban will pull purchased parts from the vendor to the stockroom, whereas normal purchase orders (suggested by traditional planning calculations) will replenish non-lean components in the stockroom. The chapter includes a separate section about managing non-lean items.

## Scenario #1a: Multilevel Product and Fixed Kanbans

Fixed kanbans also apply to a multilevel product, such as the scenario shown in Figure 3.2. Fixed manufacturing kanbans coordinate production of the end item and manufactured components. Fixed replenishment kanbans pull stocked components from the stockroom to floor stock areas. The figure also illustrates that manufactured components can be pulled from another floor stock area, as highlighted by the comment.

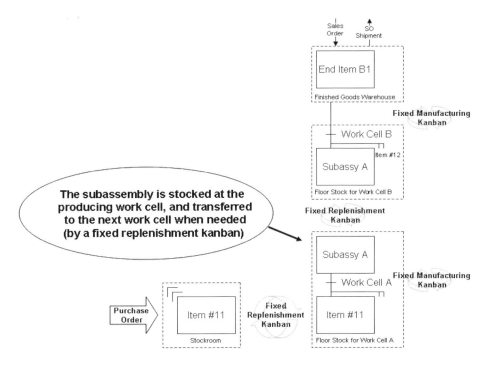

Figure 3.2 Multilevel Product and Fixed Kanbans

## S&OP Approaches for Fixed Kanbans

The S&OP game plan applies to the product family produced at the final assembly work cell illustrated in Scenario #1 and Scenario #1a. The game plan is expressed as a set of fixed kanbans for every item in the product structures, where the kanban levels reflect the anticipated rate of demand. This demand plan represents a key aspect of the S&OP approach. The demand plan for fixed kanbans can reflect three options: sales forecasts, the pipeline of actual sales orders, or both. These three options for a demand plan were previously described in the Chapter 2 subsection "S&OP Approaches for Make-to-Stock Products." The planning calculations use the demand plan to suggest planned orders that "chase the demand."

Planned orders provide the foundation for calculating kanban levels for fixed kanbans. These calculations—termed the Recalculate Kanban Level task—are performed using the planned orders within a specified set of master plan data. Figure 3.3 displays this task in terms of the two variations of a demand plan—using sales forecasts versus sales orders—and the S&OP approaches for fixed kanbans.

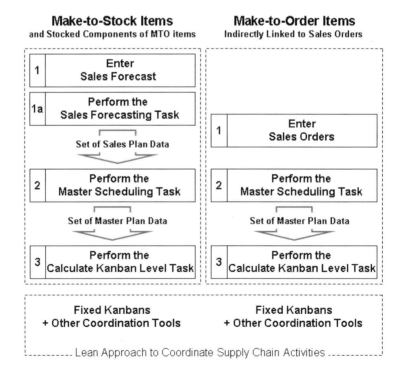

Figure 3.3 S&OP Approaches for Fixed Kanbans

The suggested kanban levels can guide the manual additions or deletions to each item's kanban orders. The fixed kanbans and their related coordination tools can then be used to coordinate supply chain activities.

The kanban level calculations reflect a rate of demand, such as a daily usage rate. Very simple math can be used to translate weekly or monthly demands (for a specific item and warehouse) into a daily usage rate, and ultimately into the number of kanbans for the item and warehouse. We will review this simple math for calculating the kanban level, and an example report generated by the Recalculate Kanban Level task.

## Calculating the Kanban Level Using Simple Math (and Little's Formula)

The number of fixed kanbans for coordinating a specific item and warehouse can be calculated by multiplying the projected daily usage rate times the item's lead time in days, and dividing the total by the normal kanban quantity. The daily usage rate can be optionally factored up by a specified percentage (termed the *alpha factor*) as a form of buffer for higher-than-expected demands. This conceptualization is commonly called Little's formula,[1] and is summarized in Figure 3.4.

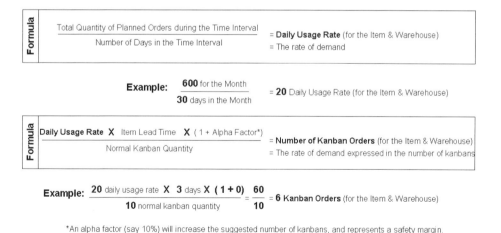

Figure 3.4  Calculating the Number of Fixed Kanbans Using Little's Formula

---

[1] Little's demand formula is based on the original formula created by John Ohno for use within the Toyota Production System.

The daily usage rate can be calculated by taking the total demand during a specified time interval (such as a 30 day interval), and then dividing the total demand by the number of days within the interval. The example in Figure 3.4 shows a total monthly demand of 600, so that a 30-day month results in a daily usage rate of 20 for the item and warehouse. The example in Figure 3.4 also shows the item's lead time of 3 days, and a normal kanban quantity of 10 units, which results in a quantity of 6 kanbans for the item and warehouse.

Most readers with AX expertise are familiar with the concept of assigning a user-defined "coverage group" to each item. For example, the coverage group contains several fields that define "period lot sizing" logic such as the number of days in a period. This information is used by the Master Scheduling task to calculate planned orders, where the run date (for the task) represents the starting point for period lot sizing logic. A similar concept applies to the calculation of kanban levels, where you assigned a user-defined "kanban group" to each item. The kanban group contains several fields that define "Little's formula" logic. In particular, you define the number of days in the interval size (termed the *forward horizon*) and an alpha factor. This information is used when performing the Recalculate Kanban Level task, where you also specify the starting date of the time interval and the desired set of master plan data (that contains planned orders).[2] For example, a starting date for an upcoming month (and a forward horizon of 30 days) would be used to calculate the number of fixed kanbans for the period.

The kanban level calculation only applies when an item's fixed kanban policies have been flagged as *dynamic* (aka the *dynamic* checkbox). For calculation purposes, the demand is represented by the planned orders with due dates during the specified time interval. The planned orders reflect independent demand for the end items, and the dependent demands for all components within the product structures.

## Example Report Generated by the Recalculate Kanban Level Task

The Recalculate Kanban Level task generates an infolog report that indicates needed changes in kanban levels, and it can optionally update each item's kanban policy concerning the number of fixed kanbans. The task does not automatically delete or add kanbans. Figure 3.5 displays an example report in terms of the current and suggested information for each lean-controlled item and warehouse, and highlights the critical information about the suggested changes in the number of kanbans.

---

[2] The specified set of data (for the Recalculate Kanban Level task) can be a set of master plan data or a set of forecast plan data.

## Fixed Kanbans

|  |  |  | Current Information | | | Suggestions | | |
|---|---|---|---|---|---|---|---|---|
| Item Number | Warehouse | Normal Kanban Quantity | Policy for Number of Kanbans | Number of Temporary Kanbans | Total Kanbans in Circulation | Calculated Demand Quantity | Calculated Number of Kanbans | Change in Number of Kanbans |
| End Item A1 | Shipping Area | 10 | 6 | 0 | 6 | 70 | 7 | +1 |
| Part-10 | Floor Stock at Cell A | 10 | 12 | 0 | 12 | 140 | 14 | +2 |
| Part-10 | Stockroom | 10 | 12 | 1 | 13 | 140 | 14 | +1 |
| Part-11 | Floor Stock at Cell A | 10 | 6 | 0 | 5 | 70 | 7 | +2 |
| Part-12 | Floor Stock at Cell A | 10 | 8 | 0 | 8 | 70 | 7 | -1 |

Legend: ① = Example of a typical suggestion
② = Example of a suggestion when temporary kanbans exist
③ = Example of a suggestion when some kanban orders have been deleted

(Critical Information)

Figure 3.5 Example Report for Recalculating Fixed Kanban Levels

Using the report illustrated in Figure 3.5, you must take additional steps to delete existing kanbans and create new kanbans that reflect the suggested kanban levels. The additional steps must also consider the current use of temporary kanbans, as illustrated by example 2 in the figure.

The Recalculate Kanban Level task should be performed periodically to understand the impact of changes in lead times, projected daily usage rates, bills of material, new products, or other factors.

The alpha factor (within Little's formula) represents one approach for increasing the number of kanbans. The use of an alpha factor will be affected by what the planned orders represent. For example, the use of a sales forecast may reflect an inflated quantity, so that the planned orders already reflect the inflated quantity and the alpha factor should be zero.

## Fixed Purchasing Kanbans

An explanation of fixed purchasing kanbans can be segmented into three basic topics: the policies for creating a kanban, the life cycle for a kanban, and the related coordination tools. Several attributes determine the nature of a fixed purchasing kanban order, and these attributes are inherited when you initially create the kanban order. Figure 3.6 summarizes the policies for creating a fixed purchasing kanban. Most of the kanban order attributes are inherited from its kanban policies. An item number and warehouse comprise the key fields for uniquely identifying kanban policies, whereas a kanban order number uniquely identifies each kanban order. The critical kanban polices are described below, along with the related prerequisite information.

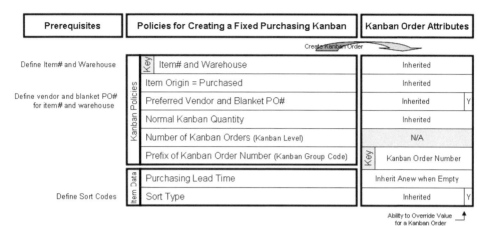

Figure 3.6 Policies for Creating a Fixed Purchasing Kanban

## Policies for Creating a Fixed Purchasing Kanban

Kanban policies are defined for an item number and warehouse using the Kanbans form. In the context of Scenario #1, for example, the purchasing kanban policies would be defined for the item "Item #10" and the "Stockroom" warehouse. An alternative approach to defining kanban policies involves the use of a kanban template, as described in the section "Variations in Using Fixed Kanbans."

**Item Information**   The critical item information includes the inventory unit of measure, an active standard cost record by site, the item's purchasing lead time, and item-related text. The printed kanban ticket can optionally include item-related text, which must be expressed as a note document for internal purposes.[3]

**Item Origin**   The item origin must be designated as purchased, regardless of the item type (item, BOM or service) assigned to the item.

**Preferred Vendor (and Alternate Vendors)**   The definition of a blanket PO for a specified item and warehouse identifies the preferred vendor (and alternate vendors).[4] The preferred vendor and blanket PO are initially

---

[3] The type of note document can be user defined, and you specify this user-defined type as the company-wide basis for item text (on the Kanban Parameters form).

[4] The traditional AX approaches for defining an item's preferred vendor do not apply to purchasing kanbans. These traditional AX approaches include the definition of an item's company-wide vendor as part of the item master data, or a warehouse-specific preferred vendor as part of the item's coverage planning policies. The traditional approaches also include the use of purchase trade agreements about price and lead time, which can be used by the master scheduling task to assign a vendor to a planned purchase order.

inherited when you create a purchasing kanban, but these values can be overridden on a specific kanban with an alternate vendor (and blanket PO).

**Blanket PO** The definition of a blanket PO for a specified item and warehouse identifies the preferred vendor, as noted above. Reporting the receipt of a purchasing kanban will automatically create a release against the blanket PO, record a receipt against this newly created PO, and print an associated packing slip. The blanket PO price applies to the receipt, and the packing slip number reflects the kanban order number.[5] Several guidelines should be considered in defining the blanket PO.

- *Single line item on a blanket PO.* Each blanket PO can only have a single line item for a specified item and warehouse. Do not use multiple line items, because this will create errors when reporting a kanban receipt.
- *Warehouse on the blanket PO.* The warehouse on the blanket PO should be the same as the warehouse for the kanban policy. It is possible to enter different warehouses in the kanban policy and the blanket PO, but a kanban receipt will be placed in the warehouse associated with the blanket PO.
- *Unit of Measure (UM) on the blanket PO.* An item's inventory unit of measure should be used on a blanket purchase order. It is possible to specify a different UM on a blanket PO, but then a kanban receipt transaction cannot be processed.

## Normal Kanban Quantity and Number of Kanbans (Kanban Level)

The normal kanban quantity and the number of kanbans (termed kanban level) will be used to initially generate the kanban orders. After initial generation, you can incrementally increase the policy concerning the number of kanbans, and generate additional kanban orders. You can also manually delete a kanban order after its creation.

The normal kanban quantity is inherited by the kanban order. A higher or lower quantity may be defined as the quantity ordered or the quantity received for a specific kanban order, but a newly emptied kanban order will revert to its normal kanban quantity. The number of fixed kanbans can be calculated for an item and warehouse, as explained earlier this chapter's section "S&OP Approaches for Fixed Kanbans."

## Prefix of the Kanban Order Number (Kanban Group Code)

A meaningful prefix provides several advantages in viewing and using kanban

---

[5] The use of the kanban order number as the packing slip number can result in duplicate packing slip numbers. Hence, you should define a company-wide policy for accepting duplicate packing slip numbers (on the Accounts Payable Parameters form).

order numbers. The prefix typically represents the buyer responsibility for the kanban orders, but it may be used for other segmentation purposes. When you create kanban orders, the system automatically assigns the user-defined prefix and a counter to the kanban order numbers. A prefix of XYZ, for example, would be used to create kanban order numbers of XYZ_000001, XYZ_000002, and so forth.

You can optionally change the prefix for all related kanban orders in circulation, which also results in a new counter. This also changes the prefix in the kanban policies. For example, a prefix change might be performed when you change the buyer responsibility for the kanban orders.

Note: The Record Id is a system-assigned internal identifier that uniquely identifies a kanban order, and is used for barcode scanning of transactions.

**Purchasing Lead Time**  The item's purchasing lead time will be inherited when you initially create a purchasing kanban order, and whenever the kanban has been emptied. This lead time is used to calculate the *required date* for an empty purchasing kanban. When the lead time is 10 days, for example, and today's inventory consumption results in an empty kanban, the kanban's required date will be 10 days from today's date. The same logic applies to an empty kanban that is newly created as of today's date.

An item's purchase lead time can be specified as a company-wide policy (within the item's default order settings for purchase orders), or as part of the item's site-specific order settings.[6]

**Sort Type**  The sort type is an optional attribute for a kanban order, and can be used for grouping or sequencing the purchasing kanbans. The sort types are user-defined, and assigned to items using the Item Sort Type form. The sort type inherited by a kanban order can be manually overridden.

**Ability to Override the Attribute Value for a Kanban Order**  Several attributes of a fixed purchasing kanban can be overridden, such as simply assigning a different sort type. You can permanently assign a different preferred vendor to a fixed purchasing kanban order; it does not revert back to the previous vendor after emptying the kanban. As noted above, you can optionally change the prefix for all related kanbans in circulation, which also results in a new counter.

**Example Ticket for a Fixed Purchasing Kanban**  The example shown in Figure 3.7 includes the bar-coded information about the Record Id

---

[6] An alternate approach to specifying an item's company-wide lead time could be based on the kanban lead time field on the item master. While it appears that a policy (termed the kanban lead time checkbox on the Kanban Parameters form) could activate logic that would use this value, my testing indicates it is not currently supported for purchasing kanbans or manufacturing kanbans.

Fixed Kanbans 37

Figure 3.7 Example Ticket for a Fixed Purchasing Kanbans

and Item Number, which are used to support scanned receipt transactions. It also includes the optional item-related text.

## Life Cycle of a Fixed Purchasing Kanban

A fixed purchasing kanban has a life cycle represented by a status, and the status is closely related to kanban order transactions. In its simplest form, a *pending* status represents an empty kanban and a requirement that must be confirmed with the supplier (by manually changing the status to *confirmed by supplier*) before you can record a receipt for the kanban order. Figure 3.8 summarizes the kanban order transactions and status, as well as related user activities and automatic updates. Figure 3.8 depicts the kanban order status using italics, and highlights use of the Kanban Purchasing form as a coordination tool.

**Prerequisite Step: Create a Kanban Order**  You create a purchasing kanban order using the Kanbans form, and it inherits the policies described in Figure 3.6. A newly created kanban order has a *pending* status; it can be termed *pending (empty)* status to emphasize the concept of an empty kanban.

**Step1: View the Empty Kanban Orders**  An empty kanban represents a requirement that must be communicated to the vendor. You can optionally assign a different approved vendor (and blanket PO) to the kanban. If needed, you can delete a kanban order with a pending status, such as reducing the number of kanbans in circulation.

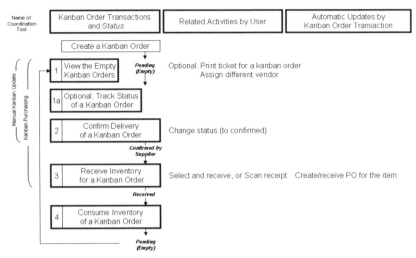

Figure 3.8 Life Cycle for a Fixed Purchasing Kanban

## Step 1a: Optionally Track Status of a Purchasing Kanban Order

Many environments need additional tracking of kanban status prior to confirmation. The variations in tracking status are shown separately in Figure 3.9, rather than incorporating them into the previous figure. The kanban order status can be manually changed from *pending* to *sent to supplier* and then to *goods dispatched,* which acts the same as the *confirmed by supplier* status for allowing a receipt transaction. Changing the status to *declined by supplier* is typically followed up by assigning a different approved vendor (and blanket PO) to the kanban order. These status changes do not have any sequencing rules.

## Step 2: Confirm Delivery of a Kanban Order

A purchasing kanban order must be confirmed with the supplier (by manually changing the status to *confirmed by supplier* or *goods dispatched*) before you can record a receipt transaction on the Kanban Purchasing form. The confirmation is not required for the barcode scanning approach to receipts.

## Step 3: Receive Inventory for a Kanban Order

The receipt can be reported via barcode scanning, or by entering data on the Purchasing Kanban form. A fixed kanban can only be received once; you cannot record multiple partial receipts.

## Step 4: Consume Inventory of a Kanban Order

The inventory associated with a purchasing kanban order is normally consumed by inventory transactions, such as transfers to a floor stock area. The pending status is automatically assigned after consuming the inventory of a kanban order.

# Fixed Kanbans 39

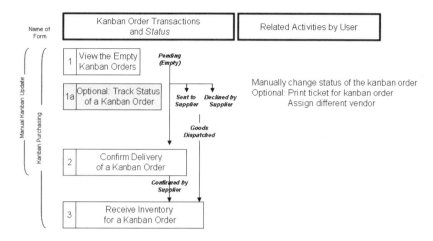

Figure 3.9  Additional Status Tracking for a Purchasing Kanban

The inventory may also be consumed by component backflushing or an explicit kanban empty transaction, as described later in this chapter in the section "Floor Stock Management Approaches."

## Coordination Tools for Fixed Purchasing Kanbans

The primary coordination tools include a list format (the Kanban Purchasing form) and a graphical format (the Stop/Go Board), and the printed kanban tickets. Each company tends to customize the graphical format for coordinating their purchasing kanbans, and one format (the Stop/Go Board) is included with out-of-the-box functionality for illustrative purposes.

**Kanban Purchasing Form**  This form displays the kanbans requiring action by the buyer, and represents the primary coordination tool. In particular, the buyer can review upcoming requirements for kanban deliveries, indicate supplier confirmations about the supplied quantity, and record actual receipt of a kanban. As illustrated in Figure 3.10, filters can help focus attention on kanbans from a specified vendor, with near-term requirement dates, or with a particular status.

Buyer responsibility can be indicated by the kanban order number prefix, as exemplified by the ANN and BOB prefix for the kanban order numbers in Figure 3.10. The typical buyer actions using the Kanban Purchasing form include the following:

❖ Identify purchasing kanbans with a *pending* status that need to be sent to the vendor, and change the status to indicate *sent to supplier*.

## Chapter 3

| | Kanban Purchasing Form | | | | | | | | | |
|---|---|---|---|---|---|---|---|---|---|---|
| | | | Filters: | Vendor | Required Date | Kanban Order Status | | | | |
| | | | | 3000 | 07/07/20XX | | | | | |
| Mark | Kanban Order Number | Item Number | Deliver To Warehouse | Vendor | Quantity Ordered | Required Date | Kanban Order Status | Quantity Supplied | Confirmed Quantity | Confirmation Date |
| ☐ | ANN_000035 | Part-15 | Stockroom | 3000 | 100 | 07/06/20XX | Pending | | | |
| ☐ | ANN_000036 | Part-15 | Stockroom | 3000 | 100 | 07/07/20XX | Pending | | | |
| ☐ | ANN_000112 | Part-3 | Stockroom | 3000 | 25 | 07/05/20XX | Sent to Supplier | | | |
| ☐ | ANN_000150 | Part-22 | Stockroom | 3000 | 50 | 07/06/20XX | Goods Dispatched | | 50 | |
| ☐ | ANN_000193 | Part-17 | Stockroom | 3000 | 100 | 07/06/20XX | Confirmed by Supplier | | 100 | 07/03/20XX |
| ☐ | BOB_000010 | Part 101 | Stockroom | 3000 | 10 | 07/07/20XX | Confirmed by Supplier | | 9 | 07/03/200X |

Data can be entered or changed

Figure 3.10  Example of the Kanban Purchasing Form

- ❖ Identify purchasing kanbans with a *sent to supplier* status that need to be updated to a status of *confirmed by supplier*.
- ❖ Identify purchasing kanbans with a past-due required date.
- ❖ Indicate supplier confirmations by changing the kanban order status to *confirmed by supplier (*or *goods dispatched*), and entering the confirmed quantity/date. If known, the supplied quantity can also be entered at this time.
- ❖ Print (or reprint) a ticket for a purchasing kanban.
- ❖ Delete a pending (empty) kanban.
- ❖ Identify kanbans with a *declined by supplier* status that need to be reassigned to another approved vendor.
- ❖ Identify or change the sort type associated with a kanban (if specified) to support sequencing or grouping of purchasing/receiving activities. This field is not shown in Figure 3.10.
- ❖ Assign a different approved vendor to a purchasing kanban.
- ❖ Select (mark) and receive a confirmed kanban.

The form does not display received kanbans because they do not require further action. Kanbans with a received status (and any other status) can be viewed on the Manual Kanban Update form; this form supports all of the above-mentioned buyer actions except the last two.

**Stop/Go Board**   Various graphical formats are typically used for coordinating purchasing kanbans, and one format is included with out-of-the-box functionality. The Kanban Stop/Go Board form (aka Stop/Go Board) provides a graphical representation of all purchasing kanbans currently in circulation, with grouping based on the assigned kanban policy for Kanban Display Group. Each kanban order is displayed as an icon on the Stop/Go

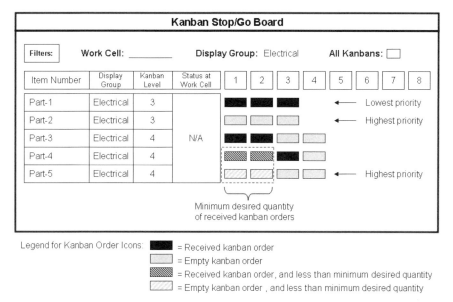

Figure 3.11  Example of the Stop/Go Board for Purchasing Kanbans

Board, with a color that designates current status such as received and empty.[7] The display information is constantly being refreshed with the latest status changes, thereby providing an up-to-date visualization. Figure 3.11 displays an example of a Stop/Go Board for purchasing kanbans for items that represent electrical parts.

Two kanban policies impact the effectiveness of the Stop/Go Board for visualizing the status of fixed purchasing kanbans:  the Kanban Display Group and the Minimum Quantity.

❖ *Kanban Display Group.*  The effectiveness of the Stop/Go Board can be increased by the assignment of a user-defined Kanban Display Group as one of the kanban policies.  For example, the Kanban Display Groups could reflect the types of purchased material, such as electrical and fabricated parts.
❖ *Minimum Desired Quantity of Received Kanbans.*  The minimum inventory quantity only provides reference information for visualization purposes, where the colored icons are shown with hash marks to indicate the minimum quantity. The minimum is typically expressed in multiples of the normal kanban quantity. Figure 3.11 displays the minimum desired quantity for two different items. Each item has a minimum quantity that corresponds to twice its normal kanban quantity, so that two icons are displayed with hash marks.

---

[7] The icon colors for each kanban order status are defined on the Kanban Parameters form.

## Variations in Using Fixed Purchasing Kanbans

The variations include direct delivery to a floor stock area and customer supplied material, as described below. Additional variations are explained later in this chapter's section "Variations in Using Fixed Kanbans," such as reporting scrap, barcode scans for reporting receipts, and temporary kanbans.

**Delivery of a Purchasing Kanban to a Floor Stock Area**   Delivery of a purchasing kanban can be to a floor stock area (rather than a stockroom), as defined by the warehouse in its kanban policies. However, a purchasing kanban cannot be directly received into a floor stock warehouse designated as a black hole, since this would create problems in accounting for the purchase. A later section, "Floor Stock Management Approaches," provides further explanation of black hole warehouses.

**Handling Customer Supplied Material via Fixed Kanbans**   When handing customer supplied material via fixed kanbans, you can indicate the customer identifier as part of the kanban policies. For example, the kanban policy that specifies the customer number would be assigned to newly created kanbans.

# Fixed Replenishment Kanbans (for Component Picking Purposes)

Replenishment kanbans are used for component picking purposes so that floor stock inventory is replenished from the stockroom or from other floor stock areas. In contrast, PTO replenishment kanbans are used for component picking purposes and for shipping purposes, as described in Chapters 6 and 7 respectively. For example, the PTO replenishment kanbans can reflect component picking for producing a fixed manufacturing kanban.

An explanation of fixed replenishment kanbans can be segmented into three basic topics: the policies for creating a kanban, the life cycle for a kanban, and the related coordination tools. Several attributes determine the nature of a fixed replenishment kanban, and these attributes are inherited when you initially create the kanban order. Figure 3.12 summarizes the policies for creating a fixed replenishment kanban. Most of the kanban order attributes are inherited from its kanban policies. An item number and warehouse comprise the key fields for defining kanban policies, whereas a kanban order number uniquely identifies each kanban. The critical kanban polices are described below, along with the related prerequisite information.

# Fixed Kanbans 43

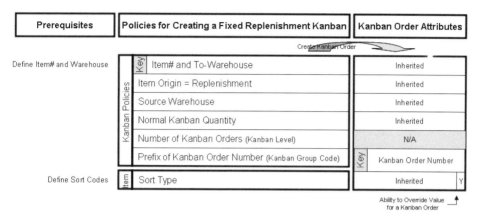

Figure 3.12  Policies for Creating a Fixed Replenishment Kanban

## Policies for Creating a Fixed Replenishment Kanban

Kanban policies are defined for an item number and warehouse using the Kanbans form. In the context of Scenario #1, for example, the replenishment kanban policies would be defined for moving the item "Item #10" from the "Stockroom" to a "Floor Stock Area" warehouse. An alternative approach to defining kanban policies involves the use of a kanban template, as described later in the section "Variations in Using Fixed Kanbans."

**Item Information**   The critical item information includes the inventory unit of measure and an active standard cost record by site. An active standard cost record must be defined for two sites when the warehouses reflect two AX sites.

**Item Origin**   The item origin is designated as replenished; it does not matter what item type (item or BOM) is assigned to the item.

**Source Warehouse**   The source warehouse is typically a stockroom or a floor stock area. For example, a completed item may be stocked at the producing cell, and transferred to a relevant floor stock area as needed.

**Normal Kanban Quantity and Number of Kanbans (Kanban Level)**
The normal kanban quantity and number of kanbans (termed *kanban level*) will be used to initially generate the kanbans. After initial generation, you can incrementally increase the policy concerning the number of kanbans, and generate additional kanban orders. The number of fixed kanbans can be calculated for an item and warehouse, as explained earlier in this chapter's section "S&OP Approaches for Fixed Kanbans."

**Prefix of the Kanban Order Number (Kanban Group Code)** A meaningful prefix provides several advantages in viewing and using kanban order numbers. The prefix typically represents the responsibility for the kanbans, but it may be used for other segmentation purposes. When you create kanban orders, the system automatically assigns the user-defined prefix and a counter to the kanban order numbers.

You can optionally change the prefix for all related kanbans in circulation, which also results in a new counter for each kanban order. This also changes the prefix in the kanban policies.

Note: The Record Id is a system-assigned internal identifier that uniquely identifies a kanban order, and is used for barcode scanning of transactions.

**Sort Type** The sort type is an optional attribute for a kanban order, and can be used for grouping or sequencing the replenishment kanbans. The sort types are user-defined, and assigned to items using the Item Sort Type form.

**Lead Time** The lead time for a replenishment kanban is always assumed to be zero. This lead time consideration is not displayed in Figure 3.12.

**Ability to Override the Attribute Value for a Kanban Order** Most attributes of a fixed replenishment kanban order cannot be overridden. The sort type can be overridden. As noted above, you can optionally change the prefix for all related kanbans in circulation, which also results in a new counter for each kanban order number.

**Example Ticket for a Fixed Replenishment Kanban** The example shown in Figure 3.13 includes the bar-coded information about the Record Id and Item Number, which are used to support scanned receipt transactions.

Figure 3.13 Example Ticket for a Fixed Replenishment Kanban

# Fixed Kanbans 45

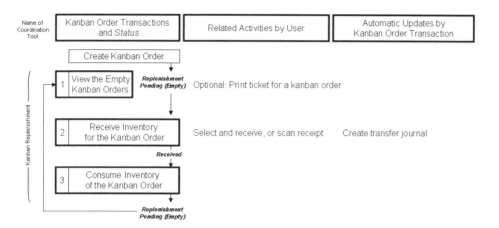

Figure 3.14    Life Cycle for a Fixed Replenishment Kanban

## Life Cycle of a Fixed Replenishment Kanban

A fixed replenishment kanban has a life cycle represented by a status, and the status is closely related to kanban order transactions. In its simplest form, a *replenishment pending* status represents an empty kanban and the requirement to move inventory. Receiving the kanban will automatically update the status to *received*, and consumption of its inventory will automatically update the status back to *replenishment pending*. Figure 3.14 summarizes the kanban order transactions and status, as well as related user activities and automatic updates. Figure 3.14 depicts the kanban order status using italics, and highlights use of the Kanban Replenishment form as a coordination tool.

**Prerequisite Step: Create a Kanban Order**    You create a replenishment kanban order using the Kanbans form, and it inherits the policies described in Figure 3.12. A newly created kanban has a *replenishment pending* status; it can be termed *replenishment pending (empty)* status to emphasize the empty status.

**Step 1: View the Empty Kanban Orders**    An empty kanban represents a requirement to move inventory from one warehouse to another warehouse.

**Step 2: Receive Inventory for a Kanban Order**    The receipt can be reported via barcode scanning, or by entering data on the Replenishment Kanban form. A fixed kanban can only be received once; you cannot record multiple partial receipts.

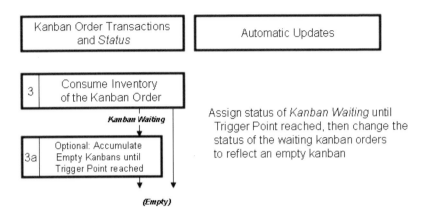

Figure 3.15 Accumulate Empty Kanbans Until Trigger Point Reached

**Step 3: Consume Inventory of a Kanban Order** The inventory associated with a replenishment kanban (for component picking purposes) is normally placed in a floor stock area. This kanban inventory can be consumed by component backflushing or an explicit kanban empty transaction, as described in a subsequent section "Floor Stock Management Approaches."

**Optional Step 3a: Accumulate Empty Kanbans until a Trigger Point Has Been Reached** Some scenarios will accumulate empty kanbans to reach a critical mass prior to communicating the requirement to replenish inventory at the point of use. A trigger point policy defines the desired number of empty kanbans that need to be accumulated. These empty kanbans will be automatically assigned a *kanban waiting* status until the trigger point has been reached, and then the status will be automatically changed to *replenishment pending*. If needed, you can also manually change the status from kanban waiting to replenishment pending (using the Manual Kanban Update form). Figure 3.15 illustrates the key difference in the life cycle of a fixed replenishment kanban.

**Coordination Tools for Fixed Replenishment Kanbans**

The primary coordination tools consist of the Kanban Replenishment form and the printed kanban tickets. The Kanban Replenishment form displays the kanbans requiring transfers from one warehouse to another. In particular, the form displays upcoming requirements for kanban replenishment, and is used to record actual kanban receipts. As illustrated in Figure 3.16, filters can help focus attention on kanbans for a specified warehouse, with near-term requirement dates, or with a printed status.

Fixed Kanbans   47

| Kanban Replenishment Form ||||||||||
| --- | --- | --- | --- | --- | --- | --- | --- | --- | --- |
| | | Filters: | From Warehouse | To Warehouse | | Days Ahead Horizon | | Printed Status | |
| | | | Stockroom | | | 3 | | All | |
| Inventory Available | Mark | Kanban Order Number | Item Number | From Warehouse | Deliver To Warehouse | Quantity Ordered | Required Date | Quantity Received | Printed | Kanban Order Status |
| Yes | ☐ | RON_000202 | Part-15 | Stockroom | Work Cell A | 10 | 07/07/20XX | | Yes | Replenishment Pending |
| Yes | ☐ | RON_000545 | Part-15 | Stockroom | Work Cell A | 10 | 07/07/20XX | | Yes | Replenishment Pending |
| No | ☐ | RON_000310 | Part-3 | Stockroom | Work Cell A | 25 | 07/08/20XX | | Yes | Replenishment Pending |
| Yes | ☐ | RON_000450 | Part-22 | Stockroom | Work Cell A | 50 | 07/06/20XX | | Yes | Replenishment Pending |
| Yes | ☐ | WES_000010 | Part-17 | Stockroom | Work Cell B | 100 | 07/09/20XX | | No | Replenishment Pending |
| Yes | ☐ | WES_000010 | Part-101 | Stockroom | Work Cell B | 10 | 07/07/20XX | | Yes | Replenishment Pending |

⌣ Data can be entered or changed

No change is needed for kanban order status

Figure 3.16  Example of the Kanban Replenishment Form

The primary responsibility for replenishment kanbans can be indicated by the prefix of the kanban order number, as exemplified by RON and WES for the kanban order numbers in Figure 3.16. The responsibility could also be associated with a warehouse. Typical actions using the Kanban Replenishment form include the following:

❖ Print (or reprint) a replenishment kanban ticket.
❖ Change the quantity ordered or the confirmed quantity.
❖ Identify replenishment kanbans with a past-due required date.
❖ Identify the sort type associated with a kanban (if specified) to support sequencing or grouping of replenishment activities. This field is not shown in Figure 3.16.
❖ Identify replenishment kanbans that have not yet been printed.
❖ Identify replenishment kanbans with required dates within a days ahead horizon.
❖ Identify availability of the from-warehouse inventory for a replenishment kanban, as shown in the far left column of Figure 3.16. An icon (a green hand or a red hand) communicates the same information about inventory availability.
❖ Select (mark) and receive a replenishment kanban.

The form does not display received kanbans because they do not require further action, nor does it support deletion of an empty kanban. Kanbans with the received status (and any other status) can be viewed on the Manual Kanban Update form. This form also supports deletion of an empty replenishment kanban.

## Fixed Manufacturing Kanban

An explanation of fixed manufacturing kanbans can be segmented into three basic topics: the policies for creating a kanban, the life cycle for a kanban, and the related coordination tools. An additional topic involves component backflushing, as covered in the section "Floor Stock Management Approaches." Several attributes determine the nature of a fixed manufacturing kanban, and these attributes are inherited when you initially create the kanban, as summarized in Figure 3.17. Most of the kanban order attributes are inherited from its kanban policies. An item number and warehouse comprise the key fields for uniquely identifying kanban policies, whereas a kanban order number uniquely identifies each kanban. The critical kanban polices are described below, along with the related prerequisite information.

### Policies for Creating a Fixed Manufacturing Kanban

Kanban policies are defined for an item number and warehouse using the Kanbans form. In the context of Scenario #1, for example, the manufacturing kanban policies would be defined for the item "End Item A1" and the "Finished Goods" warehouse. An alternative approach to defining kanban policies involves the use of a kanban template, as described in the section "Variations in Using Fixed Kanbans."

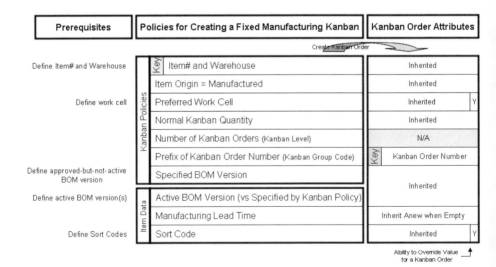

Figure 3.17 Policies for Creating a Fixed Manufacturing Kanban

**Item Information** The critical item information includes the inventory unit of measure, an approved and active BOM version by site, an active standard cost record by site, the item's manufacturing lead time, and item-related text. The printed kanban ticket can optionally include item-related or BOM-related text, which must be expressed as a note document for internal purposes.[8]

**Item Origin** An origin of manufacture can only be assigned to manufactured items (with item type of BOM).

**Work Cell** The work cell assigned to a manufacturing kanban must be predefined. One work cell policy identifies the calendar assigned to the work cell. The assigned calendar defines the working days (and working hours) and non-working days for the work cell.

A second work cell policy determines how manufacturing kanban receipts will be handled by traditional AX functionality. A manufacturing kanban receipt can be handled with an orderless approach (via a BOM Journal) or an order-based approach (via a production order). These approaches apply to detailed tracking and general tracking of floor stock inventory, as described in the section "Floor Stock Management Approaches." Other work cell policies only apply to a lean order schedule, as described in Chapter 10.

A manufacturing kanban order supports coordination of production activities, but it does not support cost accumulation for actual costing purposes. When order-based costing is required, each receipt of a manufacturing kanban can automatically generate an associated production order (based on the work cell policy described above). The autodeduction of components (and routing data) for this production order supports the actual costing capabilities within AX.

**Normal Kanban Quantity and Number of Kanbans (Kanban Level)**
The normal kanban quantity and number of kanbans (termed *kanban level*) will be used to initially generate the kanbans. After initial generation, you can incrementally increase the policy concerning the number of kanbans, and generate additional kanban orders. The number of fixed kanbans can be calculated for an item and warehouse, as previously explained in the section "S&OP Approaches for Fixed Kanbans."

**Prefix of the Kanban Order Number (Kanban Group Code)** A meaningful prefix provides several advantages in viewing and using kanban order numbers. The prefix typically represents the planner responsibility for

---

[8] The type of note document can be user defined, and you specify this user-defined type as the company-wide basis for item text (on the Kanban Parameters form).

the kanbans, but it may be used for other segmentation purposes. When you create kanban orders, the system automatically assigns the user-defined prefix and a counter to the kanban order numbers.

You can optionally change the prefix for all related kanbans in circulation, which also results in a new counter for each kanban order. This also changes the prefix in the kanban policies.

Note: The Record Id is a system-assigned internal identifier that uniquely identifies the kanban, and is used to support barcode scanning of transactions.

**Specified BOM Version Versus Active BOM Version**   A newly created fixed manufacturing kanban normally inherits the item's active BOM version as of the creation date.[9] However, you can specify use of a different BOM version as part of the kanban policies. It must be predefined, typically as an approved-but-not-active BOM version. The inherited BOM version will stay with a manufacturing kanban order. In order to assign a different BOM version, you must delete the kanban order(s) and create new kanbans with the desired BOM version.

The components within the inherited BOM version define the basis for component backflushing at the time of kanban receipt. The nature of component backflushing depends on the desired option for floor stock management, as described in this chapter's section "Floor Stock Management Approaches." The desired option determines whether backflushing applies to the components' quantities or values, or whether there is no backflushing.

**Manufacturing Lead Time**   The item's manufacturing lead time is used to calculate the future *required date* for an empty kanban. When the lead time is 10 days, for example, and today's inventory consumption results in an empty kanban, the kanban's required date will be 10 days from today's date. The same logic applies to an empty kanban that is newly created as of today's date.

An item's manufacturing lead time can be specified as a company-wide policy (as part of the item's default order settings for inventory), or as part of the item's site-specific order settings.[10] It typically represents the frequency of delivery and the elapsed time to produce an average lot size. For

---

[9] A manufactured item can have multiple active BOM versions that reflect different sites, non-overlapping validity periods, and/or different quantity breakpoints. The active BOM version assigned to a newly created manufacturing kanban ticket will reflect the creation date and the normal kanban quantity. Other scenarios apply to BOM versions with quantity breakpoints, such as a specified kanban quantity for creating a temporary kanban ticket, or the sales order quantity for creating a PTO manufacturing kanban ticket.

[10] An alternate approach to specifying an item's company-wide lead time could be based on the kanban lead time field on the item master. While it appears that a policy (termed the *kanban lead time* checkbox on the Kanban Parameters form) could activate logic that would use this value, my testing indicates it is not currently supported for purchasing kanbans or manufacturing kanbans.

example, daily deliveries may be modeled with a manufacturing lead time of 1 day. A fixed manufacturing kanban will inherit the item's manufacturing lead time each time it is emptied.

**Sort Type**   The sort type is an optional attribute for a kanban order, and can be used for grouping or sequencing the replenishment kanbans. The sort types are user-defined, and assigned to items using the Item Sort Type form.

**Ability to Override the Attribute Value for a Kanban**   Some attributes of a fixed manufacturing kanban can be overridden, such as simply changing the sort type. You can also temporarily assign a different work cell to a manufacturing kanban; it reverts to the normal work cell after the fixed kanban has been emptied. As noted above, you can optionally change the prefix for all related kanbans in circulation.

**Example Ticket for a Fixed Manufacturing Kanban**   The example shown in Figure 3.18 includes the bar-coded information about the Record Id and Item Number, which are used to support scanned receipt transactions. The printed information can include the optional text, which can be item-

Figure 3.18  Example Ticket for a Fixed Manufacturing Kanban

related or BOM-related text.[11] The printed ticket can also include optional information about the components of the manufactured item.[12]

## Life Cycle for a Fixed Manufacturing Kanban

A fixed manufacturing kanban has a life cycle represented by a status, and the status is closely related to kanban order transactions. In its simplest form, an *internal order* status represents an empty kanban and the requirement to produce the item at the work cell. Receiving the kanban will automatically update the status to *received*, and inventory consumption of the kanban order will automatically update the status back to *internal order*. Figure 3.19 summarizes the kanban order transactions and status, and the related user activities and automatic updates. It depicts the kanban order status using italics, and also highlights use of the Kanban Manufacturing form as a coordination tool.

**Prerequisite Step: Create a Kanban Order**  You create a manufacturing kanban order using the Kanbans form, and it inherits the policies described in Figure 3.17. A newly created kanban has an *internal order* status; it can be termed *internal order (empty)* status to emphasize the empty status.

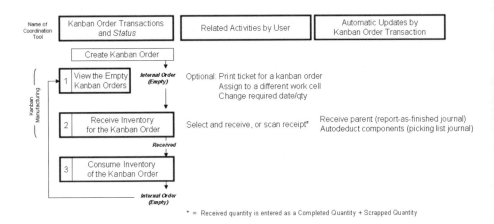

Figure 3.19  Life Cycle for a Fixed Manufacturing Kanban

---

[11] A company-wide policy (specified on the Kanban Parameters form) determines what type of text will be printed on a manufactured kanban.

[12] A company-wide policy (specified on the Kanban Parameters form) determines whether component information will be printed, and the number of BOM levels that will be printed.

**Step 1: View the Empty Kanban Orders** An empty kanban represents a requirement to produce the item at the work cell. You can optionally print or delete the kanban order, temporarily assign it to a different work cell, or change the required date/quantity.

**Step 2: Receive Inventory for a Kanban Order** The receipt can be reported via barcode scanning, or by entering data on the Manufacturing Kanban form. The received quantity is reported as a completed quantity plus a scrapped quantity. A fixed kanban can only be received once; you cannot record multiple partial receipts. Receipts provide the basis for takt time metrics, as described in the Chapter 5 section "Takt Time Metrics for a Work Cell."

An additional step may be necessary to end the production order associated with a manufacturing kanban receipt. This step is only necessary when the work cell policy for handling kanban receipts will result in a production order with a finished status.

The impact of a receipt on inventory transactions will depend on the floor stock management approach, as described in this chapter's section "Floor Stock Management Approaches." The right side of Figure 3.19 displays the inventory transactions based on a detailed tracking approach. When the work cell policy for receipt transactions is based on a production order (rather a BOM journal), the user will need to perform a follow-up step to end the production order.

**Step 3: Consume Inventory of a Kanban Order** A manufacturing kanban may be for an end item or for a manufactured component (as illustrated in Scenario #1a) with different approaches to inventory consumption. Sales order shipments normally consume inventory of the end item's kanban orders. The manufacturing kanban orders for a manufactured component are normally placed in a floor stock area. This kanban inventory can be consumed by component backflushing or an explicit kanban empty transaction, as described in this chapter's section "Floor Stock Management Approaches."

**Optional Step 3a: Accumulate Empty Kanbans until a Trigger Point Has Been Reached** Some scenarios will accumulate empty kanbans to reach a critical mass prior to communicating the requirement to replenish inventory at the point of use. For example, the work cell's optimal batch size may require multiple kanbans. A trigger point policy defines the desired number of empty kanbans that need to be accumulated. These empty kanban will be automatically assigned a *kanban waiting* status until the trigger point has been reached, and then the status will be automatically changed to *replenishment pending.* If needed, you can also manually change the status from kanban waiting to replenishment pending (using the Manual Kanban Update form). Figure 3.15 illustrated the key difference in the life cycle of a fixed kanban.

## Coordination Tools for Fixed Manufacturing Kanbans

The primary coordination tools include a list format (the Kanban Manufacturing form), a graphical format (the Stop/Go Board), and the printed kanban tickets. The takt time metrics also provide a coordination tool, as described in the Chapter 5 section "Takt Time Metrics for a Work Cell."

**Kanban Manufacturing**  This form displays the manufacturing kanbans requiring action by the planner. In particular, the planner can review upcoming requirements for kanban deliveries, and record actual receipt of a kanban. As illustrated in Figure 3.20, a filter can help focus attention on kanbans for a specified work center.

The Kanban Manufacturing displays one of the takt time metrics for a specified work cell: the required takt time. The Takt Time Board displays all of the metrics. The required takt time (express in minutes) reflects the remaining minutes within today's working hours divided by the remaining units within today's schedule. The example in Figure 3.20 shows 5.90 minutes per unit. It is continuously updated as time elapses, and as you report kanban receipts. In comparison to the target takt time, it indicates the work cell must run at a faster rate (or slower rate) to complete today's total scheduled quantity by end of working day. A comparison of 5.90 minutes to

### Kanban Manufacturing

Filter: **Work Cell** Work Cell A    Required Takt Time: 5.90 minutes

| Components Available | Mark | Kanban Order Number | Item Number | Deliver To Warehouse | Quantity Ordered | Required Date | Confirmed Quantity | Production Start Date | Sort Type | Kanban Order Status |
|---|---|---|---|---|---|---|---|---|---|---|
| Yes | ☐ | ANN_000020 | End Item A1 | Shipping Area | 10 | 07/07/20XX |  | 07/05/20XX | Large | Internal Order |
| Yes | ☐ | ANN_000021 | End Item A1 | Shipping Area | 10 | 07/08/20XX |  | 07/06/20XX | Large | Internal Order |
| No | ☐ | ANN_000219 | End Item A3 | Shipping Area | 10 | 07/08/20XX |  | 07/04/20XX |  | Internal Order |
| Yes | ☐ | ANN_000367 | End Item A2 | Shipping Area | 10 | 07/06/20XX |  | 07/02/20XX |  | Internal Order |
| Yes | ☐ | ANN_000422 | End Item A4 | Shipping Area | 25 | 07/09/20XX | 25 | 07/08/20XX | Small | Internal Order |
| Yes | ☐ | ANN_000595 | End Item A4 | Shipping Area | 10 | 07/07/20XX | 9 | 07/06/20XX | Small | Internal Order |

Data can be entered or changed — No change is needed for kanban order status

Figure 3.20  Example of the Kanban Manufacturing Form

a target takt time of 6.00 minutes per unit, for example, indicates the work cell must run at a slightly faster rate. Chapter 5 explains takt time metrics for a work cell.

The planner responsibility can be indicated by the kanban order number prefix, as exemplified by ANN for the kanban order numbers in Figure 3.20. The planner responsibility can also be associated with a work cell. The typical actions using the Kanban Manufacturing form include the following:

- Print (or reprint) a manufacturing kanban ticket.
- Delete an internal order (empty) kanban.
- Change the required date or quantity ordered.
- Identify manufacturing kanbans with a past-due required date.
- Identify the sort type associated with a kanban order (if specified) to support sequencing or grouping of manufacturing activities. The sort type for a kanban order can be manually overridden.
- View and/or assign the production start date, which initially reflects the required date minus the item's manufacturing lead time. The production start date represents reference information, and does not have any impact on system logic.
- Assign a different work cell to a manufacturing kanban.
- Identify component availability for a manufacturing kanban, as shown in the far left column of Figure 3.20. An icon (a green hand or a red hand) communicates the same information about component inventory availability.
- Use the Explode function to view component availability information in a single-level or multilevel bill of material format.
- Select and receive a manufacturing kanban, and report the actual quantity completed (and quantity scrapped, if applicable).[13]

The form does not display received kanbans because they do not require further action. Kanbans with the received status (and any other status) can be viewed on the Manual Kanban Update form; this form also supports the first four of the above-mentioned planner actions.

**Stop/Go Board for a Work Cell** A graphical format for coordinating manufacturing kanbans tends to be unique for every company, since the nature of the product and work cells can be different. An example of one graphical format is included with out-of-the-box functionality, but a customized format should be anticipated.

---

[13] As a general guideline, any scrapped inventory should be reported with the quantity completed, so that component backflushing is correctly calculated. The Scrap Kanban form can then be used to explicitly report the scrapped inventory quantity.

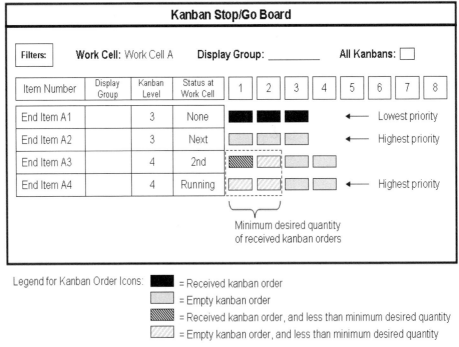

Figure 3.21 Example of the Stop/Go Board for Fixed Manufacturing Kanbans

The Kanban Stop/Go Board provides a graphical representation of all manufacturing kanbans that are currently in circulation, with grouping based on the work cell assigned to the kanban orders. Each kanban is displayed as an icon, with a color that designates current status such as received or empty.[14] The displayed information is constantly being refreshed with the latest status changes, thereby providing an up-to-date visualization. Figure 3.21 displays an example of the Stop/Go Board for a specified work cell.

A minimum inventory quantity can be specified as a kanban policy to help visualize the status of fixed manufacturing kanbans. The minimum inventory quantity only provides reference information for visualization purposes, where the icons are shown with hash marks to indicate the minimum quantity. The minimum is typically expressed in multiples of the kanban quantity.

---

[14] The icon colors for each kanban ticket status are defined on the Kanban Parameters form.

# Floor Stock Management Approaches

The inventory quantities associated with a component's kanbans are typically located in floor stock areas, where they can be used in production. These inventory quantities can be tracked on a detailed basis, a general basis, or not at all while still supporting pull signals via empty kanbans. In terms of maturity stages, a pilot project stage typically employs detailed or general tracking to support order-based costing, whereas the more mature stages employ no tracking while supporting value stream costing.

The three basic variations for managing floor stock inventory of component kanbans are summarized below.

- *Option #1: Detailed tracking with backflushing of component quantities.* Detailed tracking involves backflushing the components' inventory quantities (based on manufacturing kanban receipts) to calculate when a component's kanban order has been emptied. It can also support order-based costing.
- *Option #2: General tracking with backflushing of component value.* General tracking involves backflushing the component's value (not inventory quantities) to support order-based costing. This is termed the cost substitution concept. Since this approach does not consume component inventory, you must explicitly identify when a component's kanban order has been emptied.
- *Option #3: No tracking within black hole warehouses.* The component quantities in a black hole warehouse are not tracked, although you still identify when a kanban has been emptied and received. This option supports value stream costing as described in the chapter on lean accounting (Chapter 8).

A combination of detailed and general tracking may be used, so that some component quantities are backflushed while other components only have their value backflushed. The choice of a floor stock management option determines the impact of manufacturing kanban receipts, and use of the kanban empty transaction for floor stock components.

## Option #1: Detailed Tracking with Component Backflushing of Quantities

The receipt of a manufacturing kanban normally results in component backflushing based on the completed quantity and the inherited BOM version. Backflushing consumes the inventory of fixed kanban orders, as described in the life cycles for purchasing kanbans (Figure 3.5), replenishment kanbans (Figure 3.11), and manufacturing kanbans (Figure 3.16). Several considerations apply to component backflushing in floor stock areas.

## Inherited BOM Version of the Manufacturing Kanban Order
The inherited BOM version defines the components and their warehouse source (the floor stock area). It normally reflects the item's active BOM version but could be a specified BOM version, as described in the policies for creating a fixed manufacturing kanban (Figure 3.17) or a PTO manufacturing kanban (Figure 6.2).

## Work Cell Policy for Handling Manufacturing Kanban Receipts
A work cell policy determines how a manufacturing kanban receipt will be handled by the traditional AX functionality. It can be handled with an order-less approach (termed the BOM Journal) or a production order approach. Both approaches can trigger component backflushing, and both report the inventory consumption as a picking list journal. However, the production order approach supports order-based costing.

If you choose the production order approach (and order-based costing), then you also need to choose a company-wide policy that defines whether the resulting production order status should be finished or ended.[15] Most firms prefer the ended status to minimize additional user intervention. A resulting status of finished means an additional step must be performed to end each production order, but it also offers an opportunity to review information. Backflushing provides the basis for production order costing.[16]

## Receipt Quantity for a Manufacturing Kanban
The receipt can be reported as a completed quantity plus a scrapped quantity. However, only the completed quantity will trigger component backflushing.

## Work Cell Policy on How Receipts Will Backflush Planned Scrap
A work cell policy determines whether planned component scrap will be excluded from autodeduction when receiving a manufacturing kanban produced by the work cell. The planned scrap for a component can be expressed as a percentage and/or fixed amount, and is included in cost rollup calculations.[17]

---

[15] The company-wide policy is termed the Production Order Status field on the Kanban Parameters form.

[16] Additional backflushing considerations described in the AX 2009 book (pages 43 and 320-321) include the flushing principle assigned to items and components and the default values for update policies associated with the Report as Finished task for production orders (pages 304-307). The suggested flushing principle is *finish* (to support component backflushing), and the suggested update policies should be automatic BOM consumption based on the flushing principle.

[17] The explanation focuses on scrap related to components, since the baseline model of operations assumes routing data will not be used. When routing data is employed, a planned scrap percentage can also be expressed for a routing operation, which results in increased requirements for its related material components. An operation's scrap percentage also has a cumulative effect on previous operations in a multistep routing, and the system automatically calculates an accumulated scrap percentage for each operation.

When using production orders for handing manufacturing kanban receipts, the exclusion of planned scrap can result in favorable variances because it is included in standard cost calculations. For example, the exclusion of a component's planned scrap percentage will result in a favorable quantity variance because it appears that less material was used.

**Typical Problems with the Detailed Tracking Option**  Several types of problems impact the effectiveness of the detailed tracking option. In particular, identification of empty kanbans based on calculated consumption may not match the actual empty kanbans, and component backflushing can result in negative inventory for a component's kanban. The detailed tracking of inventory quantities for order-based costing purposes also represents waste. An alternative approach employs explicit reporting of empty kanbans to avoid these types of problems. It also employs backflushing of component value to support order-based costing. This alternative approach is covered next.

## Option #2: General Tracking with Component Backflushing of Value

General tracking means that empty kanbans in floor stock areas must be explicitly reported, since they will not be emptied through component backflushing of quantities. However, the cost substitution concept can be employed so that manufacturing kanban receipts will backflush the total value of components. This supports a simpler approach to order-based costing.

The cost substitution concept means that manufacturing kanban receipts must be handled as a production order so that the Production BOM can be automatically modified. The system automatically deletes designated components from the Production BOM, and adds a dummy item to the Production BOM with a quantity that represents the total value of designated components. This sleight of hand means that receipt of a manufacturing kanban can autodeduct the dummy item's quantity, thereby backflushing the equivalent value of components. The picking list journal (for the associated production order) contains the dummy item.

The cost substitution concept consists of two key aspects: define the dummy item used for cost substitution purposes, and designate which components will be considered for the cost substitution concept. It also involves several backflushing considerations.

**Define the Dummy Item Number Used for the Cost Substitution Concept**  You typically define the dummy item number as a service item with no tracking of physical or financial inventory (as defined in its inventory model group policies). You also define and activate a standard cost record of $1.00 for the item.

A critical step involves how to specify which item number should be used for cost substitution purposes. You can specify the dummy item as a company-wide policy, or as specific to an item group or item.[18] These three alternatives represent increasing levels of specificity, and the most specific alternative will be used as the basis for autodeducting equivalent value.

**Designate Components That Will Be Considered for the Cost Substitution Concept**  In order to backflush its equivalent value (rather than its inventory quantity), a component must be flagged as *exclude from backflush*. The special significance of this *exclude from backflush* field must be identified as a company-wide policy.[19] In some situations, a component's inventory quantity may need to be autodeducted so you should not designate the component as *exclude from backflush*.

Note: If you do not indicate the special significance of the component policy "exclude from backflush," then the component will not be backflushed and the cost substitution concept will not be used.

**Considerations about Backflushing Component Value**  The previously described considerations include the inherited BOM version of the manufacturing kanban order, the receipt quantity for a manufacturing kanban, and the work cell policy on how receipts will backflush planned scrap. The considerations also include the work cell policy for handling manufacturing kanban receipts, which should be a production order to support order-based costing.

## Option #3: No Inventory Tracking and Black Hole Warehouses

Inventory quantities are not tracked in a black hole warehouse, but you can still report received and empty kanbans to assist coordination. The policies concerning component backflushing and cost substitution do not apply.

The black hole concept is generally implemented by designating warehouses as a black hole, although it can also be implemented as a kanban policy for a specific item and warehouse. These two approaches are described below.

❖ *Warehouse Approach to Black Holes.* A warehouse designated as a black hole typically reflects the floor stock area for a work cell, so that you do

---

[18] The cost substitution item can be specified as a company-wide value (on the Lean Order Parameters form), an item group value (on the Item Group form), or an item-specific value (on the Item form). The choice depends on the need for tracking G/L account information.

[19] You designate the company-wide policy on the Lean Order Parameters form using two different fields. One field is termed *Cost Item backflushing;* the second field is termed *Lean Accounting*.

not track inventory through production. For example, you can use replenishment kanbans for transferring material into or out of a black hole warehouse. Within the black hole warehouses, the transactions related to manufacturing kanbans (such as kanban receipt and kanban empty) do not affect inventory balances.

Purchasing kanbans must be received into a normal warehouse, and sales order shipments must be from a normal warehouse, to support accounting purposes. Subcontract manufacturing also requires a normal warehouse for tracking inventory at the subcontractor.

* *Kanban Approach to Black Holes.* The kanban policies for a replenishment kanban can indicate a black hole for just the "destination warehouse," just the "source warehouse," or for both. The kanban approach to black holes is typically employed when a given warehouse must also support inventory tracking, so that the warehouse approach cannot be used.

The scenario shown in Figure 3.22 illustrates the black hole concept in a multilevel product.

### Scenario #1b: Multilevel Product and the Black Hole Concept

The scenario shown in Figure 3.22 illustrates the black hole concept in a multilevel product. It also highlights four key aspects of using black hole warehouses, as numbered in the figure and described below. The four aspects include receiving stocked items into a normal warehouse, transferring these to a floor stock area designated as a black hole warehouse, reporting received and empty kanbans within black hole warehouses, and transferring a completed end item out of a black hole warehouse.

1. *Receive stocked material into a normal warehouse.* The stocked material can be received against a purchase order, a purchasing kanban order, or any other supply order. A purchasing kanban must be received into a normal warehouse and then transferred into a black hole warehouse; it cannot be received directly into a warehouse designated as a black hole.
2. *Replenishment kanban received into a floor stock area designated as a black hole warehouse.* The receipt will reduce stockroom inventory of the kanban via an inventory journal, with an offsetting ledger entry for the value issued to work in process.
3. *Report receipts and empty kanbans within black hole warehouses.* The receipt only updates the kanban order status for coordination purposes; it does not impact inventory balances or ledger transactions.

4. *Report transfers from a black hole warehouse into a normal warehouse.* In this scenario, the transfer reflects a PTO replenishment kanban that pulls completed end items to a shipping area (a normal warehouse) from the black hole warehouse. The receipt will increase the finished goods inventory of the end item's manufacturing kanban (via the report as finished journal).

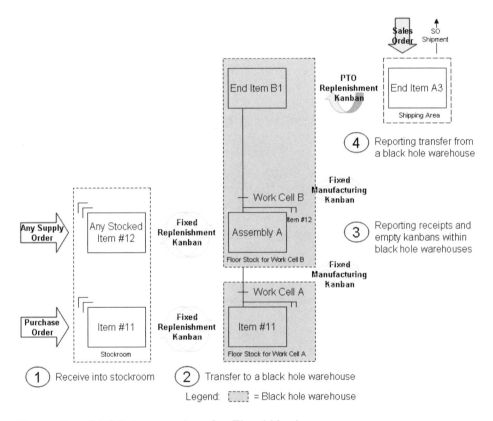

Figure 3.3 S&OP Approaches for Fixed Kanbans

## Summarizing the Impact of Floor Stock Management Approaches

The floor stock management approach determines the impact of manufacturing kanban receipts, and use of the kanban empty transaction for floor stock components. It also reflects a choice of order-based costing versus value stream costing. The life cycle for a manufacturing kanban provides one way to summarize the impact, as illustrated in Figure 3.23 and described below.

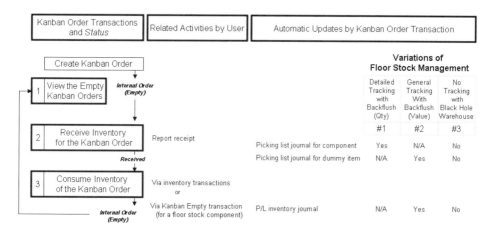

Figure 3.23 Summarizing the Impact of Floor Stock Management Approaches

The previously described life cycle steps for a manufacturing kanban (see Figure 3.19) focused on detailed tracking of component floor stock inventory. This represented an example of Option #1, where a manufacturing kanban receipt generates a report-as-finished journal for the parent item, and a picking list journal for the backflushed components. Figure 3.23 displays this impact for Option #1. The general tracking approach with backflushing of the component value (Option #2) generates a picking list journal for the dummy item. Option #3 employs no tracking of inventory quantities, and therefore generates no accounting entries.

In terms of reporting consumption, the Kanban Empty transaction only applies to component kanbans in floor stock areas, and only when the floor stock management option involves general tracking or no tracking.

## Managing Engineering Changes When Using Fixed Kanbans

The ability to manage changes is critical, especially when you embrace a philosophy of continuous improvements. The following topics represent engineering changes and other changes that need to be managed.

### Initial Cutover for Using Fixed Kanbans

The kanban policy for an active status provides one approach to support an initial cutover, since you can create fixed kanbans with an inactive status and then change the status to active at the cutover time. The intent of an inactive status is that the newly created kanbans will not appear on the kanban coordination tools. An additional intent is that you can manage replenishment with traditional supply orders (for the designated item and warehouse) prior to cutover.

## New Items and Obsolete Items

Some limitations may apply to new items or obsolete items, such as limiting the ability to purchase or produce an item. Two item-related policies will limit kanban transactions: a stopped flag for purchases and a stopped flag for inventory transactions. The item's stopped flag for purchases will prevent creation of a blanket purchase order, and prevent reporting of kanban receipts. The stopped flag for inventory transactions will prevent reporting of any kanban receipts and consumption.

## Managing Ongoing Changes for Fixed Kanbans

Ongoing changes are often driven by a philosophy of continuous improvement, such as changes to purchasing and manufacturing practices, or changes to factory layout. Each change requires slightly different considerations.

**Change in Lead Time** A change to an item's lead time will be inherited by the next empty kanban, which is used to calculate its required date.

**Change in the Preferred Vendor for a Purchasing Kanban** You can assign a different preferred vendor (with an associated blanket PO) to the kanban policy, and also to existing kanbans. The assigned vendor stays with the kanban order.

**Changes to Other Inherited Attributes of a Kanban** Changes to the following attributes must be implemented by deleting the existing-and-empty kanbans (that inherited the old value) and then creating new kanbans (that will inherit the new value). If deletion of existing-but-not-empty kanbans is desired, you can scrap the kanban inventory before deletion, and then reload the inventory for the new kanbans (via the P/L journal).

- *Change in the Normal Kanban Quantity*
- *Change in the Item Origin.* As an alternative, a manufacturing kanban can be temporarily changed to a subcontract manufacturing kanban.
- *Change in the Work Cell for a Manufacturing Kanban.* As an alternative, a manufacturing kanban can be temporarily assigned to a different work cell.

❖ *Change in the BOM Version for a Manufacturing Kanban.* The new version can reflect the item's active BOM Version or the kanban policy for a specified BOM version.

**Changes to Component Information in a BOM Version**   Changes to the component information typically require a change to the kanbans associated with the components.

❖ Add/delete Components to the BOM Version
❖ Change Quantity of a Component
❖ Change Planned Scrap for a Component
❖ Change the Warehouse Source of a Component
❖ Change a Component's Autodeduction Policy

**Change in the Planning Bill for Forecasting a Product Family**
The changes typically represent adjustments to mix percentages due to changing demand patterns, or to additions/deletions of items within the product family. A common solution approach is to create a new planning bill (aka a new *item allocation key*), which can then be specified for sales forecasting purposes. Alternatively, you can modify the existing planning bill.

# Variations in Using Fixed Kanbans

A wide variety of lean scenarios can be addressed by out-of-the-box functionality for fixed kanbans. Some of the variations described in this section include the use of kanban templates, intermittent subcontracting, temporary kanbans, and scrap reporting. Chapter 10 describes additional variations to the baseline model of operations described in Chapter 1, such as the use of bin locations within a warehouse and quality orders.

## Kanban Templates for Fixed Kanbans

The template concept provides an alternative to defining fixed kanban policies for each item and warehouse. It only applies to fixed replenishment kanbans and manufacturing kanbans. It does not apply to purchasing kanbans because each one requires a unique blanket purchase order. For example, a template might be used for similar components that must be pulled to a work cell area from a stockroom, or for similar manufactured items produced at a work cell. The template concept consists of a dummy item and its associated kanban template for a destination warehouse, and the assignment of this dummy item to the relevant item numbers. Using the template concept involves the following three steps.

1. *Define a Dummy Item on the Item Master.* The identifier and description should clearly indicate the item's purpose for a kanban template. As an example for a manufacturing kanban, the description could be "kanban template for producing manufactured items at work cell A and placing them in the finished goods warehouse." The dummy item will require the minimal information about an inventory unit of measure, an inventory model group, and item group. However, none of this information applies to its usage as a kanban template. The dummy item can be assigned a stopped flag for inventory transactions.
2. *Define the Kanban Policies for the Dummy Item Using the Kanban Template Form.* The kanban policies are defined for the dummy item and destination warehouse (such as the floor stock area) using the Kanban Template form. These policies were previously summarized for a replenishment kanban and manufacturing kanban, and the same policies are defined on the Kanban Template. As an example for a manufacturing kanban template, you would specify the item origin (manufactured), the destination warehouse (finished goods), the normal kanban quantity, and an active status.
3. *Assign the Dummy Item to Relevant Items.* The dummy item is assigned to relevant items using the field labeled *Kanban Template Group*.

The kanban policies associated with the dummy item will apply to all assigned items, such as the same prefix for kanban ticket identifiers, the same policy for the normal kanban quantity, and the number of kanbans.

## Intermittent Subcontract Manufacturing for a Normally Manufactured Item

A fixed manufacturing kanban reflects an item that is normally manufactured at an internal work cell. In some situations, the item may need to be manufactured by a subcontractor on an intermittent basis, which requires a temporary conversion to a subcontract manufacturing kanban. You can convert to subcontracting on the Kanban Manufacturing form, which represents an optional life cycle step as illustrated in the Figure 3.24. As part of this step, you indicate the desired subcontractor and the outside operation component, and the warehouse associated with the subcontractor. You can optionally specify a different BOM version defining the supplied components, since the components may differ from those used in internal manufacturing. The supplied components can then be sent to the subcontractor, and the parent item received as a manufacturing kanban. Chapter 4 provides more detailed explanations of using manufacturing kanbans with subcontract manufacturing.

# Fixed Kanbans

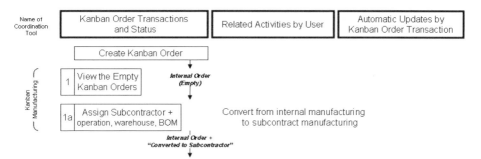

Figure 3.24 Convert a Fixed Manufacturing Kanban to Subcontracting (Discrete Kit)

## Temporary Fixed Kanbans

Temporary fixed kanbans (termed *temporary kanbans* for short) provide an alternative approach for modeling a one-time demand spike or a period of higher demand. They can be created for all types of fixed kanbans—such as purchasing, replenishment, manufacturing and subcontract manufacturing—using the Kanbans form.[20]

The key characteristic is an ending validity date, so that a temporary kanban will be automatically deleted when its inventory has been completely consumed (emptied) after its ending validity date. The ending validity date supports two conceptual variations of temporary kanbans, which can be termed the one-time usage approach and the validity-period usage approach.

❖ *One-time usage of a temporary kanban.* A newly created temporary kanban has an ending validity date equal or prior to today's date, so that it is only used once. It will be automatically deleted after being emptied. This approach is typically used in conjunction with fixed kanbans to model an anticipated spike in demand, because it avoids the problem of creating additional fixed kanbans that must be manually deleted.

❖ *Validity-period usage of a temporary kanban.* A newly created temporary kanban has an ending validity date in the future, such as the last day of a monthly period. The kanban will be used throughout the validity period just like a fixed kanban, and then automatically deleted when emptied after the ending validity date. This approach is typically used in conjunction with fixed kanbans to model a period of higher demand. Alternatively, it can be used without fixed kanbans so that the temporary kanbans represent the entire demand for the period.

---

[20] A temporary kanban cannot be created for fixed kanbans with a kanban policy of *dynamic*, since this indicates that the number of kanbans will be calculated (rather than manually increased with temporary kanbans). A separate section deals with calculating the number of fixed kanbans.

The ending validity date can be manually overridden on each temporary kanban. For example, you may initially create a temporary kanban with today's date as the ending validity date, and then change it to a future date. Hence, the two conceptual variations provide a simplification for explanatory purposes.

In addition to an ending validity date, a temporary kanban differs slightly from a fixed kanban in terms of its creation policies and its life cycle. These two differences are summarized below.

### Differences in Kanban Policies for Creating Temporary Kanbans

The kanban policies for creating a fixed kanban have been described elsewhere for purchasing (see Figure 3.6), replenishment (Figure 3.12), manufacturing (Figure 3.17), and subcontract manufacturing (Figure 4.2). The differences in kanban policies for creating temporary kanbans are summarized in Figure 3.25 and described below.

After defining the kanban policies for a fixed kanban, you can define the additional fields concerning creation of temporary kanbans. The three additional fields include the following:

❖ *Temporary Kanban Quantity*. The value initially defaults to the normal kanban quantity but it can be overridden.
❖ *Number of Temporary Kanbans*. The desired number of kanbans will be created.

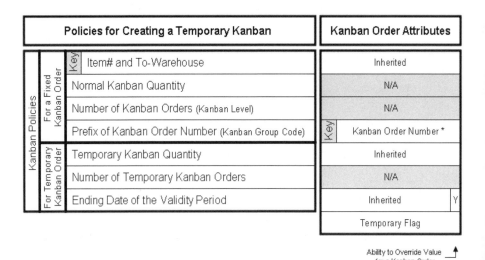

Figure 3.25  Policies for Creating a Temporary Kanban

❖ *Ending Date of the Validity Period.* The ending date should correspond to the concept of one-time usage (such as entering today's date) or validity-period usage (such as entering a future date). An additional field concerning the start date of the validity period can be entered, but it only provides reference information and has no impact on creating or using kanbans.[21] After creating a temporary kanban, you can manually override the ending validity date.

This information is used to create temporary kanbans after you click the *create kanban tickets* button. The identifier of the newly created kanban order number has a "t" included in the prefix, thereby signifying a temporary kanban. It is also identified on various forms by the checkbox for a temporary kanban, shown as a separate attribute in Figure 3.25 for the kanban order attributes.

You can incrementally create additional temporary kanbans by changing the value of the temporary kanban quantity and the ending validity date, and clicking the *create kanban tickets* button.

**Differences in the Life Cycle for a Temporary Kanban** A temporary kanban has the same life cycle as fixed kanban with one exception. It is automatically deleted when its inventory has been reported as consumed after the ending validity date. Hence, the concept of one-time usage means that a temporary kanban order is only used once, whereas the concept of validity-period usage means it will continue to be assigned an "empty" status after reporting consumption. Figure 3.26 summarizes this life cycle difference in comparison to the life cycles described elsewhere for purchasing (see Figure 3.8), replenishment (Figure 3.14), manufacturing (Figure 3.19), and subcontract manufacturing(Figure 4.4) kanbans. These other life cycles employ different terms for the empty status, such as pending, replenishment pending, and internal order.

In the special case where you have a temporary kanban with an empty status, and the passage of time goes beyond the ending validity date, you can chose to (1) fill the empty kanban or (2) manually delete the empty kanban. When you have many temporary kanbans in a similar situation, you can mass delete them using the Reorganize Kanban task.

---

[21] The fields for a starting and ending validity date can also be entered for a fixed kanban ticket, but they have no impact on system logic or the kanban ticket life cycle.

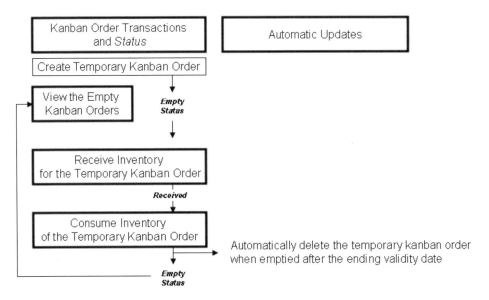

Figure 3.26 Life Cycle for a Temporary Kanban

**Coordination Tools for Temporary Kanbans**   The coordination tools for fixed kanbans also apply to temporary kanbans. For example, you would use the Manufacturing Kanban form and the Stop/Go Board to coordinate both types of kanbans, where the prefix of "t" in the kanban order number indicates a temporary kanban. Some firms view temporary kanbans as a higher priority than a fixed kanban.

## Barcode Scanning for Fixed Kanban Receipts

The barcode scanning approach employs the Record Id of the kanban being received, where the Record Id is printed on the kanban ticket as a value and as a barcode. There are two variations of the bar code scanning form. In one case, you merely enter the Record Id and confirm (or override) the quantity received. In the second case, you enter both the Record Id and the Item Number, and then confirm (or override) the quantity received. The second case can provide greater accuracy in reporting receipts. Figure 3.27 summarizes the two variations of the barcode scanning form. You cannot perform a bar code receipt when the kanban has been fully received.

## Reporting Scrap for a Fixed Kanban

The inventory for a fixed kanban (with a status of *received*) can be reported as partially or completely scrapped using the Kanban Quantity Adjustment

| Name of Form | Enter Information |
|---|---|
| Kanban Barcode Scanning | Enter the Record Id of Kanban Order<br>Confirm (or enter) quantity received |
| Kanban/Item Barcode Scanning | Enter the Record Id of Kanban Order<br>Enter the Item# for the Kanban Order<br>Confirm (or enter) quantity received |

Figure 3.27 Barcode Scanning for Fixed Kanbans Receipts

form or the Scrap Kanban form. It can also be completely scrapped using the Empty Kanban Barcode Scanning form. A final option is to report scrap with a negative quantity on a P/L inventory journal, which requires the user to specify the relevant kanban order number. These alternative methods for reporting scrap are also summarized in a subsequent section for Figure 3.28.

You report a completed quantity when entering a receipt for a manufacturing kanban; you can optionally enter an additional scrapped quantity. However, this scrapped quantity does not trigger component backflushing, it does not explicitly identify scrap for management reporting purposes, and it precludes the ability to report reusable scrap (as described in the next point). A general guideline is to receive all material as a completed quantity, and then explicitly report the scrapped quantity (if any).

The same guideline applies to receipts for fixed kanbans related to purchasing or replenishment. That is, receive all material and then explicitly report the scrapped quantity (if any).

## Reporting Reusable Scrap for a Fixed Kanban

Some situations allow usage of scrapped material, where the reusable scrap must be identified by a different item number. For example, different item numbers may represent different grades of material, so that regrading one item's inventory can be modeled by scrapping one item number and obtaining a different item number as reusable scrap. A plastic parts manufacturer, as a second example, may scrap a plastic part and then reuse the regrind in the next manufacturing batch. The concept of reusable scrap generally applies to a fixed manufacturing kanban rather than a fixed purchasing or replenishment kanban.

In order to employ the reusable scrap functionality for an item's kanbans, the item number must have a policy for *scrap replacement*.[22] This scrap replacement policy enables you to optionally identify a different item number as reusable scrap when you report scrap for a fixed kanban. You also identify the quantity and warehouse placement for the reusable scrap. This additional functionality only works when reporting scrap using the Scrap Kanban form, or using the Kanban Quantity Adjustment form to partially empty a kanban. The resulting inventory transactions reflect a quantity decrease for the scrapped item number, and a quantity increase for the item number specified as the reusable scrap. The reusable scrap is not assigned to a kanban.

## Alternative Methods for Reporting Inventory Consumption of Fixed Kanbans

Inventory of a fixed kanban is typically consumed by normal inventory transactions, such as sales order shipments, transfers, or component backflushing. However, the component backflushing transactions reflect an assumption about which kanbans get consumed. The assumption is based on the kanban order number, so that the lowest identifier for the kanban order number will be consumed first.

There are several alternative methods for explicitly reporting the inventory consumption of a fixed kanban, as summarized in Figure 3.28. For each method, the figure shows the name of the form and the information to be entered. Each method is described below.

- *Scrap Kanban form.* Use this form to completely empty a fixed kanban, thereby reducing inventory quantity via an inventory journal.
- *P/L Inventory Journal form.* Use this form to reduce (or increase) the inventory quantity for a specified kanban order number. This form provides the primary approach for initially loading the inventory for each kanban.
- *Kanban Quantity Adjustment form.* Use this form to completely or partially empty a fixed kanban, thereby reducing inventory quantity via an inventory journal. The same form can also be used to increase the inventory quantity by entering a negative quantity when partially emptying a kanban.
- *Empty Kanban Barcode Scanning form.* Use this form to report consumption against the Record Id of the fixed kanban; it will completely

---

[22] A company-wide policy on the Kanban Parameters form (termed the *Scrap Replacement in Use* checkbox) enables the *scrap replacement* field to be displayed on the item master.

|  | Name of Form | Enter Information |
|---|---|---|
| Normal | Normal inventory transactions consume the kanban order inventory (e.g., shipments, component backflushing) | The normal transactions will consume inventory based on a usage assumption of kanban order numbers |
| Manual Entry | Scrap Kanban (Completely Empty the Kanban Order) | Select the kanban order number |
| Manual Entry | P/L Inventory Journal | Enter the kanban order number Allocate qty change to a kanban order |
| Manual Entry | Kanban Quantity Adjustment (Partially Empty the Kanban Order) | Select the kanban order number Enter the quantity change Allocate qty change to a kanban order |
| Manual Entry | Kanban Quantity Adjustment (Completely Empty the Kanban Order) | Select the kanban order number |
| Scan | Empty Kanban Barcode Scanning (Completely Empty the Kanban Order) | Enter the Record ID of kanban order |

Figure 3.28  S&OP Approaches for Fixed Kanbans

empty the kanban. The Record Id is printed on the kanban ticket as a value and as a barcode. This reduces inventory quantity via an inventory journal.

When using the black hole concept, the manufacturing kanbans within a black hole are simply reported as received and emptied, and inventory is not tracked within the black hole. In most cases, you use the barcode scanning approach to receive and empty these kanbans.

## Swap Inventory of Fixed Kanbans

You can swap the inventory of two fixed kanbans for the same item, typically to correct a mistake. Use the Swap Kanban form to enter the kanban order numbers for the two kanbans.

The assumptions about inventory consumption of fixed kanbans (described in the previous point) can result in mistakes. However, the field experience in non-batch tracking environments indicates that swapping inventory of two kanbans does not provide significant advantages. The problem self-corrects itself as you continue to report kanban receipts and consumption.

### Generic Fixed Kanbans for Modeling Color/Size Variations

A generic fixed kanban provides one approach for indicating variants (such as color and size) on a kanban order. The approach provides an additional attribute for a kanban order. With this approach, you define the fixed kanban policies for an item, and then create kanban orders (using the Create Generic Kanbans function) with a specified value for the attribute. The attribute cannot be overridden on a kanban order, and it is not reflected in inventory balances or bill of material information.

The attribute is termed the Kanban Generic Number, and the possible values must be predefined by the user. For example, the values could be "black" and "white." When creating a generic kanban, you specify the desired value along with the desired kanban quantity and number of kanbans. For example, you could create some kanban orders for "white" and some for "black." The attribute can be printed on kanban tickets, and displayed on the relevant coordination tools.

The sort type field provides an alternative approach for modeling color/size variations, as described in the next point. The sort type can be overridden on a kanban order.

### Using the Sort Type for Fixed Kanbans

A sort type can be optionally assigned to a fixed kanban by selecting it from a list of user-defined values, and the kanban order keeps the assigned sort type as an attribute. A sort type can be assigned to items using the Item Sort Type form, so that a newly created kanban order inherits the item's sort type.

A sort type typically supports sequencing or grouping purposes, but more creative purposes can be considered. For example, the sort type could represent an additional characteristic of the item (such as color or size), a planner responsibility, a problem area, or a material handling requirement. The sort type attribute can be overridden on a kanban order, but it is not reflected in inventory balances or bill of material information.

## Managing Non-Lean Items

Many manufacturers with lean scenarios will purchase material without using kanbans because the suppliers are not yet ready for lean approaches. In this case, the traditional approaches for using planned purchase orders and the related coordination tools will coordinate purchasing activities.[23] The purchased material can be delivered to a stockroom, and then consumed by fixed replenishment kanbans for moving material to a floor stock area. Alternatively, the purchased material can be consumed as a result of component backflushing triggered by receipts of fixed manufacturing kanbans.

A lean scenario may also involve other types of supply orders for stocked components, such as production orders or transfer orders. In this case, the traditional approach for using planned production orders, planned transfer orders, and the related coordination tools will coordinate supply chain activities.

The same S&OP game plan used to calculate kanban levels can also be used to coordinate replenishment of non-lean items. The S&OP game plan and the critical planning data for purchased items, manufactured items, and transfer items were described in Chapter 2. It is especially important to clearly assign buyer/planner responsibility for these items, so that attention can be focused on non-lean items.

Information about planned orders can be filtered to view just the non-lean items. You can firm up the planned orders for non-lean items. You cannot firm up the planned orders for lean items, since they are already being managed by kanban orders.

## Case Studies

**Case 3: Automotive Parts Manufacturer**  An automotive parts manufacturer produced several variations of a windshield wiper at a final assembly work cell. The customer provided forward visibility of actual demand via a sales schedule, so that the number of fixed manufacturing kanbans reflected the anticipated rate of demand. Each product had a three-level bill of material, and finished goods were stocked in a finished goods warehouse. The company was currently using a home-grown system to calculate and manage these fixed kanbans, and was considering Dynamics AX as an alternative solution approach. The following explanation describes the solution approach:

The demand plan of actual sales orders is entered into Dynamics AX by importing the sales schedule from the customer. After performing the master scheduling task, the planned orders are used to calculate the number of fixed kanbans for every item within the product structures. The recalculation of kanban quantities is performed periodically to reflect the latest demand plan. The recalculation is also performed when the product structure changes, such as a change in wiper design for new car models.

---

[23] The traditional approaches for coordination of purchasing activities are described on pages 251-256 in the AX 2009 book.

The existing number of fixed kanbans for each item is manually adjusted to reflect the suggested kanban level. For example, new kanban orders (and printed kanban tickets) are generated as needed, and some kanban orders are deleted (and the tickets removed from the floor). The printed kanban tickets provide a primary coordination tool, and the bar-coded information on the printed ticket is used to report kanban receipts and empty kanbans via bar-code transactions.

Fixed manufacturing kanbans act as the pull signal for the final assembly work cell, and for the supporting work cells that produce components. A graphical schedule board like the Stop/Go board is used to coordinate production at a work cell. Purchasing kanbans coordinate deliveries from suppliers. The purchased components are received into a stockroom, and moved to the relevant floor stock area based on replenishment kanbans. The floor stock areas are treated as black hole warehouses, so that inventory is not tracked through production. An explicit kanban empty transaction (and a kanban receipt transaction) are used to report and coordinate production activities. The manufacturing kanban receipt for the end item triggers autodeduction of component value, and a financial dimension supports value stream costing.

**Case 4: Vendor Portal for Purchasing Kanban Coordination** A consumer products company wanted to use purchasing kanbans and a vendor portal in their next maturity stage of lean manufacturing. The vendor portal would be used by vendors to view purchasing kanbans with a kanban status of *sent to supplier*, and to update the kanban status to *confirmed by supplier* and *goods dispatched*. The vendor would also indicate the quantity actually sent and print the kanban tickets. With subcontract manufacturing, the vendor would view the manufacturing kanbans with a status of *sent to subcontractor*, and possibly update the quantity and date for expected delivery. The company wanted the vendor portal to be integrated directly through the .NET framework into Microsoft Dynamics AX, where all business logic and data access occur.[24]

**Case 5: Calculation Options for the Number of Fixed Kanbans** A food products manufacturer was considering different options to calculate the kanban level for fixed kanbans. Existing calculations were based on Little's formula and the planned orders that reflected projected demand. Some of the other options being considered focused on an item's historical daily usage (within a date range), which could be added to the standard

---

[24] See eBECS.com for information about their Lean Manufacturing Vendor Enterprise Portal.

deviation or factored by a multiplier. Another option focused on the planned orders generated by projected demand, and the consideration of on hand inventory and current pending kanbans.[25]

## Executive Summary

Fixed kanbans can coordinate supply chain activities for make-to-stock products, or make-to-order products with indirect linkage to sales order demand. The number of fixed kanbans can be calculated for each item within the product structure based on a demand plan for the near-term horizon. Different sources of supply are reflected in the three types of fixed kanbans: purchasing, manufacturing, and replenishment (for component picking purposes). Each kanban type has different creation policies, a different life cycle, and different coordination tools. The receipts of manufacturing kanbans provide the basis for takt time metrics of a work cell.

The component inventory in floor stock areas can be managed with different approaches. One approach involves detailed tracking of floor stock inventory, where manufacturing kanban receipts trigger autodeduction of component quantities that ultimately result in empty kanbans. This supports order-based costing but creates waste in the number of backflushing transactions. A second approach employs backflushing of component value rather than quantities (using the cost substitution concept) to support order-based costing and reduce waste. This requires an explicit kanban empty transaction for components in floor stock areas. A third approach employs black hole warehouses so that component inventory is not tracked in floor stock areas, but the kanban receipt and empty kanban transactions still coordinate replenishment.

There are many variations in using fixed kanbans. These include kanban templates, intermittent subcontract manufacturing, temporary fixed kanbans, and scrap reporting. Purchased components may be obtained through traditional purchase orders because the suppliers are not ready for kanban coordination, especially in early maturity stages of lean manufacturing. Other situations may also require replenishment via traditional supply orders rather than fixed kanbans.

---

[25] See eBECS.com for information about calculation options within their Lean Manufacturing II add-on module.

# Chapter 4

# Fixed Kanbans with Subcontract Manufacturing

Subcontract manufacturing involves an outside operation using supplied components. The use of outside operations often reflects specialized processing, capacity constraints, virtual manufacturing, or off-shore production. The wide variety of subcontract manufacturing environments can be distilled into several basic variations for using fixed kanbans. The basic variations reflect two factors: the approach for handling the supplied components and the nature of the outside operation within the manufacturing process. Within Dynamics AX, these factors are termed the *subcontract kanban type* and the *subcontract policy* respectively. Figure 4.1 summarizes the variations related to these two factors, and highlights the two variations (labeled Scenario #2 and Scenario #2a) that represent the simplest approaches for handling subcontract manufacturing. These two scenarios involve a single outside operation within the manufacturing process.

| Subcontract Policy<br>Nature of the Outside Operation within the Manufacturing Process | Subcontract Kanban Type<br>Approach for Handling the Supplied Components | |
|---|---|---|
| | Discrete Kit<br>Items Sent to Subcontractor | Consignment<br>Items Stocked at Subcontractor |
| Subcontract Only<br>Outside Operation is the only step within the process | Scenario #2 | Scenario #2a |
| Final Process<br>Outside Operation is the final step in a multi-step process | | |
| Partial Process<br>Outside Operation is an intermediate step in a multi-step process | | |

Figure 4.1 Basic Variations for Subcontract Manufacturing

A *subcontract policy* for a manufacturing kanban indicates whether the outside operation is the only step within the item's manufacturing process, or an intermediate or final step within a multistep process. A second policy (termed the *subcontract kanban type*) indicates whether you send a discrete kit of components to the subcontractor with each manufacturing kanban, or stock the consigned inventory of components at the subcontractor site. The parent item's bill of material defines the supplied components and the warehouse source of these components.

Subcontracting represents incremental functionality that builds on the foundation of fixed manufacturing kanbans. Subcontracting can also apply to PTO manufacturing kanbans covered in Chapter 7. Two company-wide policies determine whether the incremental functionality can be used, so that the incremental functionality will only apply when a company has outside operations.[1]

Subcontracting also builds on some aspects of traditional AX functionality for modeling an outside operation using the concept of an outside operation component. An outside operation component within a BOM supports the costing and purchasing aspects of subcontract manufacturing.[2] The lean approach for using the outside operation component differs slightly from the traditional approach within AX. These differences include the method for defining an approved vendor for the outside operation component, the method for handling variations in supplied components, and the method for reporting completion of an outside operation. Subsequent sections describe these methods in more detail.

Further explanation focuses on the two scenarios identified in Figure 4.1. Other major variations will be explained in a separate section. This chapter consists of three major sections:

❖ Subcontract Manufacturing with a Discrete Kit of Supplied Components
❖ Subcontract Manufacturing with Consigned Inventory of Supplied Components
❖ Variations of Subcontract Manufacturing

The explanations focus on the incremental differences with fixed manufacturing kanbans. The previous chapter explained fixed manufacturing kanbans in terms of the policies for creating a kanban (Figure 3.14), an

---

[1] One company-wide policy (the *Create Subcontract Kanbans* policy on the Kanban Parameters form) determines whether subcontract manufacturing kanbans can be used. A second company-wide policy (termed the *Convert Kanbans to Subcontract* policy on the Kanban Parameters form) enables a normally manufactured kanban to be temporarily converted to an outside operation. This second policy also provides additional functionality when assigning a subcontract manufacturing kanban to a different subcontractor.

[2] The concept of an outside operation component within a bill of material is described on pages 68-71 and 317-318 in the AX 2009 book. The book's description focuses on the traditional approaches for using an outside operation component in bills of material and production orders.

example kanban ticket (Figure 3.15), the life cycle for a kanban (Figure 3.16), and the coordination tools such as the Kanban Manufacturing form (Figure 3.17). The same information applies to subcontract manufacturing.

## Subcontract Manufacturing with a Discrete Kit of Supplied Components

A common scenario for subcontract manufacturing involves a discrete kit of supplied components, and a single outside operation within the manufacturing process. This section starts with a description of the scenario, and then explains the policies for creating a kanban order, the life cycle for a kanban order, and the coordination tools.

> **Scenario #2: Subcontract Manufacturing with a Discrete Kit of Supplied Components**

This scenario involves a single level product produced from stocked components, as shown in Figure 4.2. The scenario illustrates three warehouses:

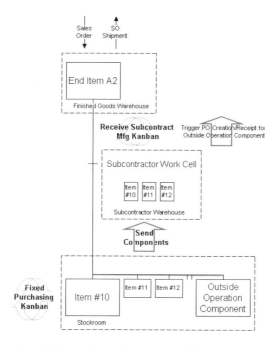

Figure 4.2 Subcontract Manufacturing with a Discrete Kit of Supplied Components

the stockroom (for stocked components), the subcontractor warehouse (for tracking supplied components), and a finished goods area (as the destination warehouse). The end item's bill of material defines the supplied components and their stockroom warehouse source. It also contains the outside operation component to support cost rollup calculations. This same item number is identified within the end-item's kanban policies to support subcontracting purposes.

The subcontractor is identified as the supplier of the outside operation component, as a warehouse, and as a work cell.

When an empty kanban exists for the end item, you *send components* to the subcontractor and optionally print the *subcontract order* that displays the end item and the list of supplied components. The system tracks component inventory at the subcontractor warehouse. The subsequent receipt of the subcontract manufacturing kanban will autodeduct components from the subcontractor warehouse, and also trigger the creation and receipt of a purchase order for the outside operation component.

## Policies for Creating a Manufacturing Kanban with Subcontracting

Kanban policies are defined for an item number and warehouse using the Kanbans form. In the context of Scenario #2, for example, the manufacturing kanban policies would be defined for the "End Item A2" and the "Finished Goods" warehouse. An alternative approach to defining kanban policies involves the use of a kanban template, as described in this chapter's section "Variations of Subcontract Manufacturing."

The kanban policies are inherited by a newly created kanban order. Figure 4.3 summarizes the kanban policies for creating a fixed manufacturing kanban with subcontracting, and highlights (via shading) the additional policies related to subcontract manufacturing.

The additional kanban policies for subcontract manufacturing are described below. They include the subcontract policy, the item number representing the outside operation, the preferred vendor and blanket PO for this item number, the subcontractor warehouse for tracking the supplied components, the method for handling supplied components, and the method for moving the end item from the subcontractor to its destination warehouse.

**Subcontract Policy** This scenario focuses on a single step in an item's manufacturing process, which is termed *subcontract only*. Other subcontract policies involving an intermediate or final step in the manufacturing process are described in a subsequent section "Variations of Subcontract Manufacturing."

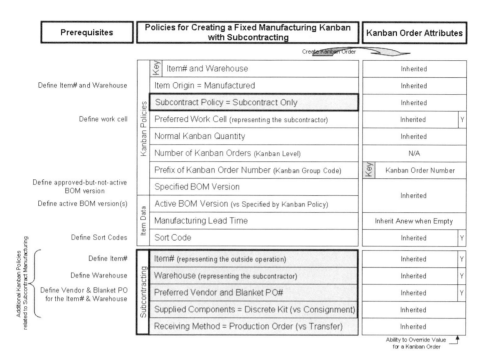

Figure 4.3  Policies for Creating a Fixed Manufacturing Kanban with Subcontracting

## Item Number Representing the Outside Operation

The item number typically reflects the outside operation component employed in the parent's bill of material for cost calculation purposes. This item number and its unit of measure define the payment basis for the outside operation. It is also termed the *payment item*. It typically has an item type of service and an actual costing method. It also has an active standard cost record so that the parent's standard cost can be calculated.

## Warehouse Representing the Subcontractor

This scenario focuses on sending the supplied components (via a discrete kit) to the subcontractor's warehouse. The receipt of the manufacturing kanban can trigger component backflushing from the subcontractor's warehouse.

Note: The end item's bill of material defines the warehouse source of each component. In this scenario, the warehouse source should reflect the warehouse that will send the components to the subcontractor; it should not reflect the subcontractor's warehouse.

## Preferred Vendor and Blanket PO# for the Outside Operation Component

The definition of a blanket PO for the outside operation

item and the subcontractor's warehouse identifies the preferred vendor for subcontract manufacturing purposes. The preferred vendor and blanket PO are initially assigned when you create a kanban, but these values can be overridden with an alternate vendor (and blanket PO) for the outside operation. More than one vendor and blanket PO can be defined, thereby indicating alternate approved vendors. As a basic guideline, each blanket PO should have a single line item for the specified item and the subcontractor's warehouse.

**Method for Handling Supplied Components**   This scenario focuses on sending a discrete kit of supplied components to the subcontractor, whereas Scenario #2a covers consigned inventory stocked at the subcontractor.

**Receiving Method for Moving Inventory from the Subcontractor Warehouse to the Destination Warehouse**   The receiving method should always reflect a production order to ensure components at the subcontractor warehouse will be backflushed. There is one exception to this guideline: That is, the receiving method could be a transfer order when the scenario involves an outside operation as the last step in a multistep routing.

**Other Policies for the Manufacturing Kanban**   Subcontract manufacturing involves some minor differences in the use of several policies for manufacturing kanbans.

- *Work Cell.* The work cell represents the subcontractor. One work cell policy determines how manufacturing kanban receipts will be handled by traditional AX functionality, as previously described for fixed manufacturing kanbans.
- *Manufacturing Lead Time.* The item's manufacturing lead time represents the typical turnaround time to provide supplied components and receive the completed item, thereby accounting for the transportation time. An item's manufacturing lead time can be specified as a company-wide policy (as part of the item's default order settings for inventory), or as part of the item's site-specific order settings.
- *BOM Version.* A newly created manufacturing kanban normally inherits the item's active BOM version as of the creation date, unless you specify a different BOM version as part of the kanban policies.

An example ticket for a fixed manufacturing kanban was previously displayed in Figure 3.15. This information includes the work cell (the subcontractor), the destination warehouse, and the optional text and bill of material information. It also includes barcoded information about the Record Id and Item Number, which are used to support scanned receipt transactions.

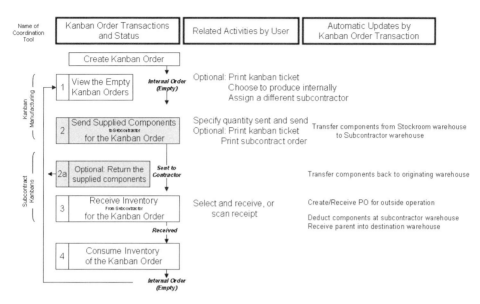

Figure 4.4 Life Cycle for a Fixed Manufacturing Kanban with Subcontracting (Discrete Kit)

## Life Cycle for a Manufacturing Kanban with Subcontracting

A manufacturing kanban with subcontracting has a life cycle represented by a status, and the status is closely related to kanban order transactions. Subcontracting involves an additional status and additional transactions in comparison to a manufacturing kanban produced internally. Figure 4.4 summarizes this life cycle, and highlights (via shading) the key differences in status and transactions. It depicts the major transactions and status (shown in italics), and use of the Kanban Manufacturing form and the Subcontract Kanban form as coordination tools.

In its simplest form, an *internal order (empty)* status represents an empty kanban and the requirement to produce the item at the subcontractor. Sending the supplied components to the subcontractor will automatically change the status to *sent to contractor*. Receiving the kanban order will automatically update the status to *received*, and inventory consumption of the kanban order will automatically update the status back to *internal order*.

**Prerequisite Step: Create a Kanban Order** You create a manufacturing kanban order using the Kanbans form, and it inherits the policies described in Figure 4.3. A newly created kanban has an *internal order* status; it can be termed *internal order (empty)* to emphasize the empty status.

**Step 1: View the Empty Kanban Orders**  An empty kanban represents a requirement to produce the item at the subcontractor work cell. View the empty kanbans using the Kanban Manufacturing form as a coordination tool. You can optionally print or delete a kanban order, or change the required date and quantity.

If needed, you can choose to internally produce a kanban order that is normally subcontracted. In this case, you simply receive the manufacturing kanban order (via the firming function) rather than proceeding with the steps to send components to the supplier.

If needed, you can temporarily assign the manufacturing kanban to a different subcontractor. The best approach for assigning a different subcontractor involves the "convert to subcontract" functionality, which forces you to specify all aspects of relevant information.[3] Other approaches only specify one aspect, such as specifying a different work cell or a different vendor. All aspects of relevant information include the specified vendor, the relevant blanket PO number (and outside operation), the relevant subcontractor warehouse, and the relevant BOM version of supplied components. Figure 4.5 highlights (via shading) this optional step in the life cycle.

An alternate vendor (and associated blanket PO for the outside operation component) must be predefined. This could be for a different outside operation. A different BOM version may be needed when the supplied components are different. The status remains *internal order*, and the kanban order is updated with the "converted to subcontract" checkbox. This optional assignment works for a scenario involving subcontract only.

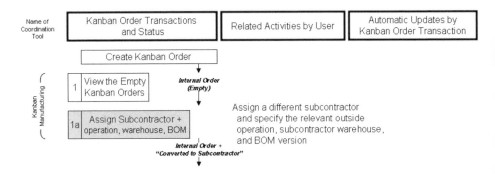

Figure 4.5  Assign a Different Subcontractor to a Manufacturing Kanban

---

[3] A company-wide policy (termed the *Convert Kanbans to Subcontract* policy on the Kanban Parameters form) enables you to assign an alternate vendor and specify the related information.

```
                        SUBCONTRACT ORDER

Send To:
Vendor Name:  ABC Company            Purchase Order:  PO-12345
Address:      123 Main Street        Return Date:     07/07/20XX
              Anytown, CA
              55555

Subcontracted
Item Number   Description                  Qty Ordered   Unit
End Item A2   Example Subcontracted Item       100        Ea


Components being supplied:
Item Number   Description                  Qty Supplied  Unit
Item #10      Item #10 Description             200        Ea
Item #11      Item #11 Description             100        Ea
Item #12      Item #12 Description             100        Ea
```

Figure 4.6 Example of a Printed Subcontract Order

**Step 2: Send Supplied Components (to the Subcontractor) for the Kanban Order** You record that supplied components have been sent using the Kanban Manufacturing form; the sent quantity must be specified. This changes the kanban status (*sent to contractor*) and transfers each component's inventory to the subcontractor's warehouse. It also moves the kanban order to a different coordination tool, so that it must be viewed on the Subcontract Kanbans form.

You can optionally print the Subcontractor Order, which displays a picking list for sending the supplied components. An example of the printed Subcontractor Order is shown in Figure 4.6. This provides an alternative approach to printing component information on the ticket for a manufacturing kanban.

**Optional Step 2a: Return the Supplied Components** If needed, you can reverse the transactions that transferred components to the subcontractor's warehouse, which will also reset the kanban ticket status to *internal order (empty)*. This transaction must be performed on the Subcontract Kanban form.

**Step 3: Receive Inventory (from the Subcontractor) for a Kanban Order** A kanban receipt can be reported via barcode scanning, or by entering data on the Subcontract Kanbans form. A fixed kanban can only be received once; you cannot record multiple partial receipts. Receipts provide the basis for takt time metrics, as described in the Chapter 5 section "Takt Time Metrics for a Work Cell."

The kanban receipt automatically triggers PO creation and receipt for the outside operation component. This purchase order reflects a release against the blanket purchase order.

An additional step may be necessary to end the production order associated with a manufacturing kanban receipt. This step is only necessary when the work cell policy for handling kanban receipts will result in a production order with a finished status.

The impact of a kanban receipt transaction depends on the chosen option for floor stock management, as described in the previous chapter's section "Floor Stock Management Approaches." Figure 4.4 displays the automatic updates for a kanban receipt transaction based on the detailed tracking option.

**Step 4: Consume Inventory of a Kanban Order** A manufacturing kanban may be for an end item or for a manufactured component. These two situations have different approaches to inventory consumption. For example, sales order shipments normally consume inventory of an end item's kanban orders. The manufacturing kanban orders for a manufactured component are normally placed in a floor stock area. This kanban inventory can be consumed by component backflushing or an explicit kanban empty transaction, as described in the previous chapter's section "Floor Stock Management Approaches." The status of the kanban order will be automatically changed to *internal order (empty)* after reporting its inventory as completely consumed.

Some scenarios will accumulate empty kanbans to reach a critical mass prior to communicating the requirement to replenish inventory at the point of use. The previous chapter described how to accumulate empty kanbans until a trigger point has been reached.

## Coordination Tools for Subcontract Manufacturing

The primary coordination tools consist of the Kanban Manufacturing form, the Subcontract Kanban form, and the printed kanban tickets and subcontract orders. The Stop/Go Board may also be used, as well as takt time metrics. Use of the Kanban Manufacturing form differs slightly in a subcontract manufacturing environment, and the Subcontract Kanbans form represents a new coordination tool, in comparison to the coordination tools for fixed manufacturing kanbans. Further explanation focuses on these two coordination tools.

**Kanban Manufacturing Form** This form displays the kanban orders requiring planner action for the subcontractor work cell. In particular, the planner can review upcoming requirements for kanban deliveries, and report the supplied components as sent. This moves the message to the Subcontract Kanbans form. An example of the Kanban Manufacturing form was previously displayed in Figure 3.17. For subcontracting purposes, the unique actions using the Kanban Manufacturing form include the following:

* Send the supplied components for a manufacturing kanban, and optionally print the Subcontract Order. After reporting the components as sent, the message moves to the Subcontract Kanban form.
* If needed, choose to internally produce a manufacturing kanban that is normally produced by a subcontractor. The manufacturing kanban can be simply received via the firming function.
* If needed, assign a different subcontractor to the manufacturing kanban. The best approach for assigning a different subcontractor involves the "convert to subcontract" functionality, as described earlier for the life cycle steps.

Other actions using the Kanban Manufacturing form include the following:

* Print (or reprint) a manufacturing kanban ticket.
* Delete an internal order (empty) kanban.
* Change the required date or quantity ordered.
* Identify manufacturing kanbans with a past-due required date.
* Identify the sort type associated with a kanban order (if specified) to support sequencing or grouping of manufacturing activities. The sort type for a kanban order can be manually overridden.
* View and/or assign the production start date, which initially reflects the required date minus the item's manufacturing lead time. The production start date represents reference information, and does not have any impact.
* Identify component availability for a manufacturing kanban
* Use the Explode function to view component availability information in a single-level or multilevel bill of material format.

The form does not display received kanbans because they do not require further action. Kanbans with the received status can be viewed on the Manual Kanban Update form.

**Subcontract Kanban Form** This form displays a manufacturing kanban after sending its components to the subcontractor. The planner can review upcoming requirements for kanban deliveries, and report a kanban as received (which removes the message). An example of the Subcontract Kanban form is displayed in Figure 4.7.

## Subcontract Kanbans

| Filter: | Supplier<br>ABC Subcontractor | | | | | | | | |
|---|---|---|---|---|---|---|---|---|---|
| Components Available | Mark | Kanban Order Number | Vendor Account | Item Number | Deliver To Warehouse | Quantity Ordered | Required Date | Confirmed Quantity | Production Start Date | Kanban Order Status |
| Yes | ☐ | ANN_000020 | ABC | End Item A1 | Finished Goods | 10 | 07/07/20XX |    | 07/05/20XX | Sent to Contractor |
| Yes | ☐ | ANN_000021 | ABC | End Item A1 | Finished Goods | 10 | 07/08/20XX |    | 07/06/20XX | Sent to Contractor |
| No  | ☐ | ANN_000219 | ABC | End Item A3 | Finished Goods | 10 | 07/08/20XX |    | 07/04/20XX | Sent to Contractor |
| Yes | ☐ | ANN_000367 | ABC | End Item A2 | Finished Goods | 10 | 07/06/20XX |    | 07/02/20XX | Sent to Contractor |
| Yes | ☐ | ANN_000422 | ABC | End Item A4 | Finished Goods | 25 | 07/09/20XX | 25 | 07/08/20XX | Sent to Contractor |
| Yes | ☐ | ANN_000595 | ABC | End Item A4 | Finished Goods | 10 | 07/07/20XX | 9  | 07/06/20XX | Sent to Contractor |

*Data can be entered or changed*

Figure 4.7  Example of the Subcontract Kanbans Form

The primary actions for using the Subcontract Kanban form include the following:

❖ Report the receipt of a kanban order, and the specified quantity received. A kanban receipt can also be scanned.
❖ If needed, return the supplied components to the originating warehouse.
❖ Print (or reprint) a manufacturing kanban ticket.
❖ Print (or reprint) a subcontract order to help in picking the supplied components.
❖ Change the required date or quantity ordered.
❖ Identify manufacturing kanbans with a past-due required date.

## Subcontract Manufacturing with Consigned Inventory of Supplied Components

Consigned inventory generally reflects direct delivery of purchased material to the subcontractor warehouse, or periodic transfers to the subcontractor. This method of handling supplied material involves a slightly different life cycle than the use of discrete kits, since the material has already been sent to the subcontractor. It also involves slightly different BOM information because the components' warehouse source must reflect the subcontractor warehouse. The following explanation focuses on these and other differences. The explanation starts with a typical scenario for subcontract manufacturing with consigned inventory of supplied components, as summarized in Figure 4.8

## Scenario #2a: Subcontract Manufacturing with Consigned Inventory of Supplied Components

This scenario involves a single level product produced from stocked components, as shown in Figure 4.8. The scenario involves just two warehouses: the subcontractor warehouse (for tracking supplied components) and a finished goods area (as the destination warehouse). The end item's bill of material defines the supplied components and the subcontractor warehouse source. It also contains the outside operation component to support cost roll-up calculations. This same item number is identified within the end-item's kanban policies to support subcontracting purposes.

In this scenario, purchase orders are used for delivering the stocked components to the subcontractor. The stocked components could also have been transferred to the subcontractor via other supply orders, such as transfer orders, production orders, or fixed manufacturing kanbans. The subcontractor is identified as the supplier of the outside operation component, as a warehouse, and as a work cell.

After completing production at the subcontractor, the manufactured kanban is received into a finished goods warehouse. The receipt will trigger the creation and receipt of a purchase order for the outside operation component, and also autodeduct components from the subcontractor warehouse.

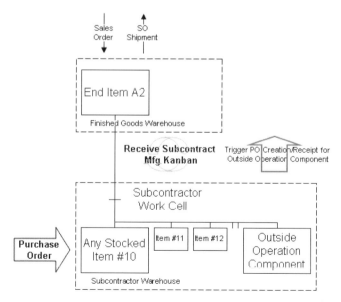

Figure 4.8 Subcontract Manufacturing with Consignment of Supplied Components

## Policies for Creating a Manufacturing Kanban with Subcontracting

The kanban policies are defined for an item and warehouse using the Kanbans form. The kanban policies described for Scenario #2 and Figure 4.3 also apply to Scenario #2a, with one exception. The method for handling supplied components (termed the *Subcontract Kanban Type*) involves consigned inventory stocked at the subcontractor. As a minor difference, the manufacturing lead time represents the elapsed days to produce the kanban and transport it to the destination warehouse.

## Life Cycle for a Manufacturing Kanban with Subcontracting

The life cycle for this scenario differs slightly from Scenario #2 because the supplied components are stocked at the subcontractor. There is no requirement for sending components or returning components. However, you still perform the life cycle step for "sending components" in order to display the kanban order on the Subcontract Kanbans form, where you can record kanban receipts. Figure 4.9 summarizes this life cycle. It depicts the major transactions and status (shown in italics), and use of the Kanban Manufacturing form and the Subcontract Kanban form as coordination tools.

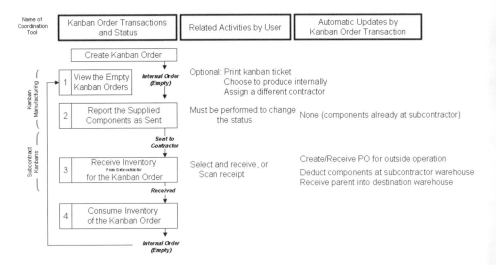

Figure 4.9 Life Cycle for Fixed Manufacturing Kanban with Subcontracting (Consigned)

In its simplest form, a kanban order with an *internal order (empty)* status indicates a requirement to produce the item at the subcontractor. As a system requirement, you report the components as sent to change the status to *sent to contractor*. Receiving the kanban will automatically update the status to *received*, and auto-deduct the components at the subcontractor warehouse. Consumption of the inventory will automatically update the status back to *internal order*. Figure 4.9 displays the use of the Kanban Manufacturing form and the Subcontract Kanban form as coordination tools.

**Prerequisite Step: Create a Kanban Order** You create a manufacturing kanban order using the Kanbans form, and it inherits the policies described in Figure 4.3. A newly created kanban has an *internal order* status; it can be termed *internal order (empty)* to emphasize the empty status.

**Step 1: View the Empty Kanban Orders** An empty kanban represents a requirement to produce the item at the subcontractor work cell. View the empty kanbans using the Kanban Manufacturing form as a coordination tool. You can optionally print or delete a kanban order, or change the required date and quantity.

If needed, you can choose to internally produce a kanban order that is normally subcontracted. In this case, you simply receive the manufacturing kanban order (via the firming function) rather than proceeding with the steps to send components to the supplier.

If needed, you can temporarily assign the manufacturing kanban to a different subcontractor. The best approach for assigning a different subcontractor involves the "convert to subcontract" functionality, which forces you to specify all aspects of relevant information. This optional step was previously described in Figure 4.5. It means that components must be sent to the newly-assigned subcontractor.

**Step 2: Report the Supplied Components as Sent** This represents an informational step; it displays the kanban order on the Subcontract Kanban form so that it can be received. The components are not actually transferred since they are already stocked at the subcontractor, and a printed Subcontractor Order does not apply.

**Step 3: Receive Inventory (from the Subcontractor) for a Kanban Order** A kanban receipt can be reported via barcode scanning, or by entering data on the Subcontract Kanbans form. A fixed kanban can only be received once; you cannot record multiple partial receipts. The kanban receipt automatically triggers PO creation and receipt for the outside operation component. This purchase order reflects a release against the blanket purchase order.

An additional step may be necessary to end the production order associated with a manufacturing kanban receipt. This step is only necessary when the work cell policy for handling kanban receipts will result in a production order with a finished status.

The impact of a kanban receipt transaction depends on the chosen option for floor stock management, as described in the previous chapter's section "Floor Stock Management Approaches." Figure 4.9 displays the automatic updates for a kanban receipt transaction based on detailed tracking of floor stock inventory.

**Step 4: Consume Inventory of a Kanban Order**   A manufacturing kanban may be for an end item or for a manufactured component with different approaches to inventory consumption, as described in the previous scenario.

## Coordination Tools for Subcontract Manufacturing

The primary coordination tools consist of the Kanban Manufacturing form, the Subcontract Kanban form, and the printed kanban tickets. The Stop/Go Board may also be used, as well as takt time metrics. The uses of these coordination tools were explained in the previous scenario.

# Variations of Subcontract Manufacturing

The two scenarios within this chapter represent two basic variations. Other variations include different subcontract policies, a multilevel product with subcontracting, multiple outside operations for a manufactured item, and converting a manufacturing kanban for intermittent subcontracting.

## Variations of the Subcontract Policy

The subcontract policy indicates whether the outside operation is the only step in the manufacturing process, or an intermediate or final step. Figure 4.1 previously highlighted these basic variations for a manufacturing kanban with subcontracting. Figure 4.10 summarizes the impact of these variations in terms of the life cycle steps for a kanban. As shown on the left side of Figure 4.10, these life cycle steps include sending the supplied components, returning the supplied components, and the need for recording one versus two receipts. Two receipts are required for an outside operation representing an intermediate step: one receipt from the subcontractor (for a partially completed item) and one receipt for the completed manufacturing kanban.

| | | Discrete Kit sent to Subcontractor | | | Consigned Inventory at Subcontractor | | |
|---|---|---|---|---|---|---|---|
| | | Subcontract Only | Final Process | Partial Process | Subcontract Only | Final Process | Partial Process |
| Steps in the Life Cycle of a Kanban Order | Send Supplied Components | Transfer components to Subcontractor [1] | Deduct components from Stockroom [2] Place parent at Subcontractor [2] | | No Impact (Components are already stocked at subcontractor) | | |
| | Return Components | Reverse above Transactions | Reverse above Transactions | | | | |
| | Receive From Subcontractor | Create/Receive PO for outside operation | | | Create/Receive PO for outside operation | | |
| | | Receive parent into stockroom [3] | | N/A | Receive parent into stockroom [3] | | N/A |
| | | Deduct components at subcontractor [4] | Deduct parent at subcontractor [3] | | Deduct components at subcontractor [4] | | |
| | Separately Receive Manufacturing Kanban | N/A | Receive parent into stockroom [3] Deduct parent at subcontractor [3] | | N/A | | Receive parent into stockroom [3] Deduct components at subcontractor [4] |

Legend: 1 = Transfer Journal   2 = P/L Journal   3 = Report as Finished Journal   4 = Picking List Journal

Figure 4.10  Comparing Basic Variations of Subcontract Manufacturing

## Multilevel Product and Subcontract Manufacturing

An outside operation may be required within a multilevel product structure. One example is shown in Figure 4.11, where the final assembly of End Item C is performed by the subcontractor. In this example, the internally produced Assembly B is received into the subcontractor's warehouse, which represents consigned inventory of the supplied component.

## Multiple Outside Operations for a Product

A product requiring multiple outside operations represents a special case of a multilevel product with subcontracting. For example, two outside operations would require two levels in the bill of materials, and the first subcontractor would transfer the completed product to the second contractor. The supplied material for the first contractor can be treated as a discrete kit or consigned inventory. The supplied material for the second contractor is typically treated as consigned inventory. The BOM information must specify the relevant warehouse source of components.

## Intermittent Subcontract Manufacturing for a Normally Manufactured Item

A fixed manufacturing kanban reflects an item that is normally manufactured at an internal work cell. In some situations, the item may need to be manu-

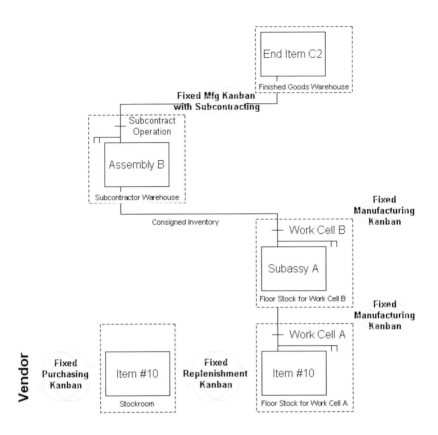

Figure 4.11 Example of a Multilevel Product with Subcontracting

factured by a subcontractor on an intermittent basis, which requires a temporary conversion to a subcontract manufacturing kanban. You can convert to subcontracting on the Kanban Manufacturing form, which represents an optional life cycle step. As part of this step, you indicate the desired subcontractor and the outside operation component, and the warehouse associated with the subcontractor. You can optionally specify a different BOM version defining the supplied components, since the components may differ from those used in internal manufacturing. The supplied components can then be sent to the subcontractor, and the parent item received as a manufacturing kanban.

## Other Variations of Fixed Kanbans

The previous chapter covered the following variations for fixed kanbans. These variations also apply to manufacturing kanbans with subcontracting.

- Temporary fixed kanbans
- Barcode scanning for kanban receipts
- Reporting scrap for a fixed kanban
- Reporting reusable scrap for a fixed kanban
- Alternative methods for reporting consumption of fixed kanbans
- Accumulating empty kanbans until a trigger point is reached
- Calculating the number of fixed kanbans

## Manage Engineering Changes for Subcontract Manufacturing

The previous chapter explained how to manage engineering changes with fixed kanbans. The use of subcontract manufacturing introduces some additional considerations, as listed below.

- Use subcontracting on a one-time or intermittent basis. This involves definition of the outside operation component, an approved vendor (and blanket PO) for the outside operations, and possibly a different BOM version that specifies the supplied components.
- Use a different subcontractor. Same as above.
- Internally produce an item that is normally subcontracted.

Changes to the following kanban order attributes must be implemented by deleting the existing kanbans (that inherited the old value) and then creating new kanbans (that will inherit the new value):

- Change the approved vendor for the outside operation
- Change the outside operation component
- Change the subcontract kanban type (Discrete Kit versus Consigned)

## Executive Summary

Subcontract manufacturing represents incremental functionality that builds on the foundation of fixed and PTO manufacturing kanbans. The wide variety of subcontract manufacturing environments can be distilled into several basic variations for using fixed kanbans. The basic variations reflect two factors: the approach for handling the supplied components and the nature of the outside operation within the manufacturing process. This chapter focused on two variations for handling the supplied components as (1) a discrete kit sent to the subcontractor with the manufacturing kanban and (2) consigned inventory stocked at the subcontractor. The chapter also covered engineering change management and other variations of subcontract manufacturing.

# Chapter 5

# Work Cell Considerations

A work cell represents a simpler alternative for modeling lean scenarios in comparison to the use of Dynamics AX work centers and routing data. You indicate the work cell for producing an item as part of the kanban policies for a fixed or PTO manufacturing kanban. The list of empty kanbans by work cell provides a coordination tool. Takt time metrics provide a measure of work cell performance, and the work cell's drumbeat can support sales order delivery promises based on available capacity.

The simpler alternative of a work cell does not currently support value-added costs related to direct manufacturing and overhead allocations. Most lean scenarios focus on direct material costs so the limitation is not an issue. However, some lean scenarios require value-added costs to support calculation of a manufactured item's cost and suggested sales price. Auto-deduction of these value-added costs supports an order-based costing approach for manufacturing kanbans. In this case, routing data must be used to support the costing purposes.

This chapter consists of the following sections:

❖ Use of Routing Data for Costing Purposes
❖ Takt Time Metrics for a Work Cell
❖ Drumbeat for a Work Cell

## Use of Routing Data for Costing Purposes

Some lean scenarios require value-added costs to support calculation of a manufactured item's cost and suggested sales price, and to support order-based costing requirements. This requires some duplicate data maintenance about work cells and work centers. In summary, a work cell can be modeled as a single work center within a work center group. A master routing must be defined with a single operation that defines the run time requirement for producing an item at the work center. The run time is typically expressed as hours per unit or units per hour. You assign a master routing to an item to indicate the applicable work center.

A work center's costing information typically reflects its direct manufacturing costs such as labor. It can be expressed as an hourly rate that reflects the average crew size and average labor rate, such as an hourly cost of $200 for a crew size of 10. Alternatively, the costing information can be expressed as a piece rate (aka cost per output unit). The overhead costs for a work center can be defined in an overhead formula. For example, the routing-related overhead can be expressed as the incremental cost per hour or per output unit.

The routing-related costs can be included in the calculation of a manufactured item's cost and suggested sales price (aka BOM calculation). In addition, the routing operation(s) can be autodeducted for a production order to support order-based costing requirements.

## Takt Time Metrics for a Work Cell

There are different variations of takt time metrics for a work cell. Within standard AX, the takt time metrics focus on today's production at a work cell. In particular, they focus on progress as of a given time within today's working hours. They provide aggregate measures of work cell progress toward completing today's scheduled production of fixed and PTO manufacturing kanban orders. Takt time metrics are typically expressed in minutes per equivalent unit, although they could be expressed as hours per unit. Other aggregate metrics of progress include percentage completion of today's total scheduled production. The takt time metrics share many similarities to traditional metrics concerning a work cell's production rate.

The *target takt time* assigned to each work cell represents its standard production rate, expressed as the standard time per equivalent unit (such as 6 minutes per unit). The target takt time represents the work cell's drumbeat. Given the previous example, a work cell may have an hourly drumbeat of 10 units per working hour, or a daily drumbeat of 80 units per working day. In a lean scenario with standardized work and balanced production, every item produced by the work cell represents one equivalent unit.

There are two aggregate measures of today's work cell performance.

❖ *Current Takt Time for Work Already Completed.* Current takt time reflects the actual elapsed time for the total units produced today. At a given moment in the day, for example, the total received kanbans could be 50 equivalent units during the elapsed time of 360 minutes. This example data would be displayed as a current takt time of 7.2 minutes per unit (360/50 = 7.2 minutes). It indicates the work cell is running behind or ahead of the target kanban time.

- *Required Takt Time for Remaining Work.* Required takt time reflects the remaining time within today's working hours and the remaining units within today's schedule. At a given moment in the day, for example, the total remaining kanbans could be 50 equivalent units and the total remaining minutes could be 240 minutes. This example data would be displayed as a required takt time of 4.8 minutes per unit (240/50 = 4.8 minutes). In comparison to the target or current takt time, it indicates the work cell must run at a faster rate (or a slower rate) to complete today's total scheduled quantity by end of working day.

The calculations for current and required takt times are constantly updated throughout the day to reflect the current time, the reported kanban receipts, and possible additions/subtractions to the manufacturing kanbans due today. The takt time calculations for a work cell are illustrated in Figure 5.1 and summarized below.

The basis for takt time calculations can be segmented into static and dynamic data. The static data includes the following fields:

- *Working hours (minutes) for today.* The calendar assigned to a work center defines the working hours for each day. The working hours for today's date, and the current time within today's date, are used to calculate elapsed minutes and remaining minutes. The example shown

| | Basis of Takt Time Calculations for a Work Cell | Example Data for Takt Time Calculations | Label of the Measurement | Significance of the Measurement |
|---|---|---|---|---|
| Static Data | Working Hours (Minutes) for Today | 10 Hours (07:00 to 17:00) 600 Minutes | Target Takt Time | |
| | Standard Time per Equivalent Unit | 6 Minutes/Unit | | |
| | Drumbeat Ratio for each Manufacturing Kanban | Drumbeat Ratio / Equivalent Unit = 1.00 | | |
| Dynamic Data | Manufacturing Kanbans Scheduled for Today (aka **Quantity Required** in Equivalent Units) | 100 Units | | Manufacturing kanbans with required date = today |
| | Current Time | 13:00 | | |
| | **Elapsed Minutes** as of Current Time | 360 Minutes = 07:00 to 13:00 | Current Takt Time | The current pace is running behind target |
| | Actual **Number Produced** as of Current Time (expressed in equivalent units) | 50 Units | | |
| | Actual Time per Equivalent Unit for Number Produced as of Current Time | 360 Minutes / 50 Units = 7.2 Minutes/Unit | | |
| | **Remaining Minutes** as of Current Time | 240 Minutes = 13:00 to 17:00 | Required Takt Time | Increase pace to complete today's quantity required |
| | **Remaining Quantity** Required for Today (expressed in equivalent units) | 50 Units = 100 - 50 | | |
| | Required Time per Equivalent Unit to produce the Remaining Quantity | 240 Minutes / 50 Units = 4.8 Minutes/Unit | | |
| | Projected Production for the Remaining Minutes based on Current Takt Time | 240 Minutes / 7.2 Minutes = 33.3 Units | Projected Production at Current Takt Time | Assume the current pace and today's remaining minutes |
| | Projected Production for the Remaining Minutes based on Target Takt Time | 240 Minutes / 6 Minutes = 40 Units | Projected Production at Target Takt Time | Assume the target pace and today's remaining minutes |

Figure 5.1 Understanding Takt Time Calculations

in Figure 5.1 reflects a 10 hour working day, which helps simplify calculations for explanatory purposes.
- ❖ *Standard time per equivalent unit.* The target takt time assigned to a work center defines the standard production rate expressed in equivalent units.
- ❖ *Drumbeat ratio for each manufacturing kanban.* In standard AX, the drumbeat ratio for each manufacturing kanban is assumed to be one, since each item is considered to be one equivalent unit. The drumbeat ratio field within the kanban policies is ignored with the current version of AX.

The manufacturing kanbans scheduled for today are used to calculate the work cell's total *Required Quantity* in equivalent units. These kanban orders can be viewed on the Kanban Manufacturing form by filtering on the work cell and on the required date field (for the value of today's date). The total required quantity reflects the equivalent units. The required date reflects an item's lead time and the date on which its manufacturing kanban was emptied. If needed, you can manually override the required date and quantity for a manufacturing kanban.

The dynamic data related to *Current Takt Time* reflects the elapsed minutes and reported receipts as of the current time. Based on the example data shown in Figure 5.1, the work cell's current takt time is calculated to be 7.2 minutes per unit. This calculated value will be continually updated to reflect the elapsed minutes and received quantities as of the current time.[1]

- ❖ *Current Time.* A current time of 13:00 is shown in Figure 5.1. The current time is used for calculating elapsed minutes and remaining minutes in the context of today's working hours.
- ❖ *Elapsed Minutes as of Current Time.* The current time is used for calculating elapsed minutes in the context of today's working hours.
- ❖ *Actual Units Produced as of Current Time.* The actual units produced reflects today's reported receipts of manufacturing kanbans up to the current time. The actual units produced can include today's receipts for manufacturing kanbans with a different required date.

The dynamic data related to *Required Takt Time* reflects the current time, working hours, and units produced (described above) to calculate the remaining minutes and remaining quantity. Based on the example data shown in Figure 5.1, the work cell's required takt time is calculated to be 4.8

---

[1] A calculated value of zero typically indicates that the current time does not fall within working hours (so that elapsed time is zero) or that no manufacturing kanban receipts for the work cell have been reported today (so that the number produced is zero).

minutes per unit. This calculated value will be continually updated to reflect the remaining minutes and quantity as of the current time.[2]

* *Remaining minutes as of current time.* The current time is used for calculating remaining minutes in the context of today's working hours.
* *Remaining quantity as of current time.* The remaining quantity reflects the units produced as of the current time, which are subtracted from today's total quantity required.

The takt time metrics can be used to calculate the projected production for the remaining minutes in the working day. The bottom two rows of Figure 5.1 illustrate the projected production assuming the current pace (current takt time) and the target pace (target takt time).

Takt times can be viewed on two different forms. The Takt Time Board form displays all of the takt time metrics for a selected work cell (as of the current time). The Kanban Manufacturing form only displays a selected work cell's required takt time (as of the current time).

## Drumbeat for a Work Cell

A work cell's drumbeat can support sales order delivery promises based on available capacity. A work cell's daily drumbeat is currently implemented with a lean order schedule, as described in Chapter 9. The use of a lean order schedule represents an advanced topic and involves greater complexity. A simpler approach to a work cell drumbeat can be handled though a customization, as described in Case 6 at the end of this chapter.

The simpler approach within Case 6 builds on the calendar of working days assigned to a work cell, and the work cell's daily drumbeat

* *Calendar.* The calendar assigned to a work cell identifies the working and non-working days, and the specified hours of operation during each working day. In the context of a daily drumbeat for each working day, a non-working day has zero minutes of working time whereas a working day can consist of 24 hours or 1 minute of working time.
* *Daily Drumbeat.* The daily drum beat provides a simple measure of a work cell's capacity in terms of equivalent units. It applies to each working day within the calendar assigned to a work cell. As part of the customization, you define a work cell's daily drumbeat (that acts as the

---

[2] A calculated value of zero typically indicates that the current time is after the working hours (so that remaining time is zero) or that the total quantity required has already been received (so that the quantity remaining is zero).

default for all working days) and optionally define a different daily drumbeat for a specified date or a range of dates. This approach reflects the same one employed by lean order schedules.

This simple approach to a work cell's daily drumbeat does not reflect actual working hours. Nor does it reflect the target takt time assigned to a work cell. The target takt time represents an hourly drumbeat, which could be applied to the working hours to provide a more realistic model of a work cell's drumbeat. As a final note, the simple approach treats all items as an equivalent unit of one. It does not consider the drumbeat consumption ratio for a manufacturing kanban.

## Case Studies

**Case 6: Work Cell Drumbeat and Delivery Promises** A lean manufacturing company produced a family of make-to-order products at a final assembly cell. The company wanted to make sales order delivery promises based on the capacity constraints (of the final assembly work cell) and material constraints. They also wanted to have PTO manufacturing kanbans consume the available capacity. The suggested solution approach involves a customization, as described below.

Material constraints can be checked using the capable-to-promise (CTP) logic within standard AX. When entering a sales order line item, for example, the CTP calculations consider the availability of on-hand inventories. When these are insufficient, the calculations consider each item's lead time. The low inventories associated with lean manufacturing (and the lack of production orders to indicate scheduled receipts) mean that lead times are often used in the CTP calculations. The calculations provide a projected completion date based on material constraints.

Capacity constraints can be checked against the work cell's available drumbeats with a customization to standard AX. When entering a sales order line item, for example, the customization can provide the earliest completion date based on available drumbeats. The definition of a work cell's daily drumbeat was previously explained. The work cell's drumbeats can be immediately consumed by each PTO manufacturing kanban associated with a sales order line item. Since the company also produced a few make-to-stock items at the same final assembly work cell, the available drumbeats can also be consumed by a fixed manufacturing kanban (using the kanban's required date as the basis for consumption). Drumbeat consumption assumes that all items represent an equivalent unit of one; it does not account for a drumbeat consumption ratio.

## Executive Summary

A work cell represents a simpler alternative for modeling lean scenarios in comparison to the use of Dynamics AX work centers and routing data. However, it does not currently support value-added costs related to direct manufacturing and overhead allocations. When required, these costing purposes can be supported by the supplemental use of routing data.

Takt time metrics provide a measure of work cell performance. The target takt time assigned to each work cell represents its standard production rate. It also represents the work cell's drumbeat, but it is not used for making sales order delivery promises. A daily drumbeat can be defined when using a lean order schedule, which supports delivery promises and consumption of the drumbeat. An alternative approach was described as a case study.

# Chapter 6

# PTO Replenishment Kanbans

A PTO replenishment kanban moves a stocked item to its point of use based on a pull signal, such as a sales order or a manufacturing kanban. It serves two different purposes related to shipping and component picking.

- *Shipping Purpose.* PTO replenishment kanbans are used to move completed end items (stocked at the final work cell based on fixed kanbans) to a shipping area to meet sales order demands. They are automatically created by a sales order. This approach can replace or supplement the concept of a sales order picking list.
- *Component Picking Purpose.* PTO replenishment kanbans are used to move stocked components (at a work cell or in a stockroom) to a floor stock area for producing a manufacturing kanban. This can be a fixed manufacturing kanban or a PTO manufacturing kanban. In a typical scenario, they are automatically created when a fixed manufacturing kanban has been emptied, or when you release the PTO manufacturing kanban for a sales order end item. The component picking purposes of a PTO replenishment kanban are conceptually similar to a production order picking list for stocked components. In contrast, fixed replenishment kanbans are conceptually similar to a consolidated picking list and provide a small buffer at the point of use.

This chapter focuses on two scenarios involving PTO replenishment kanbans. One scenario reflects the shipping purposes, and the second scenario reflects the component picking purposes (for fixed manufacturing kanbans). The next chapter covers the component picking purposes in the context of PTO manufacturing kanbans. The chapter consists of the following sections:

- PTO Replenishment Kanbans for Shipping Purposes
- PTO Replenishment Kanbans for Component Picking Purposes (for a Fixed Manufacturing Kanban)

## PTO Replenishment Kanbans for Shipping Purposes

The explanation will start with a typical scenario. In this scenario, fixed kanbans will be used to stock end items at the final work cell (rather than a finished goods warehouse), and PTO replenishment kanbans will pull the inventory to a shipping area. The same scenario also illustrates the component picking purposes of PTO replenishment kanbans in the context of a fixed manufacturing kanban, as discussed in the next section.

The explanation of PTO replenishment kanbans for shipping purposes can be segmented into three basic topics: the policies for creating a kanban, the life cycle for a kanban, and the related coordination tools.

> **Scenario #3: PTO Replenishment Kanbans for Shipping Purposes**

Scenario #3 involves a single level product and fixed manufacturing kanbans to produce and stock the end item at the work cell area. This inventory will be pulled to a shipping area to support sales order shipments. Figure 6.1 summarizes the scenario and highlights the focus on PTO replenishment kanbans for shipping purposes.

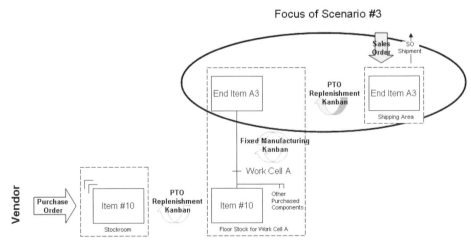

Figure 6.1 Replenishment Kanbans for Shipping Purposes

As illustrated in Figure 6.1, a sales order for the end item (at the shipping area) generates a PTO replenishment kanban for pulling the item's inventory from the floor stock area. The subsequent sales order shipment consumes the kanban inventory in the shipping area.

## Policies for Creating a PTO Replenishment Kanban (for Shipping Purposes)

Kanban policies are defined for an item and warehouse using the Kanbans form. These policies are inherited when a sales order initially creates a PTO kanban order. Figure 6.2 summarizes the policies for creating a PTO replenishment kanban. Most of these policies were previously described for fixed replenishment kanbans (see Figure 3.8). The following explanation focuses on the unique policies for creating a PTO replenishment kanban for shipping purposes.

**Sales Order Information**   Entry of a sales order automatically creates the end item's PTO replenishment kanban that reflects the sales order quan-

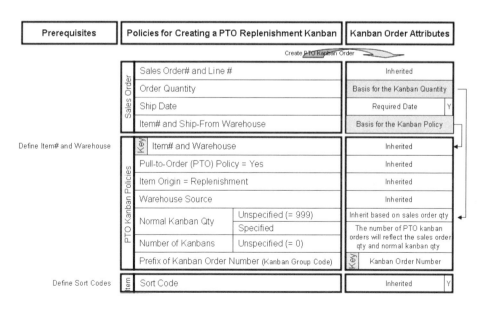

Figure 6.2  Policies for Creating a PTO Replenishment Kanban (for Shipping Purposes)

tity and ship date. Changes to the sales order quantity or ship date will automatically update the associated PTO replenishment kanban. The item and ship-from warehouse on the sales order determine the relevant kanban policies.

**Pull-to-Order (PTO) Policy**   The PTO policy indicates that a kanban order will only be created by a pull signal. In this case, a sales order acts as the pull signal for the PTO replenishment kanban. The pull signal could be from emptying a fixed manufacturing kanban (as described in the next section) or from a PTO manufacturing kanban (as described in the next chapter).

**Normal Kanban Quantity and Number of Kanban (Kanban Level)**
The normal kanban quantity is generally unspecified (as indicated by a value of "999" in the kanban policies) so that the PTO replenishment kanban inherits the sales order quantity. However, some situations require use of a specified kanban quantity, so that multiple kanban orders (for the normal kanban quantity) will be automatically created. The total matches the sales order quantity, which means that one kanban order may be less than the normal kanban quantity.

**Replenishment Lead Time**   The lead time for a replenishment kanban is always assumed to be zero, since it involves a simple move between warehouses. The lead time between warehouses can be defined within AX, but this lead time will be ignored for replenishment kanban purposes. The lead time attribute is not displayed in Figure 6.2.

**Prefix of the Kanban Order Number (Kanban Group Code)**   A meaningful prefix provides several advantages in viewing and using kanban order numbers, and you can optionally change the prefix for all related kanbans in circulation

Note: The Record Id is an internal identifier assigned to a kanban order number that supports barcode scanning of transactions. The system assigns a new Record Id when changes affect the kanban order number, such as a change to the sales order quantity that affects a PTO kanban. This approach helps avoid mistakes in barcode scanning from out-of-date paperwork, because the system will reject a transaction for the "old" Record Id.

**Example Ticket for a PTO Replenishment Kanban**   The example shown in Figure 6.3 includes the sales order information and the relevant warehouses for moving inventory. It also includes barcoded information about the Record Id and Item Number to support scanned transactions.

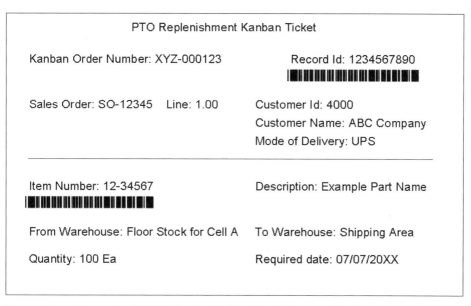

Figure 6.3 Example Ticket for PTO Replenishment Kanban

## Life Cycle of a PTO Replenishment Kanban (for Shipping Purposes)

The life cycle starts with the creation of a PTO replenishment kanban. In the context of shipping purposes, entry of a sales order for the end item automatically creates the PTO replenishment kanban. It will be automatically updated by changes to the sales order quantity or ship date, or by deletion of the sales order line, as long as other activities have not occurred such as a kanban receipt. Figure 6.4 summarizes the creation of a PTO replenishment kanban for shipping purposes.

Figure 6.4 Creating a PTO Replenishment Kanban (for Shipping Purposes)

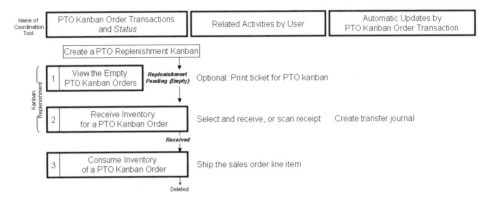

Figure 6.5 Life Cycle for a PTO Replenishment Kanban (for Shipping Purposes)

A PTO replenishment kanban (for shipping purposes) has a life cycle represented by a status that is closely related to kanban order transactions. Figure 6.5 summarizes the kanban order transactions and status, as well as related user activities and automatic updates. The figure depicts the kanban order status using italics, and highlights use of the Kanban Replenishment form as a coordination tool.

A newly created kanban order has a *replenishment pending* status; it can be termed *replenishment pending (empty)* status to emphasize the empty status.

**Prerequisite Step: Create a PTO Replenishment Kanban**  Entry of a sales order for the end item automatically creates the PTO replenishment kanban. A status of *PTO created* is assigned to the sales order line; this status communicates the production progress to sales personnel.

**Step 1: View the Empty PTO Kanban Orders**  An empty kanban order represents a requirement to move inventory from one warehouse to another warehouse. The Kanban Replenishment form displays the empty PTO replenishment kanbans, and supports printing of a kanban ticket.

**Step 2: Receive Inventory for a PTO Kanban Order**  After moving the material, the received quantity can be reported via barcode scanning or by entering data on the Replenishment Kanban form. A PTO kanban order can be received multiple times to achieve the quantity ordered. A partial receipt updates the sales order line status to *PTO Partial*. The sales order line status changes to *PTO Completed* after receiving the quantity ordered.

## Step 3: Consume Inventory of the PTO Kanban Order

The inventory associated with the PTO replenishment kanban is normally consumed by the sales order shipment, which results in automatic deletion of the kanban order and a sales order line status of *Kanban Delivered*.

## Coordination Tools for PTO Replenishment Kanbans

The primary coordination tools consist of the Kanban Replenishment form and the printed tickets for kanban orders. The Kanban Replenishment form displays the kanban orders requiring transfers from one warehouse to another. In particular, the form displays sales order requirements for PTO replenishment kanbans, as illustrated by the shaded fields in Figure 6.6. The first two examples in Figure 6.6 illustrate PTO replenishment kanbans for shipping purposes, whereas the last two examples illustrate the component picking purposes. Filters can help focus attention on kanban orders for a specified warehouse, with near-term requirement dates, or with a not-printed status. An additional filter can focus attention on PTO kanbans or fixed kanbans or both.[1] PTO replenishment kanbans are generally considered to have higher priority since they are linked to actual demands.

The typical actions using the Kanban Replenishment form include the following:

❖ Print (or reprint) ticket for a PTO replenishment kanban.
❖ Identify kanban orders with a past-due required date.

| Kanban Replenishment Form | | | | | | | | | | |
|---|---|---|---|---|---|---|---|---|---|---|
| Filters: | From Warehouse | To Warehouse | PTO vs Fixed Kanbans Both | Days Ahead Horizon 3 | Printed Status All | | | | | |
| Inventory Available | Mark | Kanban Order Number | Item Number | From Warehouse | Deliver To Warehouse | Sales Order | SO Line | Release Kanban Order Number | Quantity Ordered | Required Date | Printed |
| Yes | ☐ | RON_000202 | End Item A3 | Work Cell A | Shipping Area | SO-100 | 1.00 | | 7 | 07/07/20XX | Yes |
| Yes | ☐ | RON_000203 | End Item-A3 | Work Cell A | Shipping Area | SO-100 | 2.00 | | 18 | 07/07/20XX | Yes |
| No | ☐ | RON_000310 | Item #21 | Stockroom | Work Cell A | SO-344 | 1.00 | ANN_000555 | 15 | 07/05/20XX | Yes |
| Yes | ☐ | RON_000450 | Item #22 | Stockroom | Work Cell A | SO-387 | 1.00 | ANN-000641 | 20 | 07/05/20XX | Yes |

Examples of a PTO Replenishment Kanban for Shipping Purposes

PTO Demand Information

Examples of a PTO Replenishment Kanban for Component Picking Purposes

Figure 6.6 Example of the Kanban Replenishment Form with PTO Kanbans

---

[1] The filter attempts to differentiate between PTO kanban orders and non-PTO kanban orders, which includes fixed kanbans, fixed temporary kanbans, and target kanbans.

- Identify the sort type associated with a kanban order (if specified) to support sequencing or grouping of replenishment activities. This field is not shown in Figure 6.6.
- Identify kanban orders where a ticket has not yet been printed.
- Identify replenishment kanbans with required dates within a days ahead horizon.
- Identify availability of the from-warehouse inventory for a replenishment kanban, as shown in the far left column of Figure 6.6. An icon (a green hand or a red hand) communicates the same information about inventory availability.
- Select (mark) and receive a replenishment kanban for a specified quantity.

The form does not display received kanban orders because they do not require further action, nor does it support deletion of an empty kanban order. Kanban orders with the received status can be viewed on the Manual Kanban Update form. This form also supports deletion of an empty PTO replenishment kanban. The system prompts you to recreate the pull signal when deleting a PTO kanban.

## Variations of PTO Replenishment Kanbans for Shipping Purposes

Several variations of using PTO replenishment kanbans for shipping purposes are described below.

**Quantity Moved Exceeds the Sales Order Quantity** A PTO replenishment kanban may result in a transfer quantity greater than the sales order quantity. This larger quantity can be shipped to the customer, or the remainder can remain in the shipping area. Shipment of the larger quantity will be assumed based on a company-wide policy (termed the *update delivery remainder for PTO* checkbox on the Kanban Parameters form), and reflected in the packing slip update.

**Sales Orders Associated with Projects or RMAs** A sales order can be created for a project, or for the replacement item on an RMA. These sales orders can create a PTO replenishment kanban if the kanban policies have been defined for the item and warehouse. The ship-from warehouse for these sales orders may be the same or different than the normal shipping area.

**Alternative Method for Reporting Receipts of PTO Replenishment Kanbans (by Posting the Sales Order Picking List)** The alternative method involves posting the sales order picking list to obtain the printed document, which results in the receipt for all sales order lines with an associated PTO replenishment document. This alternative method requires a company-wide policy, termed the *update picking with replenishment* checkbox on the Kanban Parameters form.

## Template Concept for PTO Replenishment Kanban Policies

The kanban policies for PTO replenishment kanbans generally apply to all end items that must be moved to a shipping area (for shipping purposes), or to all components that must be moved to a work cell area (for component picking purposes). The template concept provides an alternative to defining kanban policies for each item and warehouse. The template concept consists of a dummy item and its associated kanban template for a destination warehouse, and the assignment of this dummy item to the relevant item numbers. Using the template concept involves the following three steps.

- *Define a Dummy Item on the Item Master.* The identifier and description should clearly indicate the item's purpose for a kanban template. In this scenario, an example description could be "kanban template for pulling items from work cell A to the shipping area." The dummy item will require the minimal information about an inventory unit of measure, an inventory model group, and item group. However, none of this information applies to its usage as a kanban template. The dummy item can be assigned a stopped flag for inventory transactions.
- *Define the Kanban Policies for the Dummy Item Using the Kanban Template Form.* The kanban policies are defined for the dummy item and destination warehouse (such as the shipping area) using the Kanban Template form. Figure 6.2 previously summarized these kanban policies for a PTO replenishment kanban, and the same policies are defined on the Kanban Template. For example, the item origin should be replenishment, the destination warehouse should be the shipping area, the warehouse source should be work cell area, and the normal kanban quantity should be unspecified (a value of 999). The kanban template must be flagged as active.

  A separate dummy item should be defined to represent each source if the shipping area can pull from different sources. Each dummy item requires a separate definition of kanban policies (using the Kanban Template form), and the same destination warehouse should be specified.
- *Assign the Dummy Item to Relevant Items.* The dummy item is assigned to relevant items using the field labeled *Kanban Template Group*.

The kanban policies associated with the dummy item will apply to all assigned items, such as the same prefix for kanban order numbers, the same policy for the normal kanban quantity, and the same source warehouse.

## PTO Replenishment Kanbans for Component Picking Purposes (for Fixed Manufacturing Kanbans)

The explanation will start with a typical scenario. In this scenario, the PTO replenishment kanbans are automatically created for an item's stocked components when a fixed manufacturing kanban has been emptied. Further explanation has been segmented into three basic topics: the policies for creating a kanban, the life cycle for a kanban, and the related coordination tools. These same topics were covered in the previous section, so the explanation highlights key differences for using PTO replenishment kanbans for component picking purposes related to fixed manufacturing kanbans.

> **Scenario #3a: PTO Replenishment Kanbans for Component Picking Purposes (for a Fixed Manufacturing Kanban)**

Scenario #3a involves a single level product and fixed manufacturing kanbans to produce and stock the end item in a finished goods warehouse. When a fixed manufacturing kanban has been emptied, it acts as a pull signal to move stocked components to the floor stock area so that the work cell can produce the manufactured item. Figure 6.7 summarizes the scenario and highlights the focus on PTO replenishment kanbans for component picking purposes.

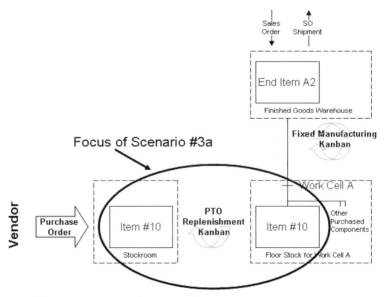

Figure 6.7 PTO Replenishment Kanbans for Component Picking Purposes (for a Fixed Manufacturing Kanban)

## Policies for Creating a PTO Replenishment Kanban (for Component Picking Purposes)

The PTO kanban policies must be defined for components of a manufactured item that is managed by fixed manufacturing kanbans. The manufactured item's bill of material indicates the warehouse source of components; the warehouse source must be reflected in the PTO kanban policies for the components. These kanban policies are assigned to the PTO replenishment kanbans that are created after emptying the fixed manufacturing kanban.

The kanban policies and the sales order information for creating a PTO replenishment kanban for shipping purposes were highlighted in Figure 6.2. The sales order information in the upper portion of Figure 6.2 does not apply to this scenario, but the kanban policies do apply.

An additional policy affects the creation of PTO replenishment kanbans in this scenario. The additional policy (defined in the BOM component information) indicates whether a PTO kanban will be automatically or manually released for a pull-to-order component. A manual release policy means that you must perform a separate step to release the fixed manufacturing kanban, which then creates the component's PTO replenishment kanban. They are created automatically (without a separate step) when you assign a policy of automatic. The concept of releasing a manufacturing kanban is discussed at length in the next chapter, so a minimal explanation is provided here. The component release policy is not shown in Figure 6.2; it is shown in Figure 7.3 for PTO manufacturing kanbans.

## Life Cycle of a PTO Replenishment Kanban (for Component Picking Purposes)

The life cycle starts with the creation of a PTO replenishment kanban. In the context of component picking purposes, the fixed manufacturing kanban must be emptied in order to automatically create the PTO replenishment kanbans for its components. An additional step may be needed (to release the fixed manufacturing kanban) when using a component release policy of manual.

The life cycle steps were previously displayed in Figure 6.5. The same steps apply to viewing and receiving a PTO replenishment kanban in this scenario, but it is deleted after receipt.

## Coordination Tools for PTO Replenishment Kanbans (for Component Picking Purposes)

The Kanban Replenishment form and printed kanban tickets act as the primary coordination tools, as previously illustrated in Figures 5.6 and 5.4.

The only difference is that the sales order information does not apply. The release kanban order number indicates the fixed manufacturing kanban requiring the component.

## Executive Summary

A PTO replenishment kanban moves a stocked item to its point of use based on a pull signal, either from a sales order or from a manufacturing kanban. It serves different purposes related to shipping and component picking.

- ❖ For shipping purposes, PTO replenishment kanbans are used to move completed end items (stocked at the final work cell) to a shipping area to meet sales order demands. This approach can replace or supplement the concept of a sales order picking list.
- ❖ For component picking purposes, PTO replenishment kanbans are used to move stocked components (at a work cell or in a stockroom) to a floor stock area for producing a fixed manufacturing kanban or a PTO manufacturing kanban. This approach represents a picking list for producing a kanban order.

The chapter focused on PTO replenishment kanbans for shipping purposes, and for component picking purposes in the context of fixed manufacturing kanbans. The explanation covered two typical scenarios, and reviewed the policies for created a kanban, the life cycle of a kanban, and the related coordination tools. It also covered several variations, such as kanban templates and alternative receipt approaches for PTO replenishment kanbans for shipping purposes.

# Chapter 7

# PTO Kanbans for Make-to-Order Items

Make-to-order products can be managed by PTO kanbans with direct linkage to the sales order. PTO kanbans are created by a pull signal, such as the sales order for the end item and the manufacturing kanbans for make-to-order components within the end item's product structure. The PTO kanbans for these components still identify the source of sales order demand. A make-to-order product is often produced from stocked components, and PTO replenishment kanbans support the component picking requirements for moving stocked items to their point of use. A make-to-order product may also require unique purchases, and PTO purchasing kanbans support these buy-to-order requirements.

This chapter focuses on two scenarios for using PTO kanbans to manage make-to-order products that reflect a single level and multilevel product structure. The previous chapter covered scenarios involving stocked items and the use of PTO replenishment kanbans for shipping purposes and component picking purposes. This chapter's scenarios also cover PTO replenishment kanbans, as well as PTO manufacturing kanbans and PTO purchasing kanbans. The first section explains the S&OP approaches for using PTO kanbans to handle make-to-order products. Subsequent sections cover each type of PTO kanban in terms of the policies for creating a kanban, the life cycle of a kanban, and the relevant coordination tools. The explanations build on information presented in previous chapters, and highlight the incremental differences rather than repeating the common information.

An understanding of fixed kanbans provides the foundation for explaining the incremental differences related to PTO kanbans. One key difference involves the creation of a PTO manufacturing kanban based on a pull signal such as the sales order for an end item. In a typical scenario, this PTO manufacturing kanban must be released in order to create the PTO kanbans for its pull-to-order components. A second key difference is that PTO kanbans are automatically deleted after consumption of their inventory.

The chapter consists of the following sections:

# Chapter 7

- ❖ S&OP Approaches for PTO Kanbans
- ❖ PTO Manufacturing Kanbans
- ❖ PTO Replenishment Kanbans (for Component Picking Purposes)
- ❖ PTO Purchasing Kanbans
- ❖ Managing Engineering Changes When Using PTO Kanbans
- ❖ Variations in Using PTO Kanbans

The use of PTO manufacturing kanbans can be supplemented with functionality associated with lean order schedules, as described in Chapter 9.

## Scenario #4: PTO Kanbans for a Single-Level Product

A single level make-to-order product provides the simplest viewpoint for illustrating PTO kanbans. Figure 7.1 depicts a single level product produced at a work cell from stocked components. The sales order for the end item automatically creates an empty PTO manufacturing kanban. When this kanban is released for production, it triggers the creation of PTO replenishment kanbans to move stocked components to the floor stock area. The components' floor stock inventory will be autodeducted based on receipts of the end item's PTO kanban into the shipping area. The sales order shipment consumes this PTO kanban inventory.

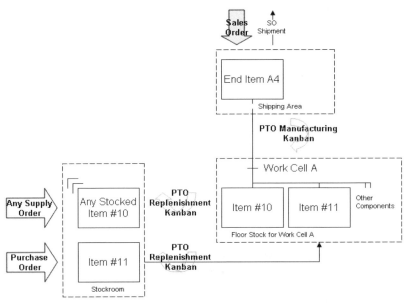

Figure 7.1 Single-Level Product and PTO Kanbans

## Scenario #4a  PTO Kanbans for a Multilevel Product

PTO kanbans also apply to a multilevel make-to-order product. Figure 7.2 depicts a multilevel product produced at multiple work cells. The sales order for the end item automatically creates an empty PTO manufacturing kanban. When this kanban is released for production, it triggers the creation of PTO kanbans for its pull-to-order components. This includes PTO replenishment kanbans to move stocked components to the floor stock area, and PTO manufacturing kanbans for make-to-order components.

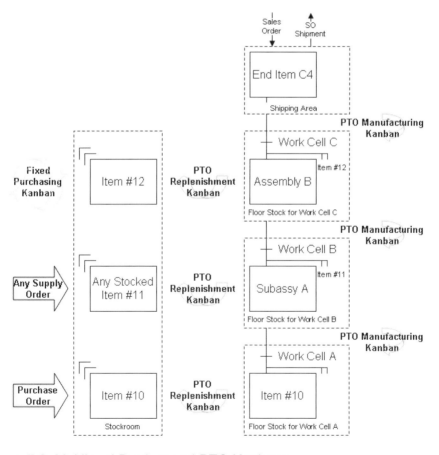

Figure 7.2  Multilevel Product and PTO Kanbans

# S&OP Approaches for PTO Kanbans

The S&OP game plan applies to the make-to-order product family produced at the final assembly work cell illustrated in Scenario #4 and Scenario #4a. The products may be completely or partially make-to order. With partially make-to-order products, the stocked components can be obtained via fixed kanbans or traditional supply orders. The S&OP approaches for traditional supply orders and fixed kanbans were explained in Chapters 2 and 3 respectively, where the demand plan is a key aspect of the S&OP approach.

The demand plan for make-to-order products consists of sales orders for end items. Each sales order line item has a corresponding PTO manufacturing kanban that represents the supply. Releasing a PTO manufacturing kanban for the end item triggers the generation of PTO kanbans for its pull-to-order components. Hence, the release step provides visibility of requirements across the product structure. Figure 7.3 summarizes the S&OP approach for make-to-order products.

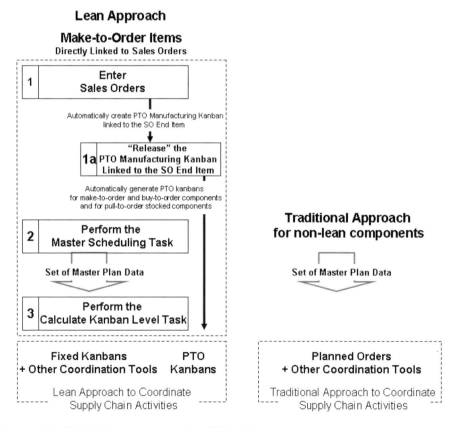

Figure 7.3 S&OP Approaches for PTO Kanbans

The replenishment of stocked components can be based on fixed kanbans or traditional supply orders. The lower left side of Figure 7.3 illustrates the use of fixed kanbans for stocked components, where the kanban levels can be calculated. The lower right side of Figure 7.3 illustrates the use of planned orders and traditional approaches for non-lean components within the product structure.

## PTO Manufacturing Kanbans

A PTO manufacturing kanban represents a logical starting point for further explanation of the scenario. It is automatically created by the sales order for a manufactured end item. In a typical scenario, releasing this PTO manufacturing kanban to production will automatically create PTO kanbans for its pull-to-order components. This includes PTO replenishment kanbans to move its stocked components to their point of use, and PTO manufacturing kanbans for its make-to-order components. Hence, PTO manufacturing kanbans can be created for an end item (based on the sales order) and for the end item's make-to-order components. The policies for creating a PTO manufacturing kanban are slightly different for these two situations.

An explanation of PTO manufacturing kanbans can be segmented into three basic topics: the policies for creating a PTO kanban, the life cycle for a PTO kanban, and the related coordination tools. An additional topic concerns the floor stock management approach, since it determines the impact of kanban receipt transactions and the use of a kanban empty transaction. It also reflects the choice between order-based versus value stream costing. The approaches were explained in the Chapter 3 section "Floor Stock Management Approaches."

The previous chapters about fixed manufacturing kanbans provide the foundation for understanding incremental differences related to PTO manufacturing kanbans. For example, fixed manufacturing kanbans were previously explained in terms of the policies for creating a kanban (Figure 3.17), an example kanban ticket (Figure 3.18), the life cycle for a kanban (Figure 3.19), and the coordination tools such as the Kanban Manufacturing form (Figure 3.20). Much of the information also applies to PTO manufacturing kanbans.

### Policies for Creating a PTO Manufacturing Kanban

Kanban policies are defined for an item and warehouse using the Kanbans form. These policies are inherited when creating a PTO manufacturing kanban for a sales order end item (termed the *SO end item* for short) or for the end item's make-to-order components. The policies for creating a PTO manufacturing kanban are slightly different for these two situations.

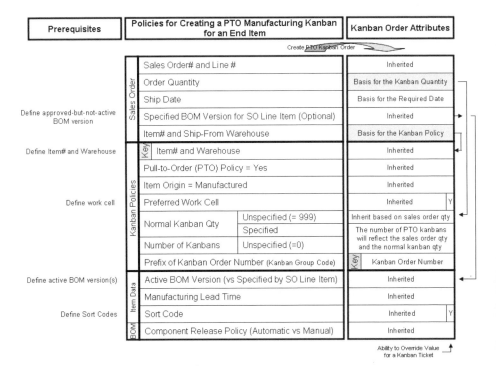

Figure 7.4 Policies for Creating a PTO Manufacturing Kanban for an End Item

We will initially focus on the policies for creating a PTO manufacturing kanban related to the sales order end item. The policies are summarized in Figure 7.4, along with the related prerequisite information. An item number and warehouse comprise the key fields for defining kanban policies, whereas a kanban order number uniquely identifies each kanban order.

**Sales Order Information**   Entry of a sales order line item for a kanban-controlled item and ship-from warehouse automatically creates a PTO manufacturing kanban. It reflects the sales order identifier, quantity, and ship date. A status of *PTO created* is assigned to the sales order line item. The sales order information is closely intertwined with several other policies, as highlighted by arrows in Figure 7.4.

- *Sales Order and the Kanban Policies for an End Item and Ship-From Warehouse.* The sales order specifies an item and ship-from warehouse, which indicate the relevant kanban policies for creating a PTO manufacturing kanban.
- *Sales Order Quantity and Normal Kanban Quantity.* A single PTO manufacturing kanban will be created when the normal kanban quantity

is unspecified. It inherits the sales order quantity. If a normal kanban quantity has been specified, a sales order for a larger quantity will result in multiple PTO manufacturing kanbans.
* *Sales Order with a Specified BOM Version.* The PTO manufacturing kanban (for the SO end item) normally inherits the item's active BOM version, unless you specified a different BOM version on the sales order line prior to saving the information. There is no impact if you enter a specified BOM version after saving the line, since the PTO manufacturing kanban has already been created.
* *Sales Order Changes and the Component Release Policy.* The choice of a component release policy applies to an end item's first level components. A manual release policy enables you to make sales order changes prior to releasing the end item's PTO manufacturing kanban to production. For example, you can change the sales order quantity, ship date or ship-from warehouse, or even delete the line. These changes will automatically update the end item's PTO manufacturing kanban.

Sales order changes cannot be entered after releasing the end item's PTO manufacturing kanban. The system prevents sales order changes because PTO kanbans have been created for pull-to-order components. You must delete all related PTO kanbans before you can make a sales order change.

**Component Release Policy (Automatic Versus Manual)** A component release policy applies to the first-level pull-to-order components of the end item in this scenario.[1] It determines whether you must perform a separate step to release the end item's PTO manufacturing kanban to production. The significance of an automatic versus manual policy is described below.

* *Automatic Release.* After a sales order creates a PTO manufacturing kanban for the end item, an automatic release policy (for first level components) means that PTO kanbans will be immediately created for this pull-to-order component. This approach makes sense when there are no expected changes to the sales orders or BOM information for the end item, and the delivery date represents a near-term requirement.
* *Manual Release.* After a sales order creates a PTO manufacturing kanban for the end item, a manual release policy (for one or more first level components) means that you decide when to release it to production. This requires a separate step to release the end item's PTO manufacturing kanban, which then creates PTO kanbans for pull-to-order components with a manual release policy. This approach makes sense

---

[1] The component release policy also applies to other scenarios, such as the release of a fixed manufacturing kanban (described in the previous chapter).

when you expect changes to the sales orders or BOM information for the end item, or the delivery date represents a longer-term requirement.

In this scenario, the ability to manually release a PTO manufacturing kanban only applies to one created for the sales order end item. It does not apply to the lower level components, since the system assumes an automatic release policy for all lower level components to support cascading creation of PTO kanbans. This applies to stocked components (with a PTO replenishment kanban), make-to-order components (with a PTO manufacturing kanban), and buy-to-order components (with a PTO purchasing kanban).

A similar concept applies to other scenarios. For example, a fixed manufacturing kanban may have pull-to-order components, where the components' release policy determines whether the fixed manufacturing kanban must be manually released to production.

**Pull-to-Order (PTO) Policy**   The PTO policy indicates that a kanban order will only be created by a pull signal. In this scenario, a sales order acts as the pull signal for the end item's PTO manufacturing. The pull signal could be from a PTO manufacturing kanban or a fixed manufacturing kanban.

**Work Cell**   The work cell assigned to a PTO manufacturing kanban must be predefined. One work cell policy identifies the calendar assigned to the work cell. The assigned calendar defines the working days (and working hours) and non-working days for the work cell.

A second work cell policy determines how PTO manufacturing kanban receipts will be handled by traditional AX functionality. A PTO manufacturing kanban receipt can be handled with an orderless approach (via a BOM Journal) or an order-based approach (via a production order). These approaches apply to detailed tracking and general tracking of floor stock inventory, as described in the Chapter 3 section "Floor Stock Management Approaches." Other work cell policies only apply to a lean order schedule, as described in Chapter 9.

A PTO manufacturing kanban order supports coordination of production activities, but it does not support cost accumulation for actual costing purposes. When order-based costing is required, each receipt of a manufacturing kanban should automatically generate an associated production order (based on the work cell policy described above). The autodeduction of components (and routing data) for this production order supports the actual costing capabilities within AX.

**Normal Kanban Quantity and Number of Kanbans**   The normal kanban quantity is generally unspecified, as indicated by a value of "999" for the kanban policy. The kanban level should be zero for a PTO kanban. In this way, a single PTO manufacturing kanban will be created that reflects the demand.

The normal kanban quantity must be specified in some situations, so that one or more PTO kanbans will be created to satisfy the sales order quantity. This means that PTO kanbans will inherit the normal kanban quantity, although one PTO kanban may be less than the normal kanban quantity so that the total matches the sales order quantity.

**BOM Version**   A PTO manufacturing kanban normally inherits the item's active BOM version as of the creation date, unless you specify a different BOM version when entering the sales order line item.[2] The inherited BOM version will stay with the PTO manufacturing kanban. In order to assign a different BOM version, you must delete the sales order line and create another line. The components within the inherited BOM version define the basis for component backflushing at the time of kanban receipt.

**Manufacturing Lead Time**   The item's manufacturing lead time is used to calculate the suggested production start date for a PTO manufacturing kanban. When the lead time is 3 days, for example, and the sales order ship

Figure 7.5  Example Ticket for a PTO Manufacturing Kanban

---

[2] A manufactured item can have multiple active BOM versions that reflect different sites, non-overlapping validity periods, and/or different quantity breakpoints. The active BOM version assigned to a PTO manufacturing kanban will reflect the creation date and the sales order quantity. With PTO manufacturing kanbans, the system ignores a BOM version specified in the kanban policies.

date is the 20th of the month, the suggested production start date would be 17th of the month. The suggested production start date is not reflected in the required date for components with PTO kanbans. Their required date reflects the required date for the PTO manufacturing kanban.

Some situations require completion of a PTO manufacturing kanban before the sales order ship date. This concept is implemented using the kanban offset field within the kanban policies, so that the required date for a PTO manufacturing kanban will be earlier than the sales order ship date.

**Example Ticket for a PTO Manufacturing Kanban**   The example shown in Figure 7.5 includes the sales order information, as highlighted by shading. It includes bar-coded information about the Record Id and Item Number, which are used to support scanned receipt transactions. The example also includes the optional item-related text and BOM information.

**Policies for Creating a PTO Manufacturing Kanban for Make-to-Order Components**   The policies for creating a PTO manufacturing kanban for a make-to-order component are slightly different. While still linked to the originating sales order, the policies reflect information about a parent item and its PTO manufacturing kanban. These policies are summarized in Figure 7.6 and described below.

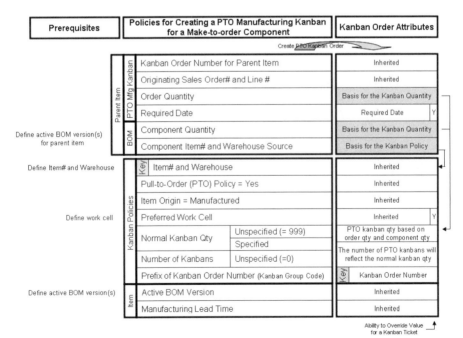

Figure 7.6  Policies for Creating a PTO Manufacturing Kanban for a Make-to-Order Component

The kanban order number for the parent item and its originating sales order define the source of demand (aka the pull signal). The demand includes an order quantity and required date. This demand is translated into component requirements based on BOM information about each component's quantity and warehouse source. The BOM information includes each component's release policy (automatic versus manual), which only applies to the first-level components of the sales order end item. A previous section described the component release policy.

## Life Cycle of a PTO Manufacturing Kanban

The creation of a PTO manufacturing kanban represents a prerequisite step to the life cycle. A single level product (such as Scenario #4) involves the creation of a single PTO manufacturing kanban for a sales order, and the choice of an automatic versus manual release approach for pull-to-order components. Figure 7.7 summarizes the creation and release of this PTO manufacturing kanban for the sales order end item.

Entry of a sales order will automatically create a PTO manufacturing kanban for the end item. It will also create a PTO kanban for first-level pull-to-order components with an automatic release policy. Alternatively, the PTO kanbans for first-level pull-to-order components (with a manual release policy) will be created when you release the end item's PTO manufacturing kanban to production. This step is labeled 1a in Figure 7.7.

With a multilevel product (such as Scenario #4a), the component release policy determines when to create a PTO manufacturing kanban for a first-level component, which then cascades through the product structure to create other PTO manufacturing kanbans for make-to-order components.

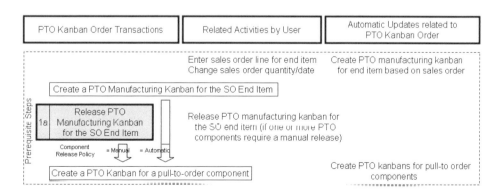

Figure 7.7 Creating and Releasing a PTO Manufacturing Kanban

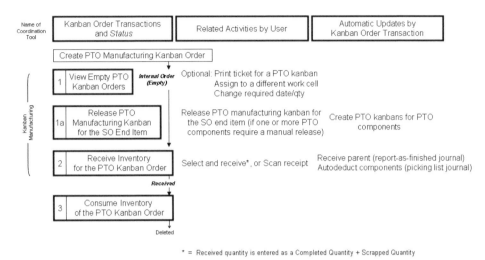

Figure 7.8 Life Cycle for a PTO Manufacturing Kanban

Figure 7.8 summarizes the life cycle for a PTO manufacturing kanban in this scenario. The life cycle includes three basic steps, and an additional step (labeled Step 1a) that applies to the manual release of a PTO manufacturing kanban for a sales order end item.

### Prerequisite Step: Create a PTO Manufacturing Kanban Order

The creation of a PTO manufacturing kanban reflects a sales order for an end item. It can also reflect a make-to-order component within the end item's product structure.

### Step 1: View the Empty PTO Kanbans

An empty kanban represents a requirement to produce the item at a work cell, and deliver it to the destination warehouse. Use the Kanban Manufacturing form to view the empty kanbans, and to optionally print a kanban ticket, to assign the kanban to a different work cell, or to change the required quantity and date.

You can optionally delete an empty PTO kanban prior to its release. You can also reset the release and delete the PTO kanban. After deletion, the system will prompt you to recreate the pull signal. If it is not recreated at this time, you can change sales order information about the quantity or date, and the PTO kanban will be automatically recreated.

### Step 1a: Release PTO Manufacturing Kanban for the SO End Item

This step must be performed when a first level component (with PTO kanban policies) has a manual release policy, as already described.

**Step 2: Receive Inventory for the PTO Kanban Order**   The receipt can be reported via bar code scanning, or by entering data on the Kanban Manufacturing form. Multiple receipts can be recorded. The kanban status changes to *received* when the kanban quantity has been fully received, and the sales order status is updated to *PTO completed*.

The impact of a receipt on inventory transactions will depend on the floor stock management approach. The right side of Figure 7.8 displays the inventory transactions based on a detailed tracking approach. When the work cell policy for receipt transactions is based on a production order (rather a BOM journal), the user may need to perform a follow-up step to end the production order.

**Step 3: Consume Inventory of the PTO Kanban Order**   The sales order shipment normally consumes inventory associated with a PTO manufacturing kanban for the sales order end item, and the status for the sales order line indicates *Kanban delivered*. Consumption results in automatic deletion of the kanban order.

The kanban inventory for a component is normally placed in a floor stock area. It can be consumed by component backflushing or an explicit kanban empty transaction, as determined by the floor stock management approach.

## Coordination Tools for PTO Manufacturing Kanbans

The primary coordination tools consist of the Kanban Manufacturing form and the printed tickets for kanban orders. PTO manufacturing kanbans are not displayed on the Stop/Go Board, so it cannot be used as a coordination tool.

The Kanban Manufacturing form displays the kanbans requiring action by the planner. In particular, the form displays the pull signal for a PTO manufacturing kanban, as illustrated by the shaded fields in Figure 7.9. The pull signal stems from a sales order in the first three examples; it stems from a fixed manufacturing kanban order in the last two examples. The planner can review upcoming requirements for kanban deliveries, and record actual receipt of a kanban. A filter can help focus attention on kanbans for a specified work cell.

The Kanban Manufacturing displays one of the takt time metrics for a specified work cell; the Takt Time Board displays all of the metrics. As one metric, the required takt time reflects the remaining minutes within today's working hours divided by the remaining units within today's schedule. The example in Figure 7.9 shows 5.90 minutes per unit. The metrics were previously explained in the Chapter 5 section "Takt Time Metrics for a Work Cell."

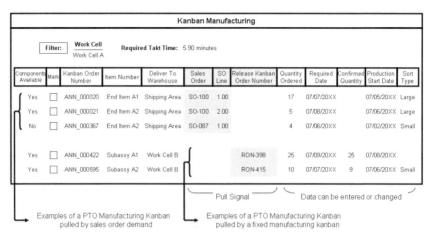

Figure 7.9  Example of the Kanban Manufacturing Form

The form can be used to select a PTO manufacturing kanban so that you can release the PTO kanbans for pull-to-order components (with a manual component release policy).  The other typical actions were described in Chapter 3, and are repeated below.

❖ Print (or reprint) a manufacturing kanban ticket.
❖ Delete an internal order (empty) kanban .
❖ Change the required date or quantity ordered.
❖ Identify manufacturing kanbans with a past-due required date.
❖ Identify the sort type associated with a kanban order (if specified) to support sequencing or grouping of manufacturing activities.  The sort type for a kanban order can be manually overridden.
❖ View and/or assign the production start date, which initially reflects the required date minus the item's manufacturing lead time.  The production start date represents reference information, and does not have any impact on system logic.
❖ Assign a different work cell to a manufacturing kanban.
❖ Identify component availability for a manufacturing kanban, as shown in the far left column of Figure 7.9.  An icon (a green hand or a red hand) communicates the same information about component inventory availability.
❖ Use the Explode function to view component availability information in a single-level or multilevel bill of material format.
❖ Select and receive a manufacturing kanban, and report the actual quantity completed (and quantity scrapped, if applicable).

The form does not display received kanban orders because they do not require further action. Kanban orders with the received status (and any other status) can be viewed on the Manual Kanban Update form.

## Template Concept as the Basis for PTO Manufacturing Kanban Policies

A PTO manufacturing kanban generally applies to every make-to-order item within the product family produced at a work cell, since every PTO kanban will be triggered by a sales order and placed in the same destination warehouse. The template concept provides an alternative to defining kanban policies for each item and warehouse. The template concept consists of a single kanban template that can be assigned to all items within a product family. Using the template concept involves the following three steps.

❖ *Define a dummy item on the item master.* The identifier and description should clearly indicate the item's purpose for a kanban template. In this scenario, an example description could be "kanban template for producing PTO end items at work cell C for delivery to the shipping area."

The dummy item will require the minimal information about an inventory unit of measure, an inventory model group, and item group. However, none of this information applies to its usage as a kanban template. The dummy item should be assigned the stopped flag for inventory transactions.

❖ *Define the kanban policies for the dummy item using the Kanban Template form (aka define a kanban template).* The kanban policies are defined for the dummy item, the work cell, and the destination warehouse (such as the shipping area). Figure 7.4 previously summarized these kanban policies for a PTO manufacturing kanban, and the same policies apply to the kanban template. For example, you need to define the item origin (manufactured), the work cell, and the destination warehouse. The the normal kanban quantity should be unspecified (a value of 999). The kanban template must be flagged as active.

❖ *Assign the dummy item to each item within the product family.* The kanban template for the dummy item and warehouse will be used to create PTO manufacturing kanbans based on sales orders for the item/warehouse. The assigned kanban template indicates a lean-controlled item/warehouse.

The above-mentioned steps for a kanban template mean that the kanban policies apply to all relevant items within the product family, such as the same prefix for kanban order numbers, the same policy for the normal kanban quantity, and the same destination warehouse.

For PTO manufacturing kanbans, an additional dummy item and kanban template should be defined for each combination of work cell and destination warehouse. For example, Scenario #4a would require a template for work cell A, work cell B, and work cell C. The dummy item can then be assigned to the relevant item numbers produced at each cell.

## PTO Replenishment Kanbans (for Component Picking Purposes)

PTO replenishment kanbans (for component picking purposes) can be driven by PTO manufacturing kanbans. They are used to move stocked components to their point of use, which typically reflects a floor stock area to support production at a work cell. Chapter 6 previously described the use of PTO replenishment kanbans driven by a fixed manufacturing kanban. The two contexts of fixed versus PTO manufacturing kanbans have slight differences in creating a PTO replenishment kanban for component picking purposes, although the life cycles are almost identical.

An explanation of PTO replenishment kanbans (for component picking purposes) can be segmented into three basic topics: the policies for creating a PTO kanban, the life cycle for a PTO kanban, and the related coordination tools.

### Policies for Creating a PTO Replenishment Kanban for Component Picking Purposes

Kanban policies are defined for an item and warehouse using the Kanbans form, where the item and source warehouse are reflected in the BOM component information. These policies are inherited when a PTO manufacturing kanban leads to the creation of a PTO replenishment kanban. The attributes of this kanban order reflect its kanban policies and the other information summarized in Figure 7.10. An item number and warehouse comprise the key fields for defining kanban policies, whereas a kanban order number uniquely identifies each kanban order.

**PTO Manufacturing Kanban for the Parent Item** The kanban order number for the parent item (and its originating sales order) define the source of demand. The demand includes an order quantity and required date. The parent's BOM information defines the components and their warehouse

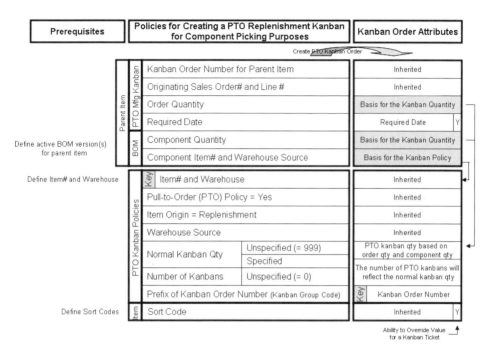

Figure 7.10  Policies for Creating a PTO Replenishment Kanban (for Component Picking Purposes)

source (which indicate the relevant kanban policies), and the component quantities. The demand for a component reflects its component quantity and the order quantity.

The parent's BOM information includes each component's release policy (automatic versus manual), which only applies to the first-level components of the sales order end item. A previous section described the component release policy.

**Pull-to-Order (PTO) Policy**   The PTO policy indicates that a kanban order will only be created by a pull signal. In this case, a PTO manufacturing kanban acts as the pull signal for the PTO replenishment kanban.

**Normal Kanban Quantity and Number of Kanban Orders**   The normal kanban quantity is generally unspecified, as indicated by a value of "999" for the kanban policy. The kanban level should be zero for a PTO kanban. In this way, a single PTO replenishment kanban will be created that reflects the demand.

The normal kanban quantity must be specified in some situations, so that one or more PTO kanbans will be created to satisfy the required quantity.

This means that PTO kanbans will inherit the normal kanban quantity, although one PTO kanban may be less than the normal kanban quantity so that the total matches the demand.

An example ticket for a PTO replenishment kanban was shown in Figure 6.3.

## Life Cycle for a PTO Replenishment Kanban

The creation of a PTO replenishment kanban for component picking purposes is directly tied to the creation of a PTO manufacturing kanban in this scenario. The previous section (and Figure 7.7) explained the creation of a PTO manufacturing kanban for the sales order end item, and the impact of releasing it to production.

The life cycle for a PTO replenishment kanban is represented by a status, and the status is closely related to kanban order transactions. This life cycle is summarized in Figure 7.11 and described below. The figure depicts the kanban order status using italics, and highlights use of the Kanban Replenishment form as a coordination tool.

**Prerequisite Step: Create a PTO Replenishment Kanban** The creation of a PTO manufacturing kanban leads to the creation of a PTO replenishment kanban for its components.

**Step 1: View the Empty PTO Kanban Orders** An empty kanban order represents a requirement to move inventory from one warehouse to another. The Kanban Replenishment form displays the empty PTO replenishment kanbans, and supports printing of a kanban ticket.

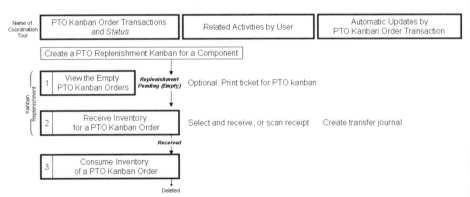

Figure 7.11 Life Cycle for a PTO Replenishment Kanban (for Component Picking Purposes)

## Step 2: Receive Inventory for a PTO Kanban Order
After moving the material, the received quantity can be reported via barcode scanning or by entering data on the Replenishment Kanban form. Multiple receipts can be recorded to achieve the quantity ordered, which changes the kanban status to received. The inventory impact of a receipt will depend on the floor stock management approach. The right side of Figure 7.11 displays the inventory transaction (a transfer journal) based on a detailed tracking approach.

## Step 3: Consume Inventory of the PTO Kanban Order
The PTO kanban inventory associated with a component can be consumed by component backflushing or an explicitly kanban empty transaction, as determined by the floor stock management approach.

## Coordination Tools for PTO Replenishment Kanbans

The primary coordination tools consist of the Kanban Replenishment form and the printed tickets for kanban orders. The Kanban Replenishment form displays the kanban orders requiring transfers from one warehouse to another, as illustrated in Figure 7.12. In the context of component picking, the form displays requirements in terms of the PTO manufacturing kanban (for the parent item) and the originating sales order. The second group of examples in the figure illustrates PTO replenishment kanbans for component picking purposes, whereas the first group of examples illustrates the shipping purposes. Filters can help focus attention on kanban orders for a specified warehouse, with near-term requirement dates, or with a not-printed status. An additional filter can focus attention on PTO kanbans or fixed kanbans or both.

| | | | Kanban Replenishment | | | | | | | |
|---|---|---|---|---|---|---|---|---|---|---|
| | | Filters: | From Warehouse | To Warehouse | PTO vs Fixed Kanbans | Days Ahead Horizon | Printed Status | | | |
| | | | | | PTO | 3 | All | | | |
| Inventory Available | Mark | Kanban Order Number | Item Number | From Warehouse | Deliver To Warehouse | Sales Order | SO Line | Release Kanban Order Number | Quantity Ordered | Required Date | Printed |
| Yes | ☐ | RON_000202 | End Item A4 | Work Cell A | Shipping Area | SO-100 | 1.00 | | 7 | 07/07/20XX | Yes |
| Yes | ☐ | RON_000203 | End Item A4 | Work Cell A | Shipping Area | SO-100 | 2.00 | | 18 | 07/07/20XX | Yes |
| No | ☐ | RON_000310 | Item #21 | Stockroom | Work Cell A | SO-344 | 1.00 | ANN_000555 | 15 | 07/05/20XX | Yes |
| Yes | ☐ | RON_000450 | Item #22 | Stockroom | Work Cell A | SO-387 | 1.00 | ANN_000641 | 20 | 07/05/20XX | Yes |

Examples of a PTO Replenishment Kanban for Shipping Purposes — Examples of a PTO Replenishment Kanban for Component Picking Purposes (PTO Demand Information)

Figure 7.12 Examples of the Kanban Replenishment Form with PTO Kanbans

Typical actions using the Kanban Replenishment form include the following:

- Print (or reprint) ticket for a PTO replenishment kanban.
- Identify kanban orders with a past-due required date.
- Identify the sort type associated with a kanban order (if specified) to support sequencing or grouping of replenishment activities. This field is not shown in Figure 7.12.
- Identify kanban orders where a ticket has not yet been printed.
- Identify replenishment kanbans with required dates within a days ahead horizon.
- Identify availability of the from-warehouse inventory for a replenishment kanban, as shown in the far left column of Figure 7.12. An icon (a green hand or a red hand) communicates the same information about inventory availability.
- Select (mark) and receive a replenishment kanban for a specified quantity.

The form does not display received kanban orders because they do not require further action. Kanban orders with the received status can be viewed on the Manual Kanban Update form.

### Template Concept for PTO Replenishment Kanbans

A PTO replenishment kanban generally applies to all components that must be pulled to a work cell area from a stockroom. The template concept can eliminate or reduce the data maintenance associated with kanban policies for every component. For example, you define a dummy item that represents "pulling to a work cell area from a stockroom," define its kanban policies using the Kanban Template form, and then assign the dummy item to relevant items.

## PTO Purchasing Kanbans

A make-to-order product is often produced from stocked components, but some products require buy-to-order components. PTO purchasing kanbans support these buy-to-order requirements.[3] This typically requires a supplier

---

[3] A PTO purchasing kanban can also reflect a sales order for a buy-to-order item. This scenario is typically handled more effectively with traditional AX functionality, which also supports direct delivery of the purchased item to the customer.

relationship that can handle kanban coordination, which reflects a more mature stage of lean manufacturing.

An explanation of PTO purchasing kanbans builds on the previous description of fixed purchasing kanbans. Chapter 3 described fixed purchasing kanbans in terms of the policies for creating a kanban (Figure 3.3), an example kanban ticket (Figure 3.4), the life cycle for a kanban (Figure 3.5), and the coordination tools such as the Kanban Purchasing form (Figure 3.7). This section will highlight the key differences in using PTO purchasing kanbans. The key differences include the policies for creating a PTO kanban and several limitations.

## Policies for Creating a PTO Purchasing Kanban

Kanban policies are defined for an item and warehouse using the Kanbans form. These policies are inherited when a PTO manufacturing kanban (and its related sales order) lead to creation of a PTO purchasing kanban. The attributes of this kanban order reflect the kanban policies and other information as summarized in Figure 7.13. An item number and warehouse comprise the key fields for defining kanban policies, whereas a kanban order number uniquely identifies each kanban order.

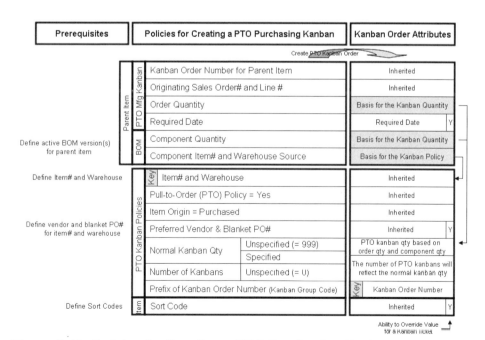

Figure 7.13 Policies for Creating a PTO Purchasing Kanbans

The information about a parent item reflects the same information presented for PTO replenishment kanbans, and is not repeated here. The sales order information is typically included on a printed ticket for a PTO purchasing kanban.

The life cycle for a PTO purchasing kanban is identical to a fixed purchasing kanban, except that it is automatically deleted after consuming the kanban inventory. You also use the Kanban Purchasing form as a primary coordination tool.

### Limitations of a PTO Purchasing Kanban

A PTO purchasing kanban can be delivered to a stockroom or directly to a floor stock area. However, the destination warehouse cannot be designated as a black hole warehouse, because this prevents proper accounting.

## Managing Engineering Changes When Using PTO Kanbans

Engineering changes often involve bill of material considerations when using PTO manufacturing kanbans. These considerations include the following:

- *Dynamically changing product structure.* The impact of a dynamically changing product structure can be postponed by using a manual release policy for all first-level components. The product structure will then be recognized when you finally release the end item's PTO manufacturing kanban to production.
- *Specified BOM version for a sales order line item.* The specified BOM version must be entered prior to saving the sales order line information, other wise the PTO manufacturing kanban will inherit the active BOM versions for the end item.
- *Changing the BOM version on the PTO manufacturing kanban for the end item.* If activities have not been reported, you can delete the sales order line and create a new line that can inherit the desired BOM version.

## Variations in Using PTO Kanbans

Several variations can be identified for PTO manufacturing kanbans. These variations include subcontract manufacturing and custom product manufacturing.

## PTO Manufacturing Kanbans with Subcontracting

Subcontract manufacturing can also be supported by PTO manufacturing kanbans. This requires kanban policies related to subcontracting, and involves the life cycle and coordination tools for subcontracting. These topics were previously covered in Chapter 4. The variations for subcontract manufacturing also apply to PTO manufacturing kanbans. These variations include the following:

- Supplying a discrete kit of components versus consigned inventory of supplied components.
- The outside operation can be the only production step, or an intermediate or final step in a multistep process.
- Use subcontracting on a one-time or intermittent basis. This involves definition of the outside operation component, an approved vendor (and blanket PO) for the outside operations, and possibly a different BOM version that specifies the supplied components.
- Use a different subcontractor. Same as above.
- Internally produce an item that is normally subcontracted.

## Custom Products and PTO Kanbans

A custom product can be defined using the rules-based product configurator within Dynamics AX, which is associated with modeling-enabled items.[4] Use of the product configurator creates a master BOM and provides two output options for assigning the master BOM to (1) the modeling enabled item or (2) to a newly-created item number. The template concept can be used as the basis for PTO manufacturing kanban policies for custom products, where you assign the dummy item (aka the template item) to the modeling-enabled item. The template concept works for the first output option. It must be customized slightly to work for the second output option that creates a new item number so that the new item inherits the template item.

## Other Variations

Other variations of using PTO kanbans include barcode scanning of receipts, and the creation of PTO manufacturing kanbans for sales orders associated

---

[4] The rules-based product configurator approach for modeling-enabled items is described on pages 94-107 in the AX 2009 book.

with projects or RMAs. These variations were previously described in Chapter 3.

## Case Studies

**Case 7: Customized Electric Motors**  An electric motor manufacturer produced custom products from stocked components and from several buy-to-order components. The factory layout involved a U-shaped final assembly work cell and several supporting work cells, as reflected in a two-level product structure. The daily production volume was approximately 500 units (a takt time of 10 minutes per unit), and the similarity of custom products meant they could be treated as equivalent units. Use of a product configurator during order entry generated a unique BOM version for the item number representing a custom product, and for the item numbers representing customized assemblies. The company currently employed a manual kanban system to coordinate supply chain activities, and wanted to replace it with electronic kanbans and Dynamics AX. The following description summarizes the prescribed solution approach, expressed in the past tense for explanatory purposes:

As a starting point, their approach to a product configurator was replaced by the capabilities associated with a modeling-enabled item within AX. The item number representing a custom product was assigned kanban policies for a PTO manufacturing kanban. The item numbers representing each customized subassembly were also assigned kanban policies for a PTO manufacturing kanban. Each sales order for a custom motor generated a corresponding PTO manufacturing kanban for the end item, although a large order quantity generated multiple PTO manufacturing kanbans that reflected the item's normal kanban quantity. A customized schedule board was developed to display these kanbans for the final assembly work cell; it also displayed the kanbans for synchronizing work at supporting work cells.

Once the final assembly schedule was agreed upon, the scheduler released the PTO manufacturing kanbans for end items, which generated the PTO manufacturing kanbans for the customized subassemblies, the PTO purchasing kanbans for buy-to-order components, and PTO replenishment kanbans for stocked components. Stocked components were purchased based on projected rates of demand, and issued from a stockroom to the relevant floor stock areas using the PTO replenishment kanbans. The receipt of a PTO manufacturing kanban resulted in the autodeduction of its component quantities, which supported order-based costing for each custom product.

## Executive Summary

PTO kanbans are typically used for make-to-order products that require direct linkage to sales order demand. A sales order for the end item automatically creates a PTO manufacturing kanban. In a typical scenario, this PTO manufacturing kanban must be released in order to create the PTO kanbans for its pull-to-order components. The release step, for example, creates PTO replenishment kanbans for pulling stocked items to their point of use, PTO manufacturing kanbans for make-to-order components, and PTO purchasing kanbans for buy-to-order components. This chapter reviewed each type of kanban in terms of its creation policies, life cycle, and coordination tools. It also covered engineering change management and other variations in using PTO kanbans, as well as a case study of make-to-order electric motors.

# Chapter 8

# Lean Accounting

Lean accounting focuses on the elimination of waste from the accounting processes and from unnecessary transactions related to manufacturing. A significant percentage of transactions represent waste in many companies; they consume management attention and do not add value. The lean accounting practices vary with the different maturity stages in lean manufacturing. For example, the first stage involving a lean pilot project generally employs an order-based costing approach, whereas the second and third stages employ value stream costing. These two costing approaches require different approaches to floor stock management. In particular, the reduced inventory quantities can lead to the elimination of detailed tracking of floor stock inventory within Dynamics AX.

Other aspects of lean accounting involve product costing, the assignment of ledger account numbers to transactions, and segmentation of kanban-related transactions by journal names. These topics provide an organizing focus for further explanation, and the chapter consists of the following sections:

- ❖ Product Costing
- ❖ Order-Based Costing
- ❖ Value Stream Costing
- ❖ General Ledger Considerations

The goals of lean accounting include support for generally accepted accounting principles (GAAP) and financial reporting, and the elimination of waste from the accounting process. These goals can be accomplished in different ways using standard functionality within Dynamics AX as well as customized extensions. This chapter focuses on the major solution approaches using standard AX functionality.

## Product Costing

Product cost information supports valuation of an item's inventory transactions using a standard cost or an actual cost method. The explanations of lean scenarios have focused on standard costing. In addition, the lean scenarios have not employed routing data for costing purposes, so that the calculation of a manufactured item's standard cost only reflects its components' direct material costs (and possibly the costs of outside operations).[1]

Some lean scenarios require landed costs for purchased items, such as freight or duty costs. In this case, the Dynamics AX functionality for miscellaneous charges can account for the landed costs after posting the vendor invoice for the purchased item.[2]

Some lean scenarios require overhead allocations for manufactured items. The definition of an overhead formula supports the calculation of a manufactured item's overhead. For example, an overhead formula can specify a surcharge percentage to calculate material-related overhead, such as applying the percentage to the value of components.[3]

Some lean scenarios require value-added costs to support calculation of a manufactured item's cost and suggested sales price. In addition, autodeduction of these value-added costs supports an order-based costing approach for manufacturing kanbans. In this case, routing data must be used to support the costing purposes, as explained in Chapter 5.

## Order-Based Costing

The pilot stage of lean manufacturing typically employs an order-based costing approach to manufacturing kanbans. This approach can keep current accounting practices largely unchanged. To support order-based costing, each manufacturing kanban receipt can generate an associated production order. This approach builds on the traditional AX functionality related to production order costing.[4] The behind-the-scenes production order supports actual costing of manufactured items.

Order-based costing requires detailed tracking or general tracking of floor stock inventory, so that costs are correctly assigned to a production order. Chapter 3 described these floor stock management approaches, but the key concepts are repeated here. The two basic variations for managing a component's floor stock inventory are summarized below.

❖ *Option #1: Detailed tracking with backflushing of component quantities.* Detailed tracking involves backflushing the components' inventory

---

[1] The explanations of standard costing and cost rollup calculations are covered on pages 111-129 in the AX 2009 book.
[2] Miscellaneous charges are explained on pages 221-222 in the AX 2009 book.
[3] Overhead formulas are covered on pages 121-124 in the AX 2009 book.
[4] Production order costing is described on pages 327-329 in the AX 2009 book. Order-based costing requires a work cell policy that indicates manufacturing kanban receipts will be handled as a production order (rather than a BOM journal).

quantities (based on manufacturing kanban receipts) to calculate when a component's kanban order has been emptied. The inventory transactions associated with detailed tracking are typically considered as waste, and have been estimated as 12 percent of transaction volume.
- *Option #2: General tracking with backflushing of component value.* General tracking involves backflushing the component's value (not inventory quantities) to support order-based costing. This is termed the cost substitution concept. Since this approach does not consume component inventory, you must explicitly identify when a component's kanban order has been emptied. General tracking helps eliminate the transactions associated with detailed tracking while still supporting order-based costing.

A combination of detailed and general tracking may be used, so that some component quantities are backflushed while other components only have their value backflushed.

# Value Stream Costing

The second and third maturity stages in lean manufacturing involve value stream costing and the use of black hole warehouses. This requires a financial dimension to represent the value stream, and the appropriate floor stock management approach for black hole warehouses. The basic idea involves tracking inventory in and out of the value stream but not within the production area, while still retaining the coordination provided by pull signals.

## Financial Dimension for a Value Stream

A financial dimension provides the basis for tracking costs by value stream.[5] There are two basic approaches for assigning a financial dimension to inventory transactions. A financial dimension can be assigned to items or warehouses or both to support value stream costing.

- *Item-related financial dimension.* Each item within a product family can be assigned the same financial dimension, thereby supporting the concept of value stream costing by product family. For example, you could use the "department" financial dimension to indicate the product families, and track purchases by product family.

---

[5] A company-wide policy (termed the Lean Accounting check box on the Lean Order Parameters form) indicates that a financial dimension will be used for value stream costing. You must also designate which financial dimension will be used, such as the department or cost center dimension.

- *Warehouse-related financial dimension.* A warehouse can represent the floor stock inventory associated with a work cell. Hence, one or more floor stock warehouses (and the associated work cells) within a value stream can be assigned a financial dimension. For example, you could use the "cost center" financial dimension to indicate the work cells within a value stream, and track material issues to the floor stock warehouses associated with the work cells.
- *Both item- and warehouse-related financial dimensions.* As an extension of the two previous examples, you could use the "department" and "cost center" financial dimensions to reflect the item- and warehouse-related ledger postings.

The assignment of different financial dimensions to other entities (such as vendors, customers, and sites) should be considered to avoid overlapping assignment of financial dimensions. Other costs can also be charged to the financial dimension associated with the value stream. These costs may include production labor, machines, support services, facilities, and maintenance.

## Black Hole Warehouses Related to Production Within the Value Stream

Value stream costing typically employs black hole warehouses for floor stock inventory, thereby eliminating inventory tracking through production. The key concept is that components are issued into black hole warehouses, and end items are received from black hole warehouses. This reflects a floor stock management approach in which inventory quantities are not tracked within black hole warehouses, but you can still report received and empty kanbans to assist coordination. The policies concerning component backflushing and cost substitution do not apply.

The black hole concept is generally implemented by designating floor stock warehouses as a black hole, as previously described in the Chapter 3 section "Floor Stock Management Approaches." Scenario #6 shown in Figure 8.1 illustrates the black hole concept in a multilevel product. It highlights two aspects of replenishment kanbans for issuing components into the value stream account, and receiving end items from the value stream account.

There are other ways to "issue material" to a black hole warehouse that are not displayed in Figure 8.1. For example, a manufacturing kanban can be received into a black hole warehouse.

The next section covers the assignment of G/L account numbers related to black hole issues and receipts. Figure 8.1 displays the T accounts related to inventory issued to (and received from) a black hole warehouse via replenishment kanbans.

# Lean Accounting 149

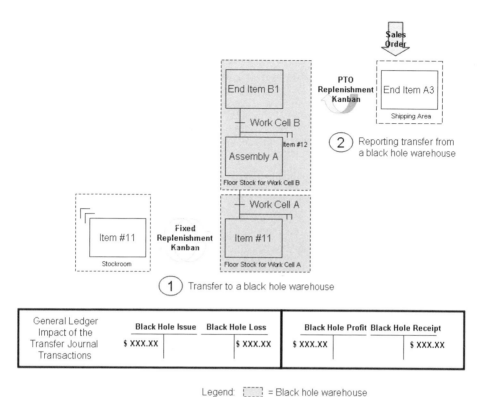

Figure 8.1 Value Stream Costing and Black Hole Warehouses

## Value Stream Costing and Black Hole Warehouses

Value stream costing typically employs black hole warehouses for floor stock inventory, thereby eliminating inventory tracking through production. The key concept is that components are issued into black hole warehouses, and end items are received from black hole warehouses. Figure 8.1 illustrates this concept in terms of a multilevel product, and highlights the two aspects of replenishment kanbans for issues to and receipts from black hole warehouses.

❖ Replenishment kanbans are used for transferring stocked items to a floor stock area designated as a black hole warehouse. This impacts the G/L accounts for a black hole issue and loss, as shown in the bottom of Figure 8.1.
❖ Replenishment kanbans are used for transferring a completed end item out of a black hole warehouse. This impacts the G/L accounts for a black hole receipt and profit.

# General Ledger Considerations

The use of kanban-related inventory transactions involves additional G/L account numbers, and segmentation of kanban-related transactions by journal name.

## G/L Account Numbers for Kanban-Related Transactions

G/L account number assignment reflects the item group assigned to an item. For example, the item group defines the G/L account numbers for inventory, cost of sales, and revenue. Additional G/L account numbers can be defined for two types of kanban-related transactions: the kanban inventory issued to or received from a black hole warehouse, and the kanban empty transaction (for the floor stock management approach to consume a fixed kanban's inventory). The four additional G/L account numbers represent an issue, receipt, loss, and profit for inventory transactions. Figure 8.1 displayed the T accounts related to these four ledger accounts for black hole warehouses.

## Segmenting Kanban-Related Inventory Transactions by Journal Name

Journal names provide one way to segment inventory transactions, especially those related to transfer journals (for replenishment kanbans) and inventory journals (for issues to and receipts from a black hole warehouse). A journal name also has an associated voucher number sequence, such as a user-defined prefix and counter that identifies inventory transactions impacting the ledger.

Most journal names reflect company-wide policies, as summarized in Figure 8.2. Two of the journal names can also be specified as kanban policies for an item and warehouse. The figure illustrates the typical kanban-related transaction for each journal name.

## Expensing Purchased Materials into the Value Stream

Some mature lean scenarios have extremely small inventories of purchased materials. You can treat the purchased material as an expense item in this case, and avoid tracking physical and financial inventory (based on the inventory model group polices assigned to the item).

| Journal Type | Journal Name | | Example of a Kanban-Related Transaction |
|---|---|---|---|
| | Company-Wide | Kanban-Specific | |
| Transfer | Transfer Journal | Yes | Receive a Replenishment Kanban |
| P/L | P/L Journal | Yes | ? |
| | Empty Kanban | | Report a Fixed Kanban as Empty |
| | Scrap Kanban | N/A | Scrap a Fixed Kanban |
| Transfer | Black Hole | | Receive a Replenishment Kanban into (or from) a Black Hole Warehouse |

Figure 8.2  Example of Journal Names for Kanban-Related Transactions

## Executive Summary

The different maturity stages in lean manufacturing have different approaches to accounting. The pilot project stage generally employs an order-based costing approach, whereas the second and third stages employ value stream costing. These two costing approaches require different approaches to floor stock management. Order-based costing requires detailed or general tracking of component inventory in floor stock areas, whereas value stream costing typically employs black hole warehouses and does not track inventory through floor stock areas. Scenario #6 illustrated value stream costing and black hole warehouses.

A value stream can be represented by a financial dimension. Various costs can be charged to this financial dimension, such as the costs for production labor, machines, support services, facilities, and maintenance. These costs are not typically included in product costs, which are comprised of direct material costs and possible outside operation costs. However, some lean scenarios may include landed costs (for purchased items) or overhead allocations (for manufactured items) in their product costs.

# Chapter 9

# Lean Order Schedules

Work cell activities can be coordinated through various forms of coordination tools. The format of a coordination tool tends to be unique for every company because of differences in the nature of the products and manufacturing processes. The format is often expressed as a graphical schedule board or a spreadsheet. The explanation to date has described two examples of out-of-the-box coordination tools. One example is the graphical Kanban Stop/Go Board for coordinating fixed manufacturing kanbans at a work cell. The second example is the Kanban Manufacturing form for coordinating fixed and PTO manufacturing kanbans at a work cell. However, these two examples did not support the concept of a work cell drumbeat for making sales order delivery promises or for work cell scheduling.

The solution approaches to a work cell drumbeat and scheduling can become very complex. One indicator of this complexity is reflected in the software packages for advanced planning and scheduling. The current version of Dynamics AX contains one solution approach termed a lean order schedule. It does not necessarily represent a common solution approach for lean manufacturing scenarios.

Dynamics AX employs an additional construct—a schedule—to support a work cell drumbeat. It is termed a *Lean Order Schedule* or *LOS* for short. There are actually two variations termed a *Booked-to-Order LOS* and a *Cumulative LOS*. You designate the desired variation when you initially define a lean order schedule. A Cumulative LOS does not use kanbans and will not be covered in this book. This chapter focuses on the Booked-to-Order LOS because it represents the most widely used approach among current users and a relatively straightforward extension of manufacturing kanbans. Rather than use the lengthy term Booked-to-Order Lean Order Schedule, or the shortened term BTO-LOS, we will simply use the term LOS because it is the only scheduling tool covered in this chapter.

A lean order schedule is typically assigned to the final assembly work cell to support make-to-order products. Each LOS line represents a sales order line item. With this approach, the primary coordination tool consists of the Lean Order Schedule form and a LOS line acts as the basis for a pull signal and printed ticket. They replace use of the Kanban Manufacturing form and PTO manufacturing kanbans. The approach involves a change in terminology as summarized in the chapter's first section. The use of a lean order schedule provides other functionality (such as engineering documentation) that is not covered in this book.

A lean order schedule defines the daily drumbeat of its associated work cell. This daily drumbeat supports delivery promises for make-to-order products produced by the associated work cell, and sales orders consume this daily drumbeat. While the primary focus of a LOS tends to be make-to-order products with PTO manufacturing kanban policies, it can optionally support stocked items with fixed manufacturing kanban policies. Stated another way, the LOS primarily supports the pull signals for sales orders and it can optionally support buffer replenishment of fixed kanbans.

The two contexts of PTO and fixed manufacturing kanbans are reflected in two sections of this chapter. The chapter starts with a typical scenario involving a final assembly work cell and a family of make-to-order products, and consists of the following sections:

- ❖ Terminology for Using a Lean Order Schedule (LOS)
- ❖ Using a LOS for PTO Manufacturing Kanbans
- ❖ Using a LOS for Fixed Manufacturing Kanbans

Lean order schedules represent an advanced topic and involve greater complexity than the manufacturing kanban constructs. The chapter is not recommended for a novice learner, and should be considered as reference material for more advanced learners.

## Lean Order Schedule for Final Assembly

A two-level product provides a simple viewpoint for illustrating a lean order schedule for final assembly. Figure 9.1 depicts the two-level product, where a lean order schedule has been assigned to the final assembly work cell. The various products produced by the work cell have been assigned to a family grouping, and the family grouping is assigned to the schedule. These products also have PTO manufacturing kanban policies that specify the final assembly work cell and the destination warehouse of a shipping area. A sales order triggers the creation of a LOS line, which acts as the pull signal for producing the end item.

A second work cell produces a component used in final assembly. The figure identifies this component as Assembly A. This second work cell does not have an assigned lean order schedule, therefore a PTO manufacturing kanban acts as the pull signal for producing Assembly A.

Lean Order Schedules 155

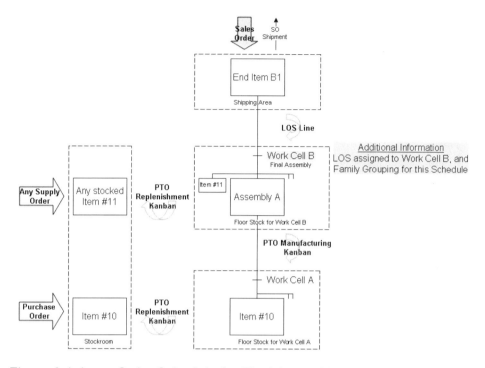

Figure 9.1  Lean Order Schedule for Final Assembly

## Terminology for a Lean Order Schedule (LOS)

Use of a lean order schedule introduces a different set of terminology. The construct of a PTO manufacturing kanban is replaced by a LOS line, and the Lean Order Schedule form acts as the primary coordination tool (rather than the Kanban Manufacturing form). Up to this point, we have consistently used kanban terminology throughout the book, as summarized in Figure 1.3. This chapter will use the LOS terminology. A comparison of terminology and other factors is summarized in Figure 9.2 and described below.

The kanban policies for creating a PTO manufacturing kanban are also used for creating a LOS line. The kanban policies define the associated work cell for a PTO manufacturing kanban. The differentiating factor is whether the work cell has an assigned lean order schedule, since this determines whether a sales order line item will create a PTO manufacturing kanban or a LOS line. A lean order schedule is typically assigned to the final assembly work cell.

Once a sales order has been entered, it creates a LOS line. The LOS line has an identifier (the sales order and line number), a status (termed the

| | Kanban versus LOS Terminology ||
| --- | --- | --- |
| | PTO Manufacturing Kanban | Lean Order Schedule (LOS) |
| Term | PTO Manufacturing Kanban or PTO Manufacturing Kanban Order | LOS Line |
| Status | Kanban Status or Kanban Order Status | Booked Status or LOS Line Status |
| Identifier | Kanban Order Number | Sales Order# and Line# |
| Printed Document | Kanban Ticket | Job Ticket |
| Name of Coordination Tool | Kanban Manufacturing form | Lean Order Schedule form |
| Kanban Policies | Kanban Policies for Creating a PTO Manufacturing Kanban ||
| Differentiating Factor within the Kanban Policies | Work cell does not have a LOS | Work cell has an assigned LOS, and the LOS family includes the item |
| Primary Focus | Any work cell | Final assembly work cell |
| Life Cycle Status | Internal Order (Empty) | Created (Empty) Released Started |
| | Received | Received Completed |

Figure 9.2 Kanban Versus LOS Terminology

*booked status*), and an optional printed document (termed a *job ticket*). The booked status reflects a multistep life cycle, starting with a created status and ending with a completed status. In addition, the booked status is displayed on the related sales order line to communicate production progress to sales personnel.

## Using a LOS for PTO Manufacturing Kanbans

A lean order schedule is typically assigned to a final assembly work cell, and typically applies to make-to-order products. The kanban policies for these make-to-order products include the specified work cell, and reflect a PTO manufacturing kanban. The products are also identified as members of a family grouping assigned to the lean order schedule. These differentiating factors mean that a sales order line will create a LOS line (rather than a PTO manufacturing kanban), and that the Lean Order Schedule form will act as the primary coordination tool.

This section starts with a summary of the Lean Order Schedule form, and then reviews the setup information for a lean order schedule. The work cell's daily drumbeat is one aspect of the LOS setup information, so we cover how to use the daily drum beat for making sales order delivery promises. The explanation reviews the policies for creating a LOS line, and the basic life cycle of a LOS line. Additional explanations cover the variations for each step of the life cycle.

## Summary of the Lean Order Schedule Form

The Lean Order Schedule form acts as the primary coordination tool for its associated work cell; it replaces use of the Kanban Manufacturing form. Each LOS line displays a sales order requirement, where the sales order number and line number act as the unique identifier (rather than a kanban order number). Figure 9.3 provides an example of the Lean Order Schedule form, and a comparison to the fields on the Kanban Manufacturing form. The planner can review upcoming requirements for production, and record updates about each LOS line. A filter can help focus attention on production for a specified work cell, time period, and destination warehouse.

The form supports several types of planner actions. The basic actions consist of releasing a LOS line (which triggers kanban creation for its pull-to-order components), and recording receipts and completion of a LOS line. These actions change a line's booked status from created to released, received, and completed, respectively. The form supports several other aspects of coordination that will be explained in a subsequent section.

Figure 9.3 Example of the Lean Order Schedule Form

## Setup Information for a Lean Order Schedule

A lean order schedule requires several aspects of setup information for its related work cell, the actual schedule, and the family grouping of items produced at the work cell.

**Work Cell Information**   Each work cell has a unique user-defined identifier, and several policies pertinent to LOS lines. These work cell policies determine whether a receipt (1) will be handled as production order or BOM journal transactions, (2) will be reserved for a sales order, and (3) will result in component backflushing that reflects the components' planned scrap. Several additional policies only apply when a lean order schedule is also used to support fixed manufacturing kanbans, as described in this chapter's section "Using a LOS for Fixed Manufacturing Kanbans."

**Lean Order Schedule**   Each lean order schedule has a unique user-defined identifier, and is assigned to a work cell. The user-defined schedule identifier is typically similar to the user-defined identifier for the work cell, thereby making it easier to understand the one-to-one relationship. The key policy (termed the *Book to Sales Order* checkbox) indicates the desired variation of a lean order schedule. Other critical polices include the following:

- ❖ *Calendar.* Each calendar has a unique user-defined identifier. A calendar identifies the working and non-working days, and the specified hours of operation during each working day. In the context of a drumbeat for each working day, a non-working day has zero minutes of working time whereas a working day can consist of 24 hours or 1 minute of working time.[1]
- ❖ *Drum Beat per Day.* The daily drum beat provides a simple measure of a work cell's capacity in terms of equivalent units. It applies to each working day within the calendar assigned to the schedule. The daily drumbeat is initially assigned when you define a lean order schedule, and it acts as the default for all working days. However, you can define a different daily drumbeat for a specified date or a range of dates, thereby reflecting changes in available capacity. These changes in available capacity are defined on the Update Schedule Drumbeat form. The daily drumbeat can be used for making delivery promises on sales orders for make-to-order items produced at the work cell, as described in the next topic about Sales Orders and Delivery Promises.

---

[1] The working time defined in a calendar does not affect the daily drumbeat, so that the daily drumbeat must be defined separately to reflect the anticipated capacity.

There are many additional policies for a lean order schedule that can help model variations in business practices. These policies will be introduced in the context of their applicability.

**Family Grouping and the Drumbeat Consumption Ratio** The products produced by a work cell with a lean order schedule must be identified twice: once for the PTO manufacturing kanban policies and also for a family grouping assigned to the schedule. A family grouping has a unique-user-defined identifier and is assigned to a schedule, as defined on the *Family Grouping* form. The user-defined family identifier is typically similar to the user-defined identifiers for the work cell and schedule, thereby making it easier to understand the one-to-one relationships.[2] A related form (termed the *Item Grouping* form) defines each family member. An item must be assigned to a family before you can define its PTO manufacturing kanban policies for the work cell.[3] You can reassign an item from one family to another to reflect a change.

The key policy for each family member includes the ratio for drumbeat consumption. A ratio of 2.0 means that a sales order for the item will consume 2 drumbeats per unit. A ratio of .5 will consume .5 drumbeats per unit. A ratio of 0.0 means that a sales order for the item will consume zero drumbeats.

In summary, manufactured items are assigned to a family, a family is assigned to a schedule, and the schedule is assigned to a work cell. As mentioned above, an item must be assigned to a family before you can define its PTO manufacturing kanban policies for the work cell.

**Sales Orders and Delivery Promises**

A sales order line item will create a corresponding LOS line. The promised delivery date can be automatically calculated based on the work cell's drumbeat or capable-to-promise (CTP) logic or both.

❖ *Delivery promise based on capable-to-promise (CTP) logic.* When entering a sales order line item, the calculations consider the availability of on-hand inventory and scheduled receipts. When these are insufficient, the calculations consider each item's lead time. The calculations display a prompt that enables you to accept or reject the suggested

---

[2] It is possible to define multiple family groups and assign them to the same schedule identifier.
[3] When using the kanban template concept, you must also assign the dummy item to the family grouping.

delivery date. The prompt is labeled a *standard ATP check*, even though the calculations actually reflect capable-to-promise logic.[4]

These CTP calculations reflect the same logic embedded in traditional AX.[5] With traditional AX, the calculations (termed an *Explosion* inquiry) must be user-initiated for each sales order line item, and the user must transfer the projected date (termed the *futures date*) back to the sales order. The calculations suggested planned orders, and the user could optionally firm these planned orders. With the lean functionality, however, the user cannot firm the planned orders and the CTP calculations are performed automatically. You can still access the Explosion inquiry to review the CTP logic.

❖ *Delivery promise based on the drumbeat for a work cell's schedule.*[6] When entering a sales order line item, the calculations display a prompt (labeled a *lean ATP check*) that enables you to accept or reject the suggested delivery date.[7] Rejecting the suggested delivery date typically results in overconsumption of the drumbeat. Consumption of the daily drumbeat is based on the concept of equivalent units, as defined by the ratio assigned to each item. Information about a schedule's drumbeat availability and consumption can be viewed on the Schedule Drumbeat Availability form (accessed from a specific lean order schedule).

The delivery promise calculations display two separate prompts when you use both approaches. The prompts will also be displayed after you change the sales order quantity or ship date.

## Policies for Creating a LOS Line

The context of a final assembly work cell means that we can focus on policies for creating a LOS line for an end item. These policies are similar to the policies for creating a PTO manufacturing kanban.[8] Both are created by a sales order, and both require definition of the kanban policies for a PTO

---

[4] A company-wide policy (termed the *MTS ATP check* checkbox on the Lean Order Parameters form) determines whether the CTP calculations will be performed automatically for all lean-controlled items, regardless of the Delivery Date Control policy. As an alternative, you can indicate that automatic calculations should only be performed when the Delivery Date Control policy is ATP. This alternative company-wide policy is termed the *Use Lead Time for MTS Items* checkbox.

[5] The explanation of CTP logic for making sales order delivery promises is covered on pages 180-183 in the AX 2009 book.

[6] A company-wide policy (termed the *Sales ATP Implemented* checkbox on the Lean Order Parameters form) determines whether the daily drumbeat will be considered when making sales order delivery promises.

[7] The consideration of drumbeat availability starts with the first date that material will be available, as calculated by the capable-to-promise logic described above.

[8] The policies for creating a PTO manufacturing kanban for a sales order end item were previously explained and summarized in Figure 6.3.

# Lean Order Schedules

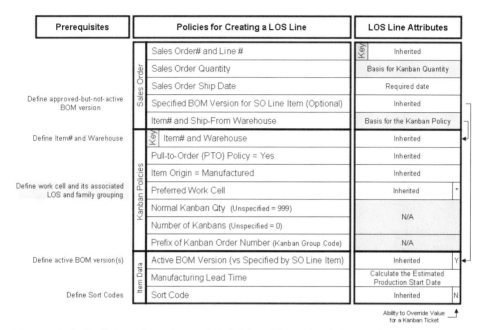

Figure 9.4  Policies Creating a LOS Line (for a PTO Manufacturing Kanban)

manufacturing kanban.  Figure 9.4 summarizes the policies for creating a LOS Line.  The following explanation reviews these policies, and highlights the differences with creation of PTO manufacturing kanbans.

**Sales Order Information**   The sales order specifies an item and ship-from warehouse which define the relevant kanban policies for creating a LOS line.  A single LOS line will be created for each sales order line, and it reflects the specified quantity and ship date.  It can optionally reflect a specified BOM version for the sales order line.

The unique identifier for a LOS line consists of the sales order number and line number.  Each LOS line is also assigned an internal Record ID.  The Record ID is printed on a job ticket for the LOS line, and used for scanned transactions such as a receipt.  The Record Id is automatically updated whenever you change the sales order quantity, date, or ship-from warehouse. This approach eliminates problems associated with scanned transactions and out-of-date paperwork, since a scanned transaction will be rejected if the Record Id no longer exists.

In contrast with a PTO manufacturing kanban, the sales order cannot trigger the automatic release of pull-to-order components.  The user must perform a separate step to release a LOS line.[9] In addition, the normal kanban quantity is always ignored in creating a single LOS line for each sales order line.

**Pull-to-Order (PTO) Policy**   The PTO policy indicates that a LOS line will only be created by sales order demand.

**Normal Kanban Quantity and Number of Kanban**   The normal kanban quantity and kanban level are always treated as unspecified, so that the kanban quantity always reflects the sales order quantity.

**BOM Version**   A LOS line normally inherits the item's active BOM version as of the creation date, unless you specify a different BOM version as part of the sales order line item.[10] The inherited BOM version can be overridden on a LOS line, typically before releasing the LOS line so that the impact will be recognized.[11] The components within the BOM version define the basis for component backflushing at the time of receipt.

**Example of a Job Ticket for a LOS Line**   The example shown in Figure 9.5 includes the sales order information, and the barcoded information about the Record Id which will be used for scanning transactions. The example includes the BOM component information. The printed job ticket can optionally include item-related or BOM-related text, which must be expressed as a note document for internal purposes.[12]

## Life Cycle for a LOS Line

The context of a final assembly work cell means that we can focus on a life cycle that starts with creation of a LOS line based on entry of a sales order. Figure 9.5 summarizes the life cycle transactions and booked status related to a LOS line, as well as the related user activities and the automatic updates by a transaction. It also highlights use of the Lean Order Schedule form as a coordination tool at each life cycle step.

---

[9] The component release policy (for first-level components) only applies to PTO manufacturing kanbans. It does not apply to LOS lines, and a LOS line always requires a separate release step.

[10] A schedule-specific policy (termed the *Use Sales Order BOM* checkbox) enables the specified BOM version to be inherited. When the active BOM version is inherited, it reflects the creation date and the sales order quantity.

[11] Changes to the BOM version after releasing a LOS line will not be recognized until you perform the Update BOM function on the lean order schedule form.

[12] The Lean Order Parameters form defines a company-wide policy (termed the Use Manufacturing Notes for Item Type field) that determines whether to print text on the job ticket. It also defines the related policy (termed Manufacturing Document Type) about which user-defined type of document should be printed. These represent a different set of policies than the ones used for printing text on manufacturing kanbans.

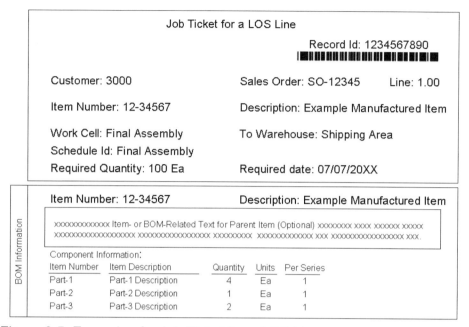

Figure 9.5 Example of a Job Ticket for a LOS Line

**Prerequisite Step: Create a LOS Line for a SO End Item**   Entry of a sales order line will automatically create a corresponding LOS line for the end item. The LOS line is assigned a booked status of *created*, which is also displayed for the sales order line item. The drumbeat of the work cell's schedule will be automatically consumed by the sales order quantity based on equivalent units (using the ratio of the item).

At the created status, changes to the sales order quantity or date will automatically update the corresponding LOS line. Conversely, you can change the LOS line's delivery date to reflect the actual production schedule, which will update the sales order delivery date.[13] Deleting the sales order line item will also delete the corresponding LOS line.

**Step 1: View the LOS Lines**   A LOS line with a created status represents a requirement to produce the item at the work cell, and deliver it to the destination warehouse. Use the Lean Order Schedule form to view LOS lines, and to optionally assign a different schedule, assign a different BOM version, or print a job ticket for a LOS line.

---

[13] A schedule-specific policy (termed the *Allow Update of Delivery Date* checkbox) determines whether changes to the delivery date can be entered on the lean order schedule form.

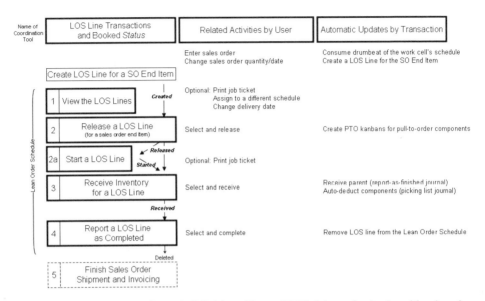

Figure 9.6 Life Cycle for a LOS Line (for a PTO Manufacturing Kanban)

**Step 2: Release a LOS Line**  Select (mark) a LOS line on the Lean Order Schedule form in order to release it. Releasing a LOS line for the end item will automatically create PTO kanbans for its pull-to-order components, which can then be acted upon. This includes PTO replenishment kanbans (to pull stocked components to their point of use), PTO purchasing kanbans for components, and PTO manufacturing kanbans throughout a multilevel product structure.

**Step 2a: Optionally Start a LOS Line**  Starting a line represents an optional step that communicates production has actually started. The step can be used to automatically print the job ticket.[14]

**Step 3: Receive Inventory for a LOS Line**  A receipt can be reported via barcode scanning, or by entering data on the Lean Order Schedule form. Multiple receipts can be recorded to achieve the quantity ordered. The booked status changes to *received* when the total received quantity matches the quantity ordered.

The impact of a receipt on inventory transactions will depend on the floor stock management approach. The right side of Figure 9.5 displays the inventory transactions based on a detailed tracking approach. When the work

---

[14] A schedule-specific policy (termed the Print Job Cards checkbox) determines whether job tickets can be printed. A related policy (termed the Automatically Print Job Cards checkbox) determines whether job tickets will be automatically printed when updating a LOS line to a booked status of Started.

cell policy for receipt transactions is based on a production order (rather than a BOM journal), the user must perform a follow-up step to end the production order.

**Step 4: Report a LOS Line as Completed**   Reporting a LOS line as completed will remove it from the Lean Order Schedule form. The booked status for the sales order will be blank, communicating the completion of production activities.

**Step 5: Finish Sales Order Shipment and Invoicing**   Shipments and invoices are normally handled with traditional AX functionality, as described below. A schedule-specific policy (termed the *Sales Order* policy) indicates whether some of these activities will be represented in the life cycle of a LOS line, as described in the section about variations to Step 5 (and illustrated in Figure 9.8).

Traditional AX functionality supports three approaches for reporting shipments. The first approach involves the packing slip update for each sales order. The other two approaches involve separate steps for picking the material prior to the packing slip update, either with an order picking list or a consolidated picking list. The Release Sales Order Picking form provides visibility of anticipated picking activities, and displays open sales order line items that should be released for picking based on actual availability.[15]

## Life Cycle Variations for a LOS Line

The variations apply to each step of the life cycle for a LOS line, so the life cycle steps provide an organizing focus for further explanation.

**Variations of the Prerequisite Step: Create a LOS Line for an SO End Item**   Several variations apply to sales order entry, such as warnings on exceptions, the use of sales schedules, and inquiries from the sales order form.

❖ *Warnings for Order Entry Exceptions.* Some environments only handle sales orders for lean-controlled items, so that a sales order for a non-lean item represents an exception. This exception can be automatically placed on hold (via the stopped flag) and a warning provided to the user, as defined by company-wide policies to perform the check and to generate a warning infolog.[16]

---

[15] The approaches for handling shipments are described in the AX 2009 book (pages 270-281).
[16] The company-wide policies for order entry exceptions are defined on the Lean Order Parameters form.

- *Impact of a Sales Schedule Containing Sales Orders.* When using a sales schedule, the customer's projected demands are imported as sales orders and sales forecasts based on time fence policies. The sales orders will create LOS lines.
- *Inquiries about a Work Cell's Schedule.* When viewing a sales order line item, you can view the status of other items within the relevant work cell's schedule (termed the *Final Assembly Schedule Structure* inquiry).
- *Create a PTO Manufacturing Kanban Rather than a LOS Line.* A work cell may produce some family members using a PTO manufacturing kanban as the pull signal rather than a LOS line.[17] This means that a PTO manufacturing kanban will be created by the sales order rather than a LOS line. This is indicated by the sales order line status of "PTO Created" rather than a booked status of "Created." The sales order does not consume drumbeats for the schedule.

**Variations to Step 1: View the LOS Lines** Several variations for analysis and status updates can be taken, such as viewing BOM component availability and updating status via barcode scanning or via a status reset.

- *View BOM Components and Availability from the Lean Order Schedule Form.* A line's BOM components can be viewed in a single-level or multilevel format, along with availability information (via the Explode function to view the Lean Order Explosion form). For each component, you can view the quantity available versus required at the relevant warehouse, an indicator whether the replenishment chain is okay or not, the pull type (such as replenished, manufactured, and non-lean), and an indicator of whether a pull has been generated. A partial format displays only those components with a problem in the replenishment chain.
- *Barcode Scan for Updating Booked Status.* A barcode scan form (termed the *Simple LOS* form) can be used to update a line's booked status based on its Record Id. It employs a user-defined value for entering the relevant status.[18]
- *Reset Booked Status from the Lean Order Schedule Form.* The booked status for a LOS line can be reset to created from a released or started status. It cannot be reset after recording a receipt for the line or its PTO components.
- *Assign a Different BOM Version from the Lean Order Schedule Form.* When assigning a different BOM version to a line, you must execute the *Update BOM* function so that the system recognizes the change.

---

[17] This item-specific policy (termed *Exclude from LOS*) is defined as part of the family grouping information.

[18] The user-defined numeric value for each booked status represents a company-wide policy as defined on the Lean Order Parameters form. For example, the numeric values of 1, 2, 3, and 4 can represent the booked status of release, start, receive, and complete.

**Variations to Step 2: Release a LOS Line**   Several variations apply to the release of a LOS line, including a mass update approach and the immediate creation of a production order associated with the LOS line.

* *Mass Update to Release Lines for a Specified Lean Order Schedule.* You can select multiple lines (via marking) to be released, or you can employ a mass update approach to release multiple lines if their delivery date falls within a user-specified range of dates. Select the desired schedule (on the Lean Order Schedule form) and perform the mass update using the Lean Schedule Release form. Only the lines with a booked status of created will be changed to a started status.
* *Barcode Scan for Releasing a LOS Line.* A barcode scan form (termed the *Simple LOS* form) can be used to update the booked status based on the Record Id for a LOS line.
* *Create Production Order When Releasing a LOS Line.* A production order represents one approach for handing a receipt transaction, as defined by a work cell's policy. A receipt transaction will normally create and then finish (or end) the production order. Some environments need to view or modify this production order prior to receipt. A company-wide policy (termed the *Create Preproduction Order* checkbox on the Lean Order Parameters form) will create the production order at the time you release a LOS line.

**Variations to Step 2a: Start a LOS Line**   Several variations apply to the start of a LOS line, including a mass update approach and the automatic printing of a job ticket associated with a LOS line.

* *Mass Update to Start Lines for a Specified Lean Order Schedule.* You can select multiple lines (via marking) to be started, or you can employ a mass update approach to start multiple lines if their delivery date falls within a user-specified range of dates. Select the desired schedule (on the Lean Order Schedule form) and perform the mass update using the Start LOS Lines form. Only the LOS lines with a booked status of released will be changed to a started status.
* *Automatically Print Job Ticket When Starting a LOS Line.* A schedule-specific policy (termed the *Automatically Print Job Cards* checkbox) determines whether job tickets will be automatically printed when updating a LOS line to a booked status of Started.
* *Barcode Scan for Starting a LOS Line* A barcode scan form (termed the *Simple LOS* form) can be used to update a line's booked status based on its Record Id.

**Variations to Step 3: Receive Inventory for a LOS Line**  Several variations apply to the receipt of a LOS line, including the ability to override the destination warehouse and to perform barcode scanning of a receipt.

- *Override the Destination Warehouse When Reporting a Receipt.* You can optionally override the destination warehouse when reporting a receipt, but only when allowed by the work cell policy (termed the *change location* policy).
- *Scanning Receipts for a LOS Line.* The barcode scanning approach employs the Record Id of the line received, where the Record Id is printed on the job ticket as a value and as a barcode. There are two variations of the barcode scanning form. In one case, you enter the Record Id and confirm (or override) the quantity received. You simply enter the Record Id in the second case; you cannot confirm or override the quantity. Figure 9.7 summarizes the variations for barcode scanning. You cannot perform a barcode receipt when a LOS line has been fully received.
- *Handling Over-Production (and Shipment) of the Item.* You can receive more than the quantity ordered. In addition, you can perform a receipt when the outstanding quantity is zero. However, you cannot perform a barcode receipt when the line has been fully received, as noted above.
- *Reserving Stock upon Receipt.* A work cell policy (termed the *Reserve Stock* checkbox) indicates whether a receipt of an end item will be reserved for the sales order line item.
- *Reporting Scrap for a Received LOS Line.* The inventory can only be scrapped by using an inventory journal to reduce the on-hand balance. A pull signal will not be generated to replace the scrapped inventory, so that inventory will not exist to ship the sales order.

| Purpose of Barcode Transaction | Name of Form | Enter Information |
|---|---|---|
| Receipt for a LOS Line | Lean Order Schedule Bar Code Entry | Enter the Record Id of the LOS Line; Confirm (or enter) quantity received |
| | Lean Order Schedule Single Bar Code Entry | Enter the Record Id of the LOS Line |
| Change the Booked Status for a LOS Line | Simple LOS | Enter the Record Id of the LOS Line and the associated numeric value for the receipt status; Confirm (or enter) quantity received |
| | | Enter the Record Id of the LOS Line and the associated numeric value for the status (such as a released, started or completed status) |

Figure 9.7 Barcode Scanning for Receipts and Status of a LOS Line

## Variations to Step 4: Report a LOS Line as Completed

The completion of a LOS line normally removes it from the Lean Order Schedule form, and a barcode scan form (termed the *Simple LOS* form) can be used to report completion. However, a completed line will remain on the schedule when you track shipping activities with the booked status, as described in the next point about Variations to Step 5.

## Variations to Step 5: Support Work Cell Responsibility for Sales Order Shipments

A schedule-specific policy (termed the *Sales Order* policy) indicates whether the lean order schedule will be used to support work cell responsibility for sales order shipments. Most scenarios will employ the policy option of *delivery*, so that the work cell personnel can post the packing list update as part of the life cycle for a LOS line, and include the printed packing slip with the shipment.[19]

The life cycle for a LOS line includes additional steps to support work cell responsibility for packing list updates, as shown in Figure 9.8 and explained below. The figure highlights the additional steps via shading; the basic steps were previously shown in Figure 9.6.

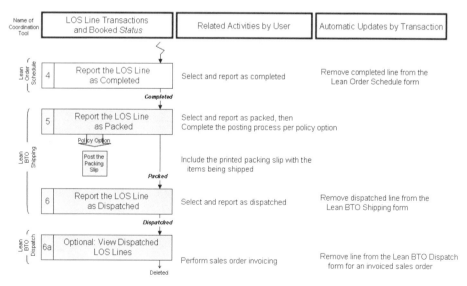

Figure 9.8 Additional Life Cycle Steps for a LOS Line

---

[19] The other policy options include invoice posting, which would typically be used when an invoice must accompany the sales order shipment. The work cell personnel will post the invoice rather than the packing slip. The policy option of picking is not used very often. It means that work cell personnel will post the picking list.

❖ S*tep 5: Report the LOS Line as Packed.* The policy option of *delivery* means that a *packed* status refers to the packing slip update. When reporting a line as packed (on the Lean BTO Shipping form), the user will actually post the packing list. The printed version is typically included with the sales order shipment. Some situations will involve multiple partial shipments via packing slip updates.

❖ *Step 6: Report the LOS Line as Dispatched.* Reporting a line as dispatched simply removes it from the Lean BTO Schedule form, thereby indicating the work cell has finished its shipping responsibilities.

❖ *Step 6a: View Dispatched LOS Lines.* The reference information about dispatched lines will be displayed (on the Lean BTO Dispatch form) until the sales order has been completely invoiced.

The Lean BTO Shipping form contains almost the same information as the Lean Order Schedule form, as illustrated in Figure 9.9. For example, one form shows component availability whereas the other form shows inventory availability of the end item. Filtering can help focus attention on a specific work cell and date range. One of the function buttons is used to pack a selected line (i.e., perform the posting of the packing slip), which can then be dispatched using the second function button (i.e., no longer display the line).

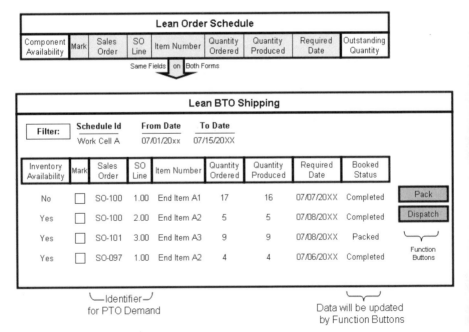

Figure 9.9 Example of the Lean BTO Shipping Form

# Using a LOS for Fixed Manufacturing Kanbans

A lean order schedule is normally only used for make-to-order products with PTO manufacturing kanban policies. It is assumed that actual demands drive all production at the final assembly work cell. In some cases, however, the final assembly work cell also produces stocked items with fixed manufacturing kanban policies. Production of these fixed manufacturing kanbans often represents filler when actual sales orders do not completely consume the work cell's drumbeat.

Using a lean order schedule for fixed manufacturing kanbans involves a dummy sales order for a specially designated internal customer, because the dummy sales order creates a LOS line. Loading a fixed manufacturing kanban on the lean order schedule creates the dummy sales order and corresponding LOS line. The approach requires some additional setup information, and a slight difference in the life cycle of a LOS line. The following explanation covers these setup and life cycle considerations.

## Setup Considerations to Support Fixed Manufacturing Kanbans

The setup considerations involve several work cell policies, and the family grouping information about stocked items that will be produced at the work cell.

**Work Cell Information**  Each work cell has three policies pertinent to the use of a lean order schedule for fixed manufacturing kanbans.

- *Enable Use of the Work Cell's Schedule to Handle Fixed Manufacturing Kanbans.* A work cell policy (labeled the *LOS Booked to Order Cell* checkbox) means that you can load fixed manufacturing kanbans on the lean order schedule for the work cell. After you load a fixed manufacturing kanban, the system creates a dummy sales order and its corresponding LOS line.
- *Manual Versus Automatic Scheduling of Fixed Manufacturing Kanbans.* Most firms will manually schedule the fixed manufacturing kanbans as filler, as reflected in the work cell policy termed *manual kanban release*. Manual scheduling involves an additional step in the life cycle of a LOS line. You drag-and-drop an empty manufacturing kanban to a date with available drumbeats (using a related form termed the *Heijunka Board*). This manual scheduling approach results in drumbeat consumption and the creation of a dummy sales order for the internal customer.

    Automatic scheduling avoids the extra life cycle step. It auto-creates the dummy sales order for delivery on the first date with drumbeat availability, and consumes the drumbeat.

❖ *Automatic Release of LOS Lines Related to Fixed Manufacturing Kanbans.* Most firms will automatically release LOS lines related to fixed manufacturing kanbans because the release step does not apply. The release step only applies to LOS lines related to make-to-order products, since it generates PTO kanbans for pull-to-order components.

The above mentioned work cell policies affect the life cycle for a LOS line, as described in the next section.

**Family Grouping and the Drumbeat Consumption Ratio**   The products produced by a work cell with a lean order schedule must be identified twice: once for the fixed manufacturing kanban and also for a family grouping assigned to the schedule. The drumbeat consumption ratio is also defined as part of the family grouping information. An item must be assigned to a family before you can define its fixed manufacturing kanban policies for the work cell. You can reassign an item from one family to another to reflect a change.

**Life Cycle for a LOS Line (for a Fixed Manufacturing Kanban)**

Loading a fixed manufactured kanban on the schedule automatically creates a dummy sales order and its corresponding LOS line. The life cycle of this LOS line is summarized in Figure 9.10 and described below. The life cycle differences reflect the additional step for manual scheduling and a parallel kanban order status for a fixed manufacturing kanban.

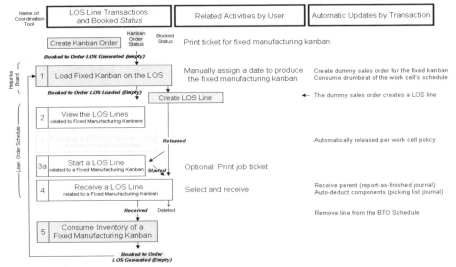

Figure 9.10 Life Cycle for a LOS Line (for a Fixed Manufacturing Kanban)

**Step 1: Load a Fixed Manufacturing Kanban on the LOS** Loading a fixed manufacturing kanban means that it is assigned a schedule date. It can be manually or automatically loaded, as determined by the work cell policy.

Manual scheduling involves an additional life cycle step. It must be performed each time a fixed manufacturing kanban has been emptied. It changes the kanban order status from "generated" to "loaded"; the status names are actually termed *Booked to Order LOS Generated* and *Booked to Order LOS Loaded*. Manual scheduling involves a separate coordination tool (termed the *Heijunka Board*) that displays empty manufacturing kanbans in a graphical format. Assigning a schedule date involves drag-and-drop, where you drag an icon representing an empty kanban and drop it on a date with available drumbeats. The breakout box on Manual Scheduling using the Heijunka Board provides further explanation.

## Manual Scheduling Using the Heijunka Board

Manual scheduling involves a separate coordination tool (termed the *Heijunka Board*) that displays a graphical format of fixed manufacturing kanbans that are now empty. Figure 9.11 displays this graphical format. You drag an icon representing an empty manufacturing kanban to a date with available drumbeats, thereby assigning a scheduled date and consuming drumbeats based on the item's ratio. The figure displays the drumbeat consumption before and after the drag-and-drop of the icon.

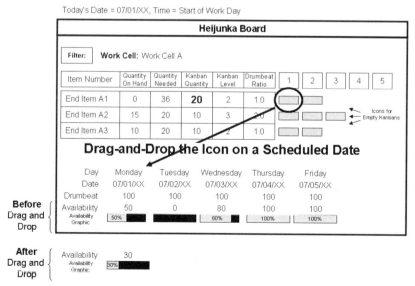

Figure 9.11 Example of Manual Scheduling with the Heijunka Board Form

Loading a fixed manufacturing kanban will consume the drumbeat. It also results in creation of a dummy sales order and its associated LOS line. The LOS line will be assigned a booked status of *created* or *released*, where a released status reflects the work cell policy for *automatic release*. Figure 9.9 displays the results of an automatic release policy.

**Step 2: View the LOS Lines** The lines can be viewed on the Lean Order Schedule form.

**Step 3: Release a LOS Line** The release step is unnecessary for a fixed manufacturing kanban because it does not have pull-to-order components that need to be released. Figure 9.9 displays the step in light grey because it illustrates the automatic release policy for the work cell.

**Step 3a: Optionally Start a LOS Line** Starting a LOS line represents an optional step that communicates production has actually started.

**Step 4: Receive Inventory for a LOS Line** The receipt can be reported via barcode scanning, or by entering data on the Lean Order Schedule form. Only one receipt can be reported against a line for a fixed manufacturing kanban. A receipt removes the LOS line from the Lean Order Schedule, and changes the kanban order status to *received*.

The impact of a receipt on inventory transactions will depend on the floor stock management approach. The right side of Figure 9.10 displays the inventory transactions based on a detailed tracking approach. When the work cell policy for receipt transactions is based on a production order (rather a BOM journal), the user may need to perform a follow-up step to end the production order.

**Step 5: Consume Inventory of a Fixed Manufacturing Kanban** The inventory consumption will result in an empty status for the fixed manufacturing kanban, and the empty kanban must again be loaded on the LOS.

## Supporting Direct Pull Decisions for a PTO Replenishment Kanban

A PTO replenishment kanban moves a stocked item to its point of use. In the context of a final assembly work cell, the stocked item would be produced by a fixed manufacturing kanban and moved from the floor stock area to a shipping area. When there is insufficient stock to be moved, it is generally preferable to create a direct pull to produce the fixed manufacturing kanban for delivery to the shipping area. This can be called a move versus make decision.

The decision to create a direct pull (and a fixed manufacturing kanban) can be manually or automatically performed when the work cell has a lean order schedule.

* *Manual Decision.* You can manually indicate the direct pull decision when viewing empty kanbans on the Kanban Replenishment form.
* *Automatic Decision.* An automatic decision reflects a rule concerning the definition of insufficient inventory, such as a sales order quantity that exceeds the available inventory at the work cell.[20]

The direct pull decision results in a fixed manufacturing kanban, which can then be loaded on the lean order schedule as described in the previous section.

## Case Studies

### Case 8: Lean Order Schedule for MTO and MTS Products

A consumer products manufacturing company produced make-to-order and make-to-stock products at the same final assembly work cell. The firm was considering the use of kanbans and a lean order schedule (LOS) to coordinate the work cell. In terms of the S&OP approaches, the demand plan consisted of sales orders for the make-to-order products, and sales forecasts for the make-to-stock products (and for stocked components of the make-to-order products). The production characteristics are summarized below.

* *Make-to-Order Products.* The make-to-order products represented more than 80 percent of the production volume, and consisted of 50,000 different configurations with 3 to 10 day lead times. Each end-item's PTO manufacturing kanban policies were defined via kanban templates. Sales order delivery promises were based on capable-to-promise logic for material availability, and drumbeat logic for capacity availability. Each sales order line generated an associated LOS line (that consumed the drumbeat), and the LOS line was released to production after checking component availability. The release step also generated the PTO kanbans for pull-to-order components in the multilevel product structure. The step for starting a LOS line generated the required paperwork for manu-

---

[20] A company-wide rule can be assigned for each context of PTO replenishment kanbans (for shipping purposes and component picking purposes). The rule is assigned on the Lean Order Parameters form.

facturing and shipping, and the step for receiving a LOS line reserved the end item for shipment.

The stocked components of these make-to-order products were managed by fixed kanbans, although purchase orders were used for many of the purchased items because the suppliers were not prepared to handle kanban coordination. The purchased components for make-to-order items were received into a stockroom, and then moved to the relevant floor stock areas based on PTO replenishment kanbans. Each work cell had its own floor stock area representing an internal supermarket.

- *Make-to-Stock Products.* The make-to-stock products represented less than 20 percent of the production volume, and consisted of 1,500 different configurations that were stocked at the final assembly work cell. Each item's fixed kanban policies were defined via kanban templates. When emptied, the fixed kanbans for end items were manually scheduled on the lean order schedule (via the Heijunka Board capability) when there was available drumbeat capacity at the final assembly work cell. The available drumbeat capacity was not previously consumed by sales orders for make-to-order products.

  The purchased components were received into a stockroom via fixed purchasing kanbans and purchase orders, and then moved to the relevant floor stock areas based on replenishment kanbans. The manufactured components were pulled directly to the relevant floor stock area. As noted above, each work cell had its own floor stock area representing an internal supermarket.

  The stocked end items were moved from the final assembly work cell to a shipping area using PTO replenishment kanbans trigged by sales orders. When stock was insufficient, the system automatically created fixed manufacturing kanbans for direct delivery to the shipping area (rather than producing the item and then moving it).

The floor stock management approach employed general tracking of components in floor stock areas, where the component value was backflushed based on the manufacturing kanban receipts. Component inventory quantities were not autodeducted. This meant that kanban empty transactions were employed to indicate an empty kanban for components in the floor stock areas.

## Executive Summary

This chapter described the use of a lean order schedule (LOS) for coordinating work cell activities and supporting a work cell drumbeat. A LOS is typically assigned to the final assembly work cell, but additional LOS can be assigned to lower-level work cells. A lean order schedule defines the daily drumbeat of its associated work cell. This daily drumbeat supports delivery promises for make-to-order products produced by the associated work cell, and sales orders consume this daily drumbeat. While the primary focus of a LOS tends to be make-to-order products with PTO manufacturing kanban policies, it can optionally support stocked items with fixed manufacturing kanban policies. Stated another way, the LOS primarily supports the pull signals for sales orders and it can optionally support buffer replenishment of fixed kanbans.

The two contexts of PTO and fixed manufacturing kanbans were reflected in two sections of this chapter. The chapter started with a typical lean scenario involving a final assembly work cell and a family of make-to-order products. It also reviewed the slight change in terminology, since a LOS line replaces a PTO manufacturing kanban as the pull signal, and the lean order schedule replaces the kanban manufacturing form as the primary coordination tool. You can optionally schedule fixed manufacturing kanbans on a lean order schedule. After you manually schedule a fixed kanban (with an empty status), the system creates a dummy sales order so that it is treated just like a make-to-order product. It consumes the work cell's daily drumbeat and the same LOS transactions apply. A case study highlighted the combination of make-to-stock and make-to-order products (with fixed and PTO manufacturing kanban policies) being produced at the same final assembly work cell.

# Chapter 10

# Alternative Approaches for the Lean Scenarios

A baseline model of operations has been used to simplify explanations. The baseline model was described in Chapter 1. It excluded several variations of manufacturing practices such as bin locations within a warehouse, batch tracking, and multisite operations. This chapter reviews the alternative approaches to the book's baseline model. It also covers alternative approaches to fixed kanbans. The alternative approaches represent advanced topics and are not recommended for novice learners.

## Alternative Approaches to the Baseline Model

This section summarizes the alternative approaches to the book's baseline model, such as the use of bin locations within a warehouse, batch tracking, and multisite operations.

### Using Bin Locations Within a Warehouse

Bin locations can be used when you always place an item in the same bin location within a warehouse area. This is termed the item's default bin location; it can be specified for issue and receipt purposes as part of the item's warehouse policies. An item's default bin locations within the from- and to-warehouse must also be specified as part of the kanban policies for a replenishment kanban.

### Quality Management Considerations

The quality management considerations about kanbans include planned and actual scrap, batch or serial tracking, quality orders, and quality signoff for a manufactured item (termed *poka-yoka signoff*).

**Planned and Actual Scrap Related to Kanbans** Planned component scrap can be defined as part of the BOM information, and automatically included in the cost calculations for a manufactured item. The component's planned scrap can be optionally considered when autodeducting components based on manufacturing kanban receipts, as defined by a work cell policy.

Actual scrap for a parent item can be reported at the time of a manufacturing kanban receipt, where you report separate quantities for completed and scrapped units. The scrapped units do not result in component backflushing. It is generally preferable to report actual scrap as a completed quantity (to correctly autodeduct components), and then explicitly scrap some or all of the kanban quantity. This approach also supports the scrap replacement concept, where the scrapped item can be reusable as a different item number. Other aspects of planned scrap were described in the Chapter 3 section "Floor Stock Management Approaches."

**Batch or Serial Tracking Related to Kanbans** Batch and/or serial tracking can be performed for end items, but the genealogy cannot be tracked across the product structure. For example, the end item's batch number can be automatically assigned upon receipt (such as a manufacturing kanban receipt), and subsequent shipment handling can specify the batch numbers being shipped.

Batch or serial tracking is not supported for components or for replenishment kanbans because the user cannot specify the batch/serial number being consumed. For example, the batch numbers cannot be specified in component backflushing.

**Quality Orders Related to Kanbans** A quality order defines the required tests for an item, and captures the actual test results.[1] The test results can be used to generate a certificate of analysis. Quality orders can be automatically or manually created for items with a kanban policy. The automatic creation policies (defined on the Quality Associations form) can be defined for the following kanban transactions:

❖ *Receipt of a purchasing kanban.* The policy should create a quality order after recording a packing slip for a purchase order, since this transaction is automatically performed as part of the kanban receipt.
❖ *Receipt of a manufacturing kanban.* The policy should create a quality order after reporting the item as finished for a production order, since this transaction is automatically performed as part of the kanban receipt.

---

[1] An explanation of product testing and quality orders is covered in the AX 2009 book (pages 290-294).

A quality order can also be generated for a sales order shipment. In this case, the automatic creation policies should create a quality order before or after a packing slip update for a sales order. The test results can be used to generate a certificate of analysis that can be sent with the shipped material.

Note: Quarantine orders are not supported for kanbans, since the material is assumed to be useable at the time of receipt.

**Poka-Yoka Sign Off**   Poka-yoka signoff represents one approach to indicate quality management signoff for a manufactured item. It only applies to manufactured items produced with a lean order schedule, where an employee can record their signoff for each step in the life cycle (such as release, start, receive, and complete). The signoff is optional, and only represents reference information. You can optionally define an item-specific policy about poka-yoka signoff and the relevant employee, so that only the specified employee can record the poka-yoka signoff.

## Actual Costing

The baseline model focused on the use of standard costing for calculating product costs and valuing inventory.[2] A lean manufacturing approach generally employs standard costing, and results in a minimum of variances related to production orders and purchase orders. The standard costing approach supports value stream costing as described in the chapter about lean accounting.

Actual costing approaches are supported in Dynamics AX.[3] From a lean manufacturing perspective, they mandate the use of an order-based costing approach because the actual costs for a production order must be collected. The actual costs can be collected by backflushing component quantities or component value.

## Multisite Operations and Lean Manufacturing

The baseline model assumed that the lean manufacturing functionality would be used in one or more autonomous sites within a single company. If transfers between these physical sites were necessary, the baseline model assumed that transfer orders would be used to coordinate the material transfers rather than kanbans. Kanban orders do not currently support transfers between physical sites. Hence, the baseline model addressed two of the

---

[2] The use of standard costing is described on pages 111-129 in the AX 2009 book.
[3] The use of actual costing approaches is described on pages 136-138 in the AX 2009 book.

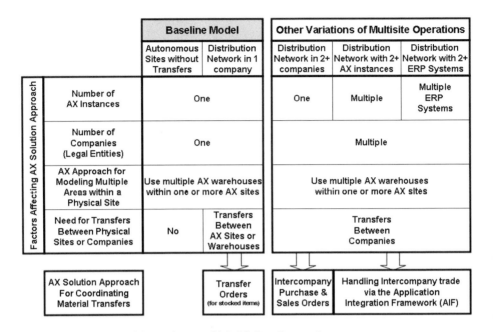

Figure 10.1 Basic Variations of Multisite Operations

basic variations in multisite operations, as summarized in Figure 10.1.[4] The baseline model allowed us to highlight the company-specific and warehouse-specific policies embedded in the lean manufacturing functionality.

The use of lean manufacturing in other multisite variations involves additional considerations. In a multicompany scenario, for example, one company may operate as a lean manufacturer while other companies operate with traditional manufacturing approaches. In this scenario, a "traditional company" could place an intercompany purchase order that creates an intercompany sales order at the "lean company." The intercompany sales order can trigger PTO manufacturing kanbans at the "lean company."

One multisite consideration involves the planning calculations that communicate requirements across multiple companies in a single AX instance.[5] The sequence for performing the master scheduling task represents one key issue, and the use of "firmed-up" purchase orders represents a second key issue. The time fence policy for automatic firming provides the visibility of requirements across a multicompany operation. This means that intercompany trade must employ traditional approaches.

---

[4] The variations for modeling multisite operations are described on pages 351-354 in the AX 2009 book.
[5] Master scheduling across a multicompany supply chain is described on page 371 in the AX 2009 book.

# Alternative Approaches to Fixed Kanbans

Some companies have difficulties in embracing the concept of kanban levels for fixed kanbans. For example, it is easier for personnel to conceptualize a min/max approach to replenishment. Target kanbans represent min/max logic. A phased target kanban represents min/max logic with a phased ramp up (or ramp down) to the desired target quantity.

## Target Kanbans

Target kanbans represent an alternative approach to fixed kanbans, and the same coordination tools apply to both. The two critical differences involve the creation of target kanbans and the automatic deletion of target kanbans after receipt.[6] Other differences are mentioned below.

**Creation of Target Kanbans** You define the kanban policies on the Target Kanbans form, which represents a different form than the Kanbans form used for fixed kanbans. This form has additional fields related to a target kanban, including the fields for a target quantity, a trigger quantity, and an automatic creation policy.

The creation of a target kanban represents min/max logic. It involves slightly different kanban policies than a fixed kanban, since you specify a *total target quantity* and a *trigger quantity* rather than a kanban level. When inventory consumption results in on-hand inventory at or below the trigger quantity, sufficient kanban orders (using the normal kanban quantity) will be automatically generated to resupply up to the total target quantity.[7] These automatically generated target kanbans have an empty status and new kanban order numbers. Figure 10.2 illustrates the life cycle of a target manufacturing kanban.

A slight variation to this approach involves a minimum quantity rather than the target and trigger quantities.[8] In this case, target kanbans will be automatically created to achieve the minimum quantity (rather than the target quantity) when the inventory balance equals zero.

---

[6] Deleting a target kanban after receipt means that inventory is not tracked by kanban, and that several kanban inventory transactions do not apply such as reporting an empty kanban or kanban scrap. It also means that the concept of accumulating empty kanbans does not apply.

[7] An additional target kanban policy (termed auto-create target kanbans) enables the min/max logic to automatically create target kanbans.

[8] The change in replenishment logic reflects an additional kanban policy (termed *create to minimum quantity*) and a value for the minimum quantity field.

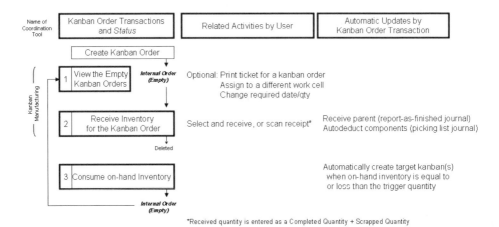

Figure 10.2  Life Cycle for a Target Manufacturing Kanban

A target kanban can also be manually created, typically to support anticipated demand spikes with additional target kanbans. The user specifies the desired kanban quantity and number of kanbans to manually create the target kanbans. These manually created target kanbans will be deleted after receipt.

**Other Differences Between Target and Fixed Kanbans**  Several other aspects of target kanban policies are different than a fixed kanban, as described below.

- *Multiple receipts for a target manufacturing kanban.*  A target kanban policy enables you to record multiple receipts rather than a single receipt, but this only applies to a target manufacturing kanban. The multiple receipts option is possible because the received inventory is not tracked by kanban order.
- *Maximum production quantity for a target manufacturing kanban.*  A target kanban policy enables you to enforce a maximum production quantity, but this only applies to a target manufacturing kanban. That is, an empty target kanban is no longer automatically generated after receipts equal or exceed the maximum (and inventory falls below the trigger quantity).
- *Date constraint for a target kanban.*  A target kanban policy enables you to enforce a date constraint for any type of target kanban. That is, an empty target kanban is no longer automatically generated after the constraint date (and inventory falls below the trigger quantity).
- *Templates cannot be defined for a target kanban.*

## Phased Target Kanbans

A phased target kanban represents a slight variation to a target kanban, since it can achieve a Total Target Quantity in phases. It is commonly used to ramp up (or ramp down) the number of target kanbans. The phases consist of user-specified dates and a percentage for each date, such as monthly dates across a 2 month horizon with percentages of 60 percent and 100 percent respectively. This means that automatic creation of the target kanban will achieve 60 percent of the total target quantity in the first month and 100 percent in the second month. These phased target kanbans can be viewed on two inquiry forms (the Phased Schedule and the Target Kanban Schedule).

Alternatively, phased target kanbans can be created from sales forecasts. The approach involves a user-defined profile of time periods, which will be used to extract the item's relevant forecast data for the specified time periods. The phased target kanbans are automatically created when the user performs the *kanban creation from profile* function as part of defining the kanban policies.

## Executive Summary

A baseline model of operations and several lean scenarios have been used to simplify explanations of lean manufacturing. This chapter reviewed several alternative approaches to the baseline model, such as the use of bin locations within a warehouse, batch tracking, and quality orders. It covered alternative approaches to fixed kanbans, such as using target kanbans to represent min/max logic. The alternative approaches represent advanced topics that are not necessary to manage typical lean scenarios.

# Chapter 11

# Summarizing the Transition to Lean

An integrated supply chain management (SCM) system represents a critical success factor for effective implementation of lean manufacturing. The SCM system must be able to manage variations in lean scenarios as well as changes associated with continuous improvement efforts and the maturity stages of lean manufacturing. This chapter summarizes the book contents and the transition to supply chain management for lean manufacturing. The chapter consists of the following sections:

- Managing the Variations in Lean Scenarios
- S&OP Approaches for Lean Scenarios
- Applicability of Traditional SCM Approaches
- Managing Components with Traditional Supply Orders
- Sales Order Delivery Promises
- Managing the Maturity Stages of Lean Manufacturing
- Initial Cutover for Using Kanbans
- Managing Continuous Improvement and Engineering Changes
- Alternative Approaches for the Lean Scenarios
- Concluding Remarks

## Managing the Variations in Lean Scenarios

Variations in lean scenarios can be broadly categorized into make-to-stock and make-to-order products. A given work cell typically produces a family of products that represent make-to-stock or make-to-order products, or both. These two variations employ fixed kanbans and PTO kanbans for supply chain coordination of purchased items, manufactured items, and transfers of stocked items. Each type of kanban differs in terms of the policies for creating a kanban, the life cycle of a kanban, and the relevant coordination tools.

In many make-to-stock scenarios, the end items are stocked at the final assembly work cell and pulled to a shipping area (via PTO replenishment kanbans) based on actual sales orders. In many make-to-order scenarios, the products consist of stocked components which can be managed via fixed kanbans. In both cases, traditional supply orders may be used for stocked components, such as using purchase orders when suppliers are not prepared to handle kanban coordination approaches.

A work cell often reflects internal manufacturing, and has an associated floor stock area for components and even completed items. A work cell can also reflect subcontract manufacturing, where the supplied components can be sent as a discrete kit to the subcontractor (with the manufacturing kanban) or stocked as consigned inventory at the subcontractor.

## S&OP Approaches for Lean Scenarios

The S&OP game plan differs for make-to-stock and make-to-order products. With make-to-stock products, the S&OP game plan is expressed as a set of fixed kanbans for every item in the product structures, where the kanban levels reflect the anticipated rate of demand. This demand plan represents a key aspect of the S&OP approach. The demand plan for fixed kanbans can reflect three options: sales forecasts, the pipeline of actual sales orders, or both. The planning calculations use the demand plan to suggest planned orders that "chase the demand," and planned orders provide the foundation for calculating kanban levels for fixed kanbans. These calculations—termed the *Recalculate Kanban Level* task—are performed using the planned orders within a specified set of master plan data. The suggested kanban levels can then be used to manually increase or decrease the number of fixed kanbans for each item.

With completely make-to-order products, the S&OP game plan is expressed as a set of PTO kanbans linked to sales orders for end items. The sales orders for end items constitute the demand plan. Each sales order line item has a corresponding PTO manufacturing kanban that represents the supply. Releasing a PTO manufacturing kanban for the end item triggers the generation of PTO kanbans for its pull-to-order components. Hence, the release step provides visibility of requirements across the product structure.

Make-to-order products may also be built from stocked components. The stocked components can be obtained via fixed kanbans or traditional supply orders.

## Applicability of Traditional SCM Approaches

Some lean manufacturing scenarios can be supported by the traditional SCM approaches within AX. Make-to-order products linked to sales orders, for example, can employ the traditional AX approaches to closely mimic PTO manufacturing kanbans using production orders for the end item and reference orders for its make-to-order components. This was illustrated in Case 1. In contrast, the traditional AX approaches for handling make-to-stock products (or make-to-order products indirectly linked to sales demand) cannot easily mimic fixed kanbans. For example, the near-term planned orders loosely mimic fixed kanbans, but they do not provide the detailed day-to-day coordination between supplies and demands in a multilevel product structure. However, the traditional approach to an S&OP game plan for make-to-stock products can still be used to calculate the number of fixed kanbans. The same S&OP game plan can also be used to generate planned orders for components not yet managed by kanban coordination.

## Managing Components with Traditional Supply Orders

Many manufacturers with lean scenarios will purchase material without using kanbans because the suppliers are not yet ready for lean approaches. In this case, the traditional approaches for using planned purchase orders and the related coordination tools will coordinate purchasing activities. The purchased material can be delivered to a stockroom, and then consumed by fixed replenishment kanbans for moving material to a floor stock area. Alternatively, the purchased material can be consumed as a result of component backflushing triggered by receipts of manufacturing kanbans.

A lean scenario may also involve other types of supply orders for stocked components, such as production orders or transfer orders. In this case, the traditional approach for using planned production orders, planned transfer orders, and the related coordination tools will coordinate supply chain activities.

The same S&OP game plan used to calculate fixed kanban levels can also be used to generate planned orders and coordinate replenishment of these non-lean items. Information about planned orders can be filtered to view just the non-lean items. You can firm up the planned orders for non-lean items. You cannot firm up the planned orders for kanban-controlled items, since they are already being managed by kanban orders.

## Sales Order Delivery Promises

Sales order delivery promises align the actual demands within the constraints of material and capacity availability. A promised delivery date can be automatically calculated based on capable-to-promise (CTP) logic or the work cell's drumbeat or both. With CTP logic, the calculations consider the availability of on-hand inventory and each item's lead time. The delivery promises based on a work cell drumbeat require the use of a lean order schedule for the work cell and only apply to make-to-order products with PTO manufacturing kanban policies. An alternative approach to a work cell's drumbeat was described as a case study.

## Managing the Maturity Stages of Lean Manufacturing

Most companies begin their lean journey with a pilot project approach, which represents the first of three maturity stages in lean manufacturing. The first stage generally employs order-based costing, and a floor stock management approach that provides detailed tracking of component inventory in floor stock areas. Detailed tracking involves backflushing of component quantities to correctly support order-based costing. An alternative approach entails backflushing of component value based on the cost substitution concept. This alternative approach requires an explicit kanban empty transaction for floor stock components, since the component quantities are not being backflushed.

With the second and third stages, the biggest change involves value stream costing, and the associated elimination of floor stock inventory tracking. A financial dimension provides the basis for value stream costing that reflects a product family and/or the internal work cells that constitute the value stream. Black hole warehouses eliminate inventory tracking through the production process, but still support the use of pull signals (via empty kanbans) to coordinate supply chain activities.

These three maturity stages are reflected in variations of using the lean manufacturing functionality within Dynamics AX. For example, the software supports the transition from traditional approaches to lean, the transition from order-based costing to value stream costing, and the transition from detailed tracking to no tracking of floor stock inventory.

## Initial Cutover for Using Kanbans

The initial cutover suggestions differ slightly for fixed and PTO kanbans. With fixed kanbans, you can use the inactive status when defining the kanban policies and creating the kanbans for each item and warehouse. An inactive status means that the kanbans will not appear on the coordination tools. As another intended purpose, you can continue using traditional approaches (such as purchase orders and production orders) prior to cutover. The status should be changed to active at the time of cutover.

With PTO kanbans, you can also use the inactive status when defining the kanban policies for each item and warehouse. This means that a sales order for the end item will not generate a PTO manufacturing kanban. You can continue to use traditional approaches for creating a corresponding production order for the sales order end item, and releasing this production order to create reference orders for make-to-order and buy-to-order components. The status should be changed to active at the time of cutover, which means a sales order will automatically create PTO manufacturing kanbans for the end item.

Some limitations may apply to new items or obsolete items, such as limiting the ability to purchase or produce an item. Two item-related policies will limit kanban transactions: a stopped flag for purchases and a stopped flag for inventory transactions. The item's stopped flag for purchases will prevent creation of a blanket purchase order, and prevent reporting of kanban receipts. The stopped flag for inventory transactions will prevent reporting of any kanban receipts and consumption.

## Managing Continuous Improvement and Engineering Changes

Ongoing changes are often driven by a philosophy of continuous improvement, such as changes to purchasing and manufacturing practices, changes to bills of material, or changes to factory layout. Each change requires slightly different considerations.

Suggestions were provided for managing changes to fixed kanbans. Some changes must be implemented by deleting the existing kanbans and then creating new kanbans. These include changes to the normal kanban quantity, item origin, and the preferred work cell or BOM version for a manufacturing kanban. Changes to the BOM component information typically require a change to the kanbans associated with the components. For example, these changes may impact a component's quantity or warehouse source, or reflect additional components in a bill of material.

Suggestions were also made for managing changes to manufacturing kanbans with subcontracting. The changes include the use of a different subcontractor and subcontracting on a one-time or intermittent basis. Some changes must be implemented by deleting the existing kanbans and then creating new kanbans. These include changing the outside operation component and changing the subcontract kanban type (discrete kit versus consigned inventory).

## Alternative Approaches for the Lean Scenarios

A baseline model of operations was used to simplify explanations thoughout the book. It excluded several variations of manufacturing practices such as the use of bin locations within a warehouse, batch tracking, quality orders, and multisite operations. A separate chapter described the approaches for handling these variations. It also covered alternative approaches to fixed kanbans.

Target kanbans represent an alternative approach to fixed kanbans. The same coordination tools apply to both. The two critical differences involve the automatic creation of target kanbans based on min/max logic and on-hand inventory balances, and the automatic deletion of target kanbans after receipt. The min/max logic is expressed as a target quantity (the maximum) and a trigger quantity (the minimum). A phased target kanban represents a slight variation to a target kanban, since it can achieve a total target quantity in phases. It is commonly used to ramp up (or ramp down) the number of target kanbans.

## Concluding Remarks

This book covered the software functionality to support lean manufacturing scenarios, as defined by functionality within the latest release of Microsoft Dynamics AX 2009. It also covered the traditional approaches to these same scenarios, as defined in a previous book, *Managing Your Supply Chain Using Microsoft AX 2009*. The book explained the incremental conceptual differences between the lean and traditional approaches. The intended objective is to help people transition from traditional to lean approaches for supply chain management of lean manufacturing.

# Appendix A

# Dynamics AX Terminology and Synonyms

System usage is shaped by the conceptual model and vocabulary that describes software functionality. This terminology includes the window titles, field labels, button titles, and menu labels within the system. This book's explanations used the Microsoft Dynamics AX terminology as much as possible, but sometimes employed alternative or generally accepted terminology to clarify understanding. In particular, the software involves new constructs concerning kanbans and work cells. These terms have been described throughout the book, and this appendix provides a summarized explanation.

**Kanbans (aka Kanban Orders)** A kanban has a unique identifier (aka kanban order number), and each variation of a kanban order has a slightly different life cycle and associated status (aka kanban order status). The terms *kanban* and *kanban order* will be used interchangeably; they both refer to a pull signal for coordinating supply chain activities. The replenishment policies for a kanban order are specific to an item, warehouse, and container.[1] The linkage to sales order demand defines the two basic types of kanbans—a fixed kanban and a pull-to-order kanban (aka PTO kanban)—which act as pull signals for replenishing stocked or pull-to-order items respectively.

- *Fixed Kanban.* A fixed kanban communicates a pull signal using a fixed container quantity and multiple containers. The fixed kanbans are not linked to actual sales orders. They reflect anticipated rates of demand based on the current sales backlog or sales forecasts for end items, plus bill of material (BOM) information for components.

---

[1] A container has other synonyms such as tote or pallet. A printed kanban ticket typically accompanies the container as part of the visible pull signal, or the kanban ticket can act as the pull signal without accompanying a physical container.

❖ *PTO Kanban.* A PTO kanban is closely linked to an actual sales order, whether it represents the end item or a component within the end-item's bill of material. It typically communicates a pull signal using the sales order quantity for a single container. It can also be expressed as multiple containers (with a fixed quantity per container) that add up to the sales order quantity.

Variations in kanban orders reflect these two basic types (fixed kanbans and PTO kanbans) and the sources of supply (manufacturing, purchasing, and replenishment). Each variation has a slightly different approach for defining replenishment policies and creating kanban orders. In addition, each variation has a slightly different life cycle of kanban order transactions and status, and different coordination tools.

The book's explanation of kanban variations employed consistent terminology to minimize possible confusion. Figure A.1 summarizes the terminology for fixed and PTO kanbans. The book sometimes shortened the terminology for fixed kanbans by dropping the word "fixed," since the alternative is already differentiated by the words "PTO kanban." The figure illustrates this shortened term by displaying the word [Fixed].

| | Kanban Terminology | |
|---|---|---|
| | **For Fixed Kanbans** | **For PTO Kanbans** |
| Term | [Fixed] Kanban or [Fixed] Kanban Order | PTO Kanban or PTO Kanban Order |
| Status | Kanban Status or Kanban Order Status | Kanban Status or Kanban Order Status |
| Identifier | Kanban Order Number | Kanban Order Number |
| Printed Document | Kanban Ticket | Kanban Ticket |
| Types Of Kanbans | [Fixed] Purchasing Kanban | PTO Purchasing Kanban |
| | [Fixed] Replenishment Kanban* | PTO Replenishment Kanban* |
| | [Fixed] Manufacturing Kanban | PTO Manufacturing Kanban |
| | [Fixed] Manufacturing Kanban with Subcontracting | PTO Manufacturing Kanban with Subcontracting |

*A Fixed Replenishment Kanban is only used for component picking purposes, whereas a PTO Replenishment Kanban can be used for component picking purposes or shipping purposes.

Figure A.1 Terminology for Kanbans

**Work Cell**  A work cell represents a simpler alternative for modeling lean scenarios in comparison to the use of Dynamics AX work centers and routing data. You indicate the work cell for producing an item as part of the kanban policies for a fixed or PTO manufacturing kanban. The list of empty kanbans by work cell provides a coordination tool. Takt time metrics provide a measure of work cell performance, and the work cell's drumbeat can support sales order delivery promises based on available capacity.

The simpler alternative of a work cell does not currently support value-added costs related to direct manufacturing and overhead allocations. Most lean scenarios focus on direct material costs so the limitation is not an issue. However, some lean scenarios require value-added costs to support calculation of a manufactured item's cost and suggested sales price. Auto-deduction of these value-added costs supports an order-based costing approach for manufacturing kanbans. In this case, routing data must be used to support the costing purposes. Chapter 5 explained several work cell considerations, including the use of routing data for costing purposes.

**List of Terms and Synonyms**  The following list of Dynamics AX terms and synonyms represents a mapping with commonly used terminology.

| DYNAMICS AX TERM | SYNONYM or DEFINITION |
|---|---|
| Black hole concept | No tracking of inventory transactions within a designated warehouse, or for a designated item |
| BOM Calculation | Calculation of costs, sales price and net weight for a manufactured item |
| BOM Item | Manufactured Item |
| BOM Line | Component |
| BOM Line Type | Component type (Normal, Phantom, Production, Vendor) |
| BOM Number | Identifier for a master bill of material |
| BOM Version | Master BOM assigned to a manufactured item |
| Configurable Item | Custom product with a bill of options, used in option selection process to define a unique bill and routing |
| Costing Version | Set of cost data containing cost records about items, cost categories, and overhead formulas |
| Coverage Code | Reordering policy, such as min/max or requirement |
| Coverage Group | Set of item planning data policies |

| DYNAMICS AX TERM | SYNONYM or DEFINITION |
|---|---|
| Demand plan | A demand plan provides the starting point for the S&OP game plan; it may consist of a sales forecast, the pipeline of sales orders, or both |
| Dimension Group | Set of policies about item identification (Item Dimension) and inventory management (Inventory Dimension) |
| Floor stock area | Placement of inventory and required resources in the production area by a work cell |
| Forecast Model | Forecast identifier |
| Forecast Data Plan | Set of forecast data generated by forecast scheduling task |
| Futures Message | Message about projected completion |
| Heijunka Board | Graphical display of manufacturing kanbans to support manual scheduling against a work cell drumbeat |
| Inventory Dimension | Inventory management policies for an item |
| Item Dimension | Basis for item identification (such as item number) |
| Item Origin | Source of supply for a kanban order (purchased, manufactured or replenishment) |
| Kanban policies | Define the source of supply and other characteristics inherited by a newly created kanban order |
| Location | Bin location |
| Master Plan Data | Set of data generated by the master scheduling task |
| Modeling-Enabled Item | Custom product with an associated product model that provides a rules-based configurator |
| Non-Inventoried Item | Inventory dimension policies indicate no tracking of physical or financial inventory |
| Operation | Master operation that provides default values when adding a operation to a routing |

| DYNAMICS AX TERM | SYNONYM or DEFINITION |
|---|---|
| Outside operation component | Item number representing an outside operation in terms of its identification and costs, which is included in a manufactured item's bill of material |
| Packing Slip Update | Sales order shipment or purchase order receipt |
| Production BOM | Order-dependent bill for a production order |
| Production Number | Production order number |
| Production Order | Work order, manufacturing order |
| Production Route | Order-dependent routing for a production order |
| Reference Order | Production (or purchase) order linked to another production order |
| Report as Finished Quantity | Production order output or parent receipt quantity |
| Route Number | Identifier for a master routing |
| Route Version | Master routing assigned to a manufactured item |
| Scheduling Method | Detailed (Job) or Rough-Cut (Operation) scheduling method |
| Site | A physical site with financial reporting requirements |
| Stop/Go Board | Graphical display of kanban orders |
| Sub-BOM | Master BOM specified for a sales order or a bill component |
| Sub-Route | Master routing specified for a sales order or a bill component |
| Takt time | Production rate for a work cell |
| Value stream | Set of activities required to bring a product from raw material to the customer possession |
| Value stream costing | Provide financial information for value stream activities; it may involve assigning a financial dimension to ledger transactions |
| Warehouse | A physical site without financial reporting requirements; examples include a stockroom, a floor stock area, and a shipping area |

| DYNAMICS AX TERM | SYNONYM or DEFINITION |
|---|---|
| Work Cell | A manufacturing cell in which equipment and work stations are arranged to facilitate small-lot continuous flow production |
| Work Center | Machine, person, tool or subcontractor |
|   - Available Capacity | Working hours (and hourly drumbeat) |

# Appendix B

# Purposes of Work Center and Routing Data

Work center and routing data serve several purposes in a traditional approach to supply chain management and the use of production orders. They include purposes related to process specifications, capacity, costing, delivery promises, scheduling, and production reporting. This appendix reviews the Dynamics AX capabilities to support several traditional purposes, as summarized in Figures B.1 and B.2. It concludes with the applicability of work center and routing data in a kanban environment, where the current design of Dynamics AX employs the parallel construct of a work cell to support manufacturing kanbans.[1] Appendix C describes the purposes of work cell data.

The explanation has been segmented into basic and additional capabilities. The basic capabilities represent the minimal definition of work center and routing data that would replicate functionality associated with the work cell construct. The additional capabilities represent work center and routing data that (1) could supplement work cell functionality, or (2) do not apply to a kanban environment.

## Basic Setup Information

Each manufacturing cell is typically modeled as a single work center within a work center group, where a single operation (within a master routing) defines the capacity requirement for producing an item at the work cell. The capacity requirement can be expressed in terms of time per unit or drumbeat consumption per unit, as described in the next section about capacity. You indicate the applicable work center by assigning a master routing to an item.

---

[1] The author anticipates that future software versions will combine aspects of the two constructs (for work centers and work cells) into a single integrated approach.

| | Purpose | Basic Capabilities | Additional Capabilities |
|---|---|---|---|
| Setup | | Define work center (and group) Define master routing Define operation in master routing | |
| Basic | Indicate work center for producing item | Assign master routing to item | |
| Capacity | Define capacity for work center | | Assign calendar of working days (and working times) to work center Define hourly drumbeat of work center |
| Capacity | Define requirement for producing item at work center | | Define master routing and an operation time (or drumbeat consumption) that reflects work center requirement |
| Capacity | Calculate capacity requirements for work center | | Use master scheduling to calculate projected capacity requirements |
| Costing | Define direct mfg costs for work center | | Assign hourly rate (or piece rate) |
| Costing | Define overhead costs for work center | | Assign routing-related overhead formula |
| Costing | Calculate costs for a manufactured item | | Use BOM calculation for labor and overhead costs |
| Costing | Calculate costs for a production order | | Costing based on reported time |

Figure B.1 Purposes of Work Center and Routing Data

## Capacity

The definition of work center capacity and an item's capacity requirements are shown in Figure B.1 as additional capabilities rather than basic. This type of information is not employed for the work cell construct, therefore we will treat it as additional capabilities for a work center and routing.

A work center's capacity is defined by a calendar of working days and the working time within each day. In addition, you can define a work center's hourly drumbeat (termed the work center capacity) representing the number of equivalent units that can be produced by the work center.

A routing operation defines the capacity requirement for producing an item at the work center. It can be expressed in terms of time per unit or drumbeat consumption per unit.

❖ *Time per unit.* The *standard* consumption can defined in terms of time per unit or units per time, such as .25 hours per unit or 4 units per hour.
❖ *Drumbeat consumption per unit.* When using a work center's hourly drumbeat as a measure of capacity, you define *capacity* consumption in

terms of equivalent units (termed the routing operation *factor*) rather than time per unit.

Both approaches can reflect the concept of consuming equivalent units. A product that would consume two equivalent units, for example, would have a time requirement or a factor that is twice as much as a product requiring one equivalent unit. Different master routings can be defined for variations in drumbeat consumption, and assigned to the relevant item numbers.

A work center's capacity can be designated as infinite or finite for the purpose of scheduling production orders. For example, you can schedule an individual production order, or perform the master scheduling task for all production orders, and account for work centers designated as having finite capacity.

A work center's projected capacity requirements can be calculated from a demand plan using the master scheduling task (with a detailed job scheduling method). The projected capacity is typically calculated without consideration of finite capacity constraints.

## Costing

A work center's costing information typically reflects its direct manufacturing costs such as labor. It can be expressed as an hourly rate that reflects the average crew size and average labor rate, such as an hourly cost of $200 for a crew size of 10. Alternatively, the costing information can be expressed as a piece rate (aka cost per output unit).

The overhead costs for a work center can be defined in an overhead formula. In this case, the routing-related overhead is expressed as the incremental cost per hour or per output unit. For example, the incremental overhead costs could be $400 per hour, which would be a 100 percent overhead rate when the direct manufacturing costs are $200 per hour.

The value-added costs associated with a work center's routing operation can be included in the calculation of a manufactured item's cost and suggested sales price (aka BOM calculation). In addition, the routing operation(s) can be autodeducted for a production order to support order-based costing requirements.

## Sales Order Delivery Promises

The basic approach to a delivery promise involves a capable-to-promise calculation (termed the explosion function) for a sales order line item. The projected completion date can be transferred back to the line item. The capable-to-promise calculation considers material and capacity availability,

| | Purpose | Basic Capabilities | Additional Capabilities |
|---|---|---|---|
| **Delivery Promises** | Support delivery promises based on capacity | | Calculate capable-to-promise date or Create/schedule production order |
| | Support finite capacity logic in revising promises | | Perform master scheduling task to calculate projected completion date of production orders |
| **Scheduling** | Link production to sales order | Create reference orders for make-to-order components | |
| | Provide coordination tool for production | Printed production order Production schedule by work center | |
| | Calculate manufacturing lead time | | Perform scheduling to calculate lead time of production orders |
| **Production Reporting** | Report completion of manufactured item | Receive finished quantity (based on last operation) | |
| | Support time reporting | | Autodeduct time based on production order receipts |
| | | | Report time against production order and its related operation |

Figure B.2 Purposes of Work Center and Routing Data

but it does not account for capacity reservations by existing production orders.

An alternative approach can account for existing capacity reservations by production orders (aka drumbeat consumption), especially for make-to-order products requiring immediate creation of a linked production order. In this case, you create and schedule the production order (using forward finite scheduling logic) to determine the completion date, which can then be manually entered on the sales order line item. The projected completion date can be continuously calculated by the master scheduling task, where a suggested change to a sales order delivery date is communicated by a futures message.

## Scheduling

The basic coordination tools consist of a production schedule by work center and the printed production orders (and their picking lists). The calculated lead time for a production order reflects the routing data and the order quantity. A fixed manufacturing lead time is used when no routing data has been defined.

A production order is typically created from a sales order line for make-to-order products requiring linkage to the demand. Scheduling this production order can automatically create reference orders for make-to-order components. In addition, these reference orders can be synchronized when the end-item's production order must be rescheduled.

## Production Reporting

The receipt of a production order represents basic production reporting. You can optionally report the finished quantity as part of reporting the last operation in a routing.

The actual time expended on a production order's routing operation may also be reported, either though autodeduction or by explicitly reporting time. In the context of a manufacturing cell, the reported time reflects the entire crew rather than individual employees.

## Applicability to a Kanban Environment

A kanban environment can be modeled using just the work cell construct in the current version of AX 2009. Work center and routing data are not required, and the information does not apply to kanban orders. Most lean scenarios do not involve routing data. A work cell can be used to designate where to produce a manufactured item, as described in Appendix C.

In some cases, work center and routing data may be used to support costing purposes. This includes the calculated costs of manufactured items, and order-based costing that is characteristic of the first maturity stage in lean manufacturing. The costing purposes require definition of a work center and an item's routing data.

In terms of delivery promises via capable-to-promise logic, the calculations do not account for drumbeat consumption of work center capacity. The alternative approaches using scheduled production orders do not apply because production orders are replaced by PTO manufacturing kanbans and fixed manufacturing kanbans. Hence, the concept of drumbeat availability for PTO manufacturing kanbans cannot be based on work center and routing information.

# Appendix C

# Purposes of Work Cell Data

Work cell data serves several basic purposes related to manufacturing kanbans. They represent a slightly different and simpler approach (in comparison to work centers) for modeling cellular manufacturing in the current version of Dynamics AX.[1] Appendix B described the purposes of work center and routing data.

The explanation of work cell purposes has been segmented into basic and additional capabilities, as shown in Figure C.1. The basic capabilities include the identification of a work cell producing an item, and the coordination of manufacturing kanbans at a work cell. The additional capabilities involve the use of a lean order schedule (LOS) to manage a work cell, which supports the definition of a work cell's daily drumbeat and delivery promises based on drumbeat availability. A lean order schedule employs LOS lines (rather than PTO manufacturing kanbans) to coordinate and report work cell activities.

The work cell functionality does not support costing purposes. As noted in Appendix B, the costing purposes must be supported by work center and routing data. This includes the calculated costs of manufactured items, and order-based costing that is characteristic of the first maturity stage in lean manufacturing.

## Basic Capabilities of a Work Cell

The basic capabilities involve simple setup information, and several tools for scheduling and reporting production at the work cell.

**Basic Setup Information**  A work cell can be minimally defined by an identifier. As part of the kanban policies, you assign this identifier to the fixed and PTO manufacturing kanbans produced at the work cell.

---

[1] The author anticipates that future software versions will combine aspects of the two constructs (for work centers and work cells) into a single integrated approach.

| | Purpose | Basic Capabilities | Additional Capabilities (with Lean Order Schedule) |
|---|---|---|---|
| Setup | | Define work cell | Define lean order schedule (LOS) Define family covered by LOS |
| Basic | Indicate work cell for producing item | Assign work cell to item's manufacturing kanban | Assign item to family covered by LOS |
| Capacity | Define capacity for work cell's schedule | | Define calendar of working days and daily drumbeat for work cell |
| | Define requirement for producing item at work cell | | Define drumbeat consumption ratio for items produced at work cell |
| Delivery Promises | Support delivery promises based on capacity | | Automatically check drumbeat during sales order entry |
| | Support finite capacity logic in making promises | | Sales orders consume available drumbeats |
| Scheduling | Link production to sales order | Create PTO manufacturing kanban(s) | Create LOS line |
| | Provide coordination tool for production | Printed kanban ticket Manufacturing kanbans by work cell | Printed job ticket Lean Order Schedule by work cell |
| Production Reporting | Report completion of manufactured item | Receive manufacturing kanban | Receive LOS line |
| | Track work cell activities | Takt time metrics | Start, complete and ship LOS line Report time against production order |

Figure C.1 Purposes of Work Cell Data

**Scheduling** The basic coordination tools consist of the manufacturing kanbans by work cell, the replenishment kanbans (for component picking purposes) to deliver stocked items to the relevant floor stock area, and the printed kanban tickets. A graphical coordination tool (termed the Stop/Go Board) applies to fixed manufacturing kanbans produced at a work cell. You can optionally assign a fixed manufacturing kanban to a different work cell.

A PTO manufacturing kanban is automatically created from a sales order line for make-to-order products requiring linkage to demand. Releasing this kanban automatically creates PTO manufacturing kanbans for its make-to-order components, and PTO replenishment kanbans for picking and delivering stocked components to the relevant floor stock area.

**Production Reporting** Production reporting involves the receipt of a PTO manufacturing kanban or a fixed manufacturing kanban. It may also involve scrapping a manufacturing kanban, or reporting reusable scrap. The kanban receipts provide a key input for a work cell's takt time metrics. Current takt time reflects the elapsed time (within today's working hours) for the total units received today. Required takt time reflects the remaining time and the remaining units within today's schedule. Further explanation is provided in the Chapter 5 section on takt time metrics.

## Additional Capabilities with a Lean Order Schedule

The additional work cell capabilities involve the use of a lean order schedule (LOS) to manage supply chain activities. These capabilities include the definition of a work cell's daily drumbeat, delivery promises based on drumbeat availability, and tracking work cell activities. A lean order schedule employs LOS lines (rather than PTO manufacturing kanbans) to coordinate and report work cell activities.

**Basic Setup Information**  The work cell must be assigned an identifier, and you assign this identifier (as part of the kanban policies) to the manufacturing kanbans produced at the work cell. These are the same steps mentioned above.

The lean order schedule must be assigned an identifier, and associated with a work cell. In addition, a family grouping must be defined and assigned to the schedule, so that you can assign items to the family covered by the lean order schedule. These items typically reflect make-to-order products (with a PTO manufacturing kanban policy), although they may include stocked items (with a fixed manufacturing kanban policy).

**Capacity**  A work cell's capacity is defined by the calendar and daily drumbeat assigned to the lean order schedule.

- *Calendar.* A calendar identifies the working and non-working days, and the specified hours of operation during each working day. In the context of a drumbeat for each working day, a non-working day has zero minutes of working time whereas a working day can consist of 24 hours or 1 minute of working time.[2]
- *Drum Beat per Day.* The daily drumbeat provides a simple measure of a work cell's capacity in terms of equivalent units. It applies to each working day within the calendar assigned to the schedule. The daily drumbeat is initially assigned when you define a lean order schedule, and it acts as the default for all working days. However, you can define a different daily drumbeat for a specified date or a range of dates, thereby reflecting changes in available capacity. These changes in available

---

[2] The working time defined in a calendar does not affect the daily drumbeat, so that the daily drumbeat must be defined separately to reflect the anticipated capacity.

capacity are defined on the Update Schedule Drumbeat form. The daily drumbeat can be used for making delivery promises on sales orders for make-to-order items produced at the work cell, as described in the next point about Sales Orders and Delivery Promises.

The requirements for producing an item at the work cell are defined by a drumbeat consumption ratio. Each item's drumbeat ratio is defined as part of the family grouping information. The drumbeat consumption applies to sales orders and delivery promises. A ratio of 2.0, for example, means that a sales order for the item will consume 2 drumbeats per unit. A ratio of .5 will consume .5 drumbeats per unit. A sales order does not consume drumbeats when the ratio is zero.

**Sales Order Delivery Promises**  A sales order line for a make-to-order product will automatically create a corresponding LOS line, and a promised delivery date can be automatically calculated based on drumbeat availability. Sales orders consume available drumbeats within the work cell's schedule.

**Scheduling**  The basic coordination tool consists of a lean order schedule for the work cell, where the LOS lines (rather than PTO manufacturing kanbans) represent the pull signal. The printed job ticket provides an additional tool.

You can optionally load fixed manufacturing kanbans on the lean order schedule. These empty kanbans are displayed on the Heijunka Board form, which also displays the available drumbeats in daily increments. The icons for these fixed manufacturing kanbans are dragged-and-dropped to the desired date.

**Production Reporting**  The receipt of a LOS line represents basic production reporting. Other aspects of production reporting include starting, completing, and even shipping a LOS line. It is also possible to create a production order associated with a started LOS line, so that you can report time against the production order's routing operation.

# Index

Accumulate empty kanbans, 46, 53-54, 97
Action messages, 15-16
Alternate vendor, see also Vendor
   for purchasing kanban, 34-35
   for subcontract manufacturing, 83-84, 86

Barcode scanning,
   for kanbans, 70-71, 97, 141
   for LOS lines, 166, 167, 168
Baseline model of operations, 8
Batch tracking, 8, 180
Bill of material (BOM)
   BOM version for a manufacturing kanban, 50, 58, 65, 84, 125, 127, 162
   warehouse source of components, 14
Bin locations, 8, 179
Black hole concept, 23-24, 60-63, 73, 148-149; see also Floor stock management approach; see also Warehouses
BOM Journal, 17, 58
Booked status, see Lean order schedules
Buy-to-order component, 21

Capable to Promise (CTP). See Delivery promises
Capacity, see Work center, Drumbeat Concept
Color, see Variants
Component backflushing for kanbans, see Floor stock management approaches
Component release policy for manufacturing kanbans, 117, 125-126
Consigned inventory method for subcontract manufacturing, 18, 90-94
Cost substitution concept, 59-60. See also Floor stock management approaches
Coverage code, 32
Custom products, 21, 141
   surgical kit, case study, 25
   transportation equipment, case study, 24-25
   electric motors, case study, 142

Delivery promises, 16, 159-160, 189-190, 201-202, 208
Demand plan, see S&OP
Discrete kit method for subcontract manufacturing, 17-18, 79-90
Drumbeat concept, 103-104
   Case study, 104-105

Empty kanban transaction, 59, 72-73; see also Floor stock management approach
Engineering changes, 63-65, 97, 140, 191
Exclude from backflush flag, 60; see also Floor stock management approach

Family grouping for LOS, 159, 172; see also Lean order schedule
Financial dimension, 23, 147-148
Floor stock management approach, 57-63, 146-147
Forecast, 14-15 See also S&OP
Forecast scheduling task, 15, 30

General ledger considerations, 150-151
Generic fixed kanban, 74

Heijunka board, 173-174

Intercompany trading, see Multisite operations
Item allocation key, 14, 65

Journals, 150-151

Kanban coordination tools, see also Lean order schedule
   kanban manufacturing form, 54-55, 88-89, 94, 131-133
   kanban purchasing form, 39-40, 140
   kanban replenishment form, 46-47, 113-114, 117-118, 137-138
   stop/go board, 40-41, 55-56
   subcontract kanban form, 89-90, 94
Kanban level calculations, 30-33, 97, 188; see also Little's formula
   calculation options, case study, 76-77
   automotive parts, case study, 75-76
Kanban quantity adjustment form, 72-73
Kanban Parameters form, 34, 36, 41, 49, 51, 56, 58, 60, 72, 80, 86, 114, 115
Kanban policies
   Dynamic, 32
   Kanban group, 32
   Normal kanban quantity, 35, 43, 49, 110, 124-125, 126-127, 135, 162
   Pull-to-order (PTO), 110, 126, 135, 162
Kanban template, 65, 115, 133-134, 138
Kanban terminology, 5-7, 193-195

209

# Index

Lead time
  manufacturing kanban, 50-51, 84, 127-128
  purchasing kanban, 36
Lean accounting, 145-151
Lean manufacturing
  applicability, 2-4
  maturity stages, 4-5, 23, 57-63, 145-147, 190
Lean order schedule (LOS), 120, 153-177
  Lean Order Parameters form, 60, 147, 160, 162, 165, 166, 167, 175, 190
  MTO and MTS products, case study, 175-176
  terminology, 155-156
Little's formula, 31-32 see also Kanban Level Calculations

Make-to-order component, 21, 128-129
Make-to-order products, 3, 19-23, 27-77, 119-143
Make-to-stock products, 3, 11-19
Master scheduling task, 15, 21-22, 122
Multisite operations, 8, 181-183

Non-lean items, 74-75

Operation. See Routing
Order-based costing, 146-147; see also Production Orders
Outside operation component, 17, 80, 83
  See also subcontract manufacturing

Phased target kanbans, 185
Picking list for sales orders, 16, 18-19
Planning calculations, 15, 21-22, 30; see also Master scheduling task
  Forecast scheduling task
Poka-Yoka signoff, 181
Preferred vendor,
  for purchasing kanban, 34-35,
  for subcontract manufacturing kanban, 83-84
Product costing, 99-100, 145-146
Production order, 24
  sales order linkage, 20-22, 24
  traditional approach, 13, 15, 188-189
Production pool, 14
Pull to order shipping area, 18-19, 107-115
Purchase order,
  blanket PO, 17, 35
  intercompany, 182
  traditional approach, 13, 15, 188-189

Quality management, 8, 180-181
Quality order, 8, 180-181

Record Id, 36, 44, 50, 51, 70, 71
Reference orders, 21
Release a manufacturing kanban, 129-130;
  see also Component release policy
Return Material Authorizations (RMAs),
Routing, 13-14, 99-100, 199-203
  outside operation, 17, 80, 83,

Sales and Operations Planning (S&OP),
  approach for make-to-stock products, 11, 14-17, 30-33, 188
  approach for make-to-order products, 21-23, 122-123, 188
Sales order, 124-125; see also Delivery promises
Sales schedule, 75, 166
Scrap,
  handling planned scrap, 58-59, 180
  reporting actual scrap, 70-71, 97, 168, 180
  reporting reusable scrap, 71-72, 97
Serial number tracking, 8, 180
Shipments, 16, 165, 169-170
Sort type for a kanban, 36, 44, 51, 74
Standard costing, 8
Stop/Go Board, see Kanban Coordination Tools
Subcontract manufacturing, 79-97, 141
  subcontract policies for kanbans, 79-80, 82, 94-95
  traditional approaches with production orders, 17-18
  intermittent subcontracting with kanbans, 66, 95
Swap kanban inventory, 73-74

Takt time board, 54, 103
Takt time metrics, 54-55, 100-103
Target kanban, 183-184, 192
Temporary fixed kanbans, 67-70, 97
Terminology/synonyms, 5-7, 193-198
Transfer order, 15

Value stream costing, 4-5, 23-24, 147-149
Variants, 8
Vendor, 34-35, 64
  Vendor portal, case study, 76

Warehouse,
  black hole, 60-63, 140, 148-149
Work cell, 6-7, 49, 99-105, 126, 158, 171-172, 205-208
  drumbeat concept, 103-105, 158
Work centers, 12, 199-203
  work center consumption logic, 14